Tom Phillips is an author and journalist. He's worked as the editor of *Full Fact* and editorial director of *BuzzFeed UK*. Books in Tom's internationally bestselling *Brief History* series have been translated into more than thirty-five languages. *A Brief History of the End of the F*cking World* is his fourth book. Tom lives in Cornwall with an exponentially growing number of spider plants.

By Tom Phillips and available from Wildfire

Truth: A Brief History of Total Bullsh*t
Humans: A Brief History of How We F*cked It All Up

By Tom Phillips and Jonn Elledge, available from Wildfire

Conspiracy: A History of Boll*cks Theories,
and How Not to Fall for Them

Praise for *A Brief History of the End of the F*cking World*:

'Superb . . . entertaining . . . Phillips traverses this sprawling terrain with energy and charm' *Telegraph*

'[A] topically valuable corrective for those who think – what with Gaza, Ukraine, floods, firestorms and fools with their fingers on world-ending buttons – we are indeed in the end times and should descend into our silos or colonise Mars . . . Fans of Phillips's earlier books *Humans: A Brief History of How we F*cked It All Up* and *Truth: A Brief History of Total Bullsh*t* will be pleased that the ex-*BuzzFeed* editor is on form, not letting the grimness of his subject spoil his gagsmithery.' *Guardian*

'A great read . . . [Phillips] fills his timeline of unfilled apocalypses with wry humour and keeps the queue of plagues and judgements accessible.' *New Scientist*

'Exceptionally funny from cover to cover, it is not only an entertaining read but also deeply researched and thoughtful . . . his research is meticulous, and he lays it out with precision . . . What sets Phillips apart from other historical writers is his ability to mix academic research with comedy. He never simply presents historical facts; he delivers them with wit, sarcasm and a deep understanding of human absurdity. His writing allows for the historical details to be engaging, and his voice shines through every word.' *Irish Independent*

Praise for the *Brief History* series:

'Tom Phillips has proven beyond a doubt that humans are goddamn lucky to be here and are doing nearly nothing to remain relevant and viable as a species – except, that is, for writing witty, entertaining and slightly-distressing-but-ultimately-endearing books about the same. And if you care to avoid orbiting the earth in a space-garbage prison of your fellow humans' design, you should probably read it.' Sarah Knight, author of *The Life-Changing Magic of Not Giving a F*ck*

'This book is brilliant. Utterly, utterly brilliant. Apart from the epilogue, which is idiotic' Jeremy Clarkson

'Uproarious . . . [Phillips and Elledge] pair the abundant good humour of this book with a warning about the corrosive effects of conspiracy theories' *Times*

'A light-touch history of moments when humans have got it spectacularly wrong . . . Both readable and entertaining' *Telegraph*

'In dark times, it's reassuring to learn that we've always been a bunch of clueless f*cking nitwits' Stuart Heritage, author of *Don't Be a Dick, Pete*

'If you find yourself looking at the news and wondering how humanity has got so many things wrong, over and over again, this book is a very funny answer to just that question' Mark Watson, comedian and author of *Eleven*

'Tom Phillips is a very clever, very funny man, and it shows. If Sapiens was a testament to human sophistication, this history of failure cheerfully reminds us that humans are mostly idiots'
Greg Jenner, historian and author of *A Million Years and a Day*

'Chronicles humanity's myriad follies down the ages with malicious glee and much wit . . . a rib-tickling page-turner'
Business Standard

'*Humans* is Tom Phillips' timely, irreverent gallop through thousands of years of human stupidity. Every time you begin to find our foolishness bizarrely comforting, Phillips adds another kick in the ribs. Beneath all this book's laughter is a serious question: where does so much serial stupidity take us?'
Nicholas Griffin, author of *Ping-Pong Diplomacy: The Secret History Behind the Game That Changed the World*

A Brief History of the End of the F*cking World

TOM PHILLIPS

First published in 2025 by Wildfire
An imprint of Headline Publishing Group Limited

This paperback edition published in 2025

2

Cataloguing in Publication Data is available from the British Library

Paperback ISBN 978 1 0354 0221 2

Typeset in Parango by CC Book Production

Printed and bound in Great Britain by Clays Ltd, Elcograf S.p.A.

Headline's policy is to use papers that are natural, renewable and
recyclable products and made from wood grown in sustainable forests.
The logging and manufacturing processes are expected to conform to
the environmental regulations of the country of origin.

Headline Publishing Group Limited
An Hachette UK Company
Carmelite House
50 Victoria Embankment
London EC4Y 0DZ

The authorised representative in the EEA is Hachette Ireland,
8 Castlecourt Centre, Dublin 15, D15 XTP3, Ireland
(email: info@hbgi.ie)

www.headline.co.uk
www.hachette.co.uk

For Ben & Ellie.

(I worry that dedicating a book about the end of the world to people could be . . . misinterpreted? It's meant to be nice.)

Contents

1.

The Sky Was Always Falling

On Easter Sunday in 1534, Jan Matthys rode out through the gates of Münster to welcome the end of the world.

This is, perhaps, not quite the situation Matthys would have expected to end up in. Until about a decade earlier, he had been a fairly unremarkable Dutch baker. And yet in the space of just a few years, seized by an enthralling and radical idea, Matthys had left behind his old life and his homeland, married an ex-nun, and risen to become one of the leaders of an apocalyptic sect.

This sect had seized control of Münster three months previously – whereupon they expelled non-believers, and set about establishing a regime that might be best described as an increasingly totalitarian proto-communist sex cult. They were now awaiting the Day of Judgement – while under siege by the massed armies of the German city's recently deposed prince-bishop, who was not best pleased about having been deposed.

In fact, Matthys and his companions had managed the impressive feat of annoying everybody so much that, at the height of Europe's bitter religious schisms, Catholic and Protestant forces had teamed up in an effort to defeat them.

Matthys and his fellow believers hadn't come to the beliefs they held about the end of days out of the blue. They were simply the latest iteration of a rolling apocalyptic fervour that had gripped much of Europe for decades at this point – in which seemingly every year was proclaimed by *somebody* to be the last one.

In the case of the Münster sect, their inspiration had come from a radical Anabaptist preacher named Melchior Hoffman. He'd proclaimed that the Second Coming would occur in 1533 in Strasbourg, where Christ would establish his New Jerusalem.

But, as tended to happen, 1533 came and went without any sign of Jesus. Strasbourg remained a stubbornly earthly city, with the only event of relevance to our tale being that the disgruntled city authorities shoved Melchior Hoffman in prison. He would die there a decade later, never having got to see the world to come – or much more of the world that was, either.

Hoffman's followers were not discouraged by this failure of prophecy, however. Rather, they reasoned, Hoffman had been in the right ballpark, but had simply erred a little in his interpretation of exactly *where* and *when* the end would begin.

Instead, Matthys now prophesied, the true New Jerusalem would be Münster. (Thanks to a relatively tolerant approach to religious dissent, Münster already had a helpfully large population of Anabaptists.) Precisely when this revised end date would occur was not immediately clear, but they knew it would be soon. Very, very soon.

And then, on the evening of Holy Saturday, Matthys had

received a divine vision that left him slumped face-down in his dinner. After extricating himself from his meal, he shakily declared that the Last Day was now at hand. And thus it was that the next morning, with a sickly sense of trepidation, but fortified by his devotional certainty, he and a small band of twelve followers rode out through the city gates to face destiny.

Now, in one sense, Matthys's prediction turned out to be absolutely right. *His* world really did come to an abrupt end that day. He and his party were quickly surrounded by the bishop's soldiers, and Jan was brutally hacked to pieces. After dismembering him, his killers nailed his genitals to the city gates to really emphasise their point.

But in another sense, of course, Jan was completely wrong – as the subsequent 490 years of the world's continued existence have helpfully proved.

Wherever you look these days, it seems hard to escape the looming spectre of apocalypse.

Our world seems to be permanently on the brink of some catastrophe. We lurch from one crisis to the next, each new disaster piling upon its predecessors to create an exponential chain reaction of chaos. Financial crisis follows war follows pandemic follows financial crisis, all of it with the steady drum beat of climate change growing ever louder in the background. Millions die in a brand-new plague; refugees huddle in fear on the streets of shattered cities, while many miles away fingers hover over nuclear buttons; at the far end of supply chains, deprivation and starvation loom for millions more. One tenth of Pakistan is left underwater by floods; wildfires rampage across America and Australia; in Kazakhstan, a glacier collapses; in Africa, a lake vanishes.

In our media, doom is everywhere. If you're tempted to distract yourself from the anxieties of the real world with a dash of escapism, well – walk into just about any multiplex, pick a film at random, and there's a good chance you'll end up watching some flavour of city-, planet-, universe- or multiverse-destroying catastrophe.

Turn on the TV news, and not only will you hear more than you can stand about the actual crises afflicting our planet, but you'll also find yourself assailed by a legion of pundits declaring that civilisation is on the verge of collapse for any number of other reasons. Too much inequality, not enough inequality, the fact that we have pronouns, whatever. Newspapers love to grasp at the merest hint of doom, rushing to report every faint possibility that, say, an asteroid might hit Earth in a hundred years' time.

And if you turn instead to social media, then it's hard to escape the impression that, frankly, we've all had enough, and we'd welcome the end times like the return of an old friend. When, inevitably, it turns out that the asteroid will actually miss us by several million miles, your timeline will become filled with lamentations. 'Noooooooo,' they will cry, 'please, friendly space rock, come and release us from this torment.'

Ours is the age of doomscrolling. We are blasted by a non-stop fire hose of apocalypse, anxiously swiping our way through a dizzying choice of possible Armageddons.

And look: we're not *wrong* to be worried about plenty of these things. There really are genuine and profound upheavals that threaten us. Moreover, we live in an age when lots of our anxieties have a far more solid foundation than they did in the past.

Since the bombs dropped in 1945, humanity has had to live

with the knowledge that we have the ability to bring atomic destruction upon ourselves in cataclysms of unprecedented scale. And as science has untangled the threads of our world, we've come to understand in painful detail how many disasters are not simply the will of distant, vengeful gods, but rather are all too often the consequences of our own actions.

But at the same time, there's something else going on here. We are, after all, far from the first age to suffer a cascading domino effect of catastrophes. Imagine we could go back to, say, the mid-sixth century, described by one historian as 'one of the worst periods to be alive', when a large part of the world was reeling under the double whammy of an unprecedented pandemic and a devastating climate crisis. If we stepped out of our time machine and tried telling the inhabitants of that era about our current woes, then honestly they'd probably just be impressed that people were still around to worry about things.

So we have many troubles, yes. The worst of the threats we face have the capacity to wreak havoc on a vast scale and fundamentally reshape our world. But it's clear that our doomsday fixation isn't simply a sober assessment that our age is uniquely troubled: a dispassionate actuarial projection of worrying trends.

Rather, the *idea* of apocalypse is one that has exerted a profound hold on the human psyche for thousands of years. The notion that disasters are not merely isolated events, but the end of all things – that the world as we know it will very soon be consumed in fire or flood or war – is one to which we seem irresistibly drawn.

This is very often a response to the anxieties and traumas of the age – a way of imposing a narrative on our fears. It's not always the most straightforward of responses, but in elevating our troubles from small, dark, local despairs into the grandest and most unequivocal of stories, the apocalypse has proven to be a captivating and seductive theme.

This book is about the history of that idea. It's about all the ways we've thought that the world would end, and about the fierce grip this concept can have on us. And it's also about the consequences of that idea – one that has led to holy wars and revolutionary uprisings, inspired both conquest and resistance, and continues to shape our feelings, our culture and our political world to this day.

It's also an idea that links Jan Matthys with, to pick just one example, Dorothy Martin – a middle-aged woman living in the arty, liberal Chicago suburb of Oak Park in the 1950s. Despite the fact that the failed medieval prophet and the suburban housewife were separated by an ocean, more than four centuries of history, and a vast universe of cultural reference points, the unshakeable impulse that drove both Matthys and Martin was fundamentally the same.

Dorothy Martin had come to believe that, through the practice of automatic writing, she had been in communication with a species of aliens from the planet Clarion. These aliens had important messages for Martin – and, through her, for the people of the Chicago metropolitan area and, more broadly, the world.

Initially they wished to share their advanced learning, and the deep understanding of the cosmos that came with existing on a different 'vibratory frequency' to humans. But over the course of a few summer months, the messages Martin received turned from hopeful talk of wisdom and enlightenment to increasingly dark warnings of 'the holocaust of the coming events'.

This eventually solidified into a very specific prediction: the apocalypse would begin on 21 December 1954. A great flood would wreak havoc – first the Chicago area would be subsumed by Lake Michigan, then the entire West Coast of the Americas would sink beneath the waves, before eventually most of North America would be drowned. Other, vaguer calamities would also occur elsewhere.

The good news – at least for the small band of people who followed Dorothy Martin's teachings, calling themselves 'the Seekers' – was that the aliens would be arriving in one of their flying saucers shortly before the flood to take them to safety. Everybody else was shit out of luck, but *they* would be okay. And so it was that, having followed the aliens' oddly specific instruction to remove every item of metal from about their persons, they all gathered in Martin's backyard on 17 December, awaiting salvation.

The aliens did not come.

Reasoning that, obviously, this simply meant it had been a test run before the *actual* rescue, the Seekers were not discouraged. And so they reassembled in the same location the next day. Once again, the aliens stubbornly failed to show. So they did it again on 21 December, and then one more time on Christmas Eve, at which point they were already three days past the point when the backyard they were standing in was supposed to have been submerged beneath the floodwaters.

For those in Martin's group, this presented something of a problem. At least, it did for those who were genuine believers – rather than the sizeable percentage of 'followers' who were actually undercover psychologists gleefully taking notes. Some of the Seekers found their belief shaken by this series of prophetic failures, questioning whether something had gone wrong. A few expressed scepticism about the authenticity of the original message telling them the saucers were coming – which had been delivered via a phone call to Martin from someone who said his name was 'Captain Video'.

But for others in the group, all this was no reason to stop believing. In fact, they doubled down on their beliefs – for a time, at least. Their coping mechanism for the failed prediction was to recommit even more strongly to Martin and the community they'd found among their fellow Seekers. Rather than being swayed by the failure, it made them double down on their beliefs.

This is another thing that links Martin with Matthys – and the innumerable others who have foreseen the imminent end of all things.

Just as Melchior Hoffman's original failed prediction hadn't discouraged Matthys in his prophesying, so Jan's gruesome fate and the failure of the end to arrive on that Easter Sunday did not spell the end for the apocalyptic rule of Münster. In fact, Jan's fellow believers became ever more extreme in their certainty, and would manage to hold the city for another year before the prince-bishop's forces retook it (with, as we'll see, an even grimmer fate awaiting Matthys's successors). All the while, they held firm to their belief that the end really was coming *this* time, honest.

The belief in apocalypse is not just common, it turns out: it's also incredibly *resilient*.

In fact, when you think about it, apocalypticism is a remarkable entry in the history of ideas. It has persisted for millennia, constantly adapting to fit the times and local circumstances. It has proved to be a potent export, able to cross geographical and cultural boundaries with ease. It can fade away from the discourse for decades, only to resurge more strongly than ever; it may be almost as popular today as it has ever been. And it's done all of this despite the fact that its predictions have – at the time of writing – an absolute 100 per cent failure rate.

This is a bit puzzling.

I mean, look. There are plenty of ideas – both secular and religious – that remain bafflingly popular despite having incredibly dodgy track records. (You can probably fill in some yourself here, according to your ideological preferences.) But even with these ideas, there's normally at least *something* that adherents can point at to justify their beliefs: some cherry-pickable evidence, some superficially persuasive analysis, some kind of tangible benefit that accrues to those who believe it or those who promote it. The ideas might be wrong, but you can see why people want them to be right.

The longevity and popularity of the apocalypse idea, by contrast, seem on the face of it harder to explain. Because it has *literally never been right*. To put it bluntly, this book you're reading shouldn't be able to exist. If you can trace the claim that history is going to end imminently across thousands of years of history, then something's clearly gone screwy somewhere.

So why has the apocalypse idea stuck around with such limpet-like stubbornness? There are plenty of possible explanations – historical, psychological, theological – but alongside these runs one relatively straightforward reason. Which is, simply, political expediency.

Throughout much of history, the end of the world has proved to be extremely useful for people wanting to achieve much more worldly ends.

* * *

When Columbus set sail in 1492 for what he thought was Asia, but would turn out to be the Americas, he was driven by many things. Ambition, certainly. Avarice, yes. Curiosity . . . ehhh, maybe?

But among these impulses was also one simple and yet overwhelming belief – the same one that would later drive Jan Matthys, and Dorothy Martin, and a legion of others throughout history.

Christopher Columbus believed that the end of the world was nigh.

Or, at least, nigh*ish*. Columbus did not think that he would live to see the end of days himself. Nonetheless, he firmly held that, within the foreseeable future, the world as it was would be swept away and replaced with a new heavenly kingdom. The clock was ticking. And he had a vital role to play in the epic events that were to unfold.

This was no mere abstract notion. Columbus had a very specific date in mind for the apocalypse: it would occur in around mid-February 1656. That's the date the interpretations of the Bible that he favoured held was precisely seven millennia after the creation. And, therefore, that's when it would all come to a crashing end.

One and a half centuries in the future may not be quite as imminent as 'tomorrow' or 'this December', but it was enough to profoundly influence Columbus and push him towards staking his claim in the New World. He went so far as to compile an entire work, the *Book of Prophecies*, a kind of scrap-book of all the apocalyptic writings that had influenced him and that he felt justified his voyages.

We don't usually think of Christopher Columbus as having been driven by apocalyptic fervour. He's one of the most famous figures in Western history, but this aspect of him has been almost entirely lost from his story. Whether you view him as a heroic explorer worthy of commemoration, or as a genocidal slave-driver with the blood of entire peoples on his hands, the idea that he was every bit as apocalyptic as the likes of Jan Matthys or Dorothy Martin simply isn't part of the Columbus narrative.

And yet this knowledge is essential to understanding what he did, and how the history of the world was fundamentally altered – not just through Columbus's voyages, but through the end-times mindset that was shared by many of those who colonised the Americas.

This tells us a few interesting things. One is that apocalyptic belief often gets written out of the historic tales we tell ourselves.

In the popular imagination, doomsday is usually a fringe belief, the preserve of weird cults and ranting oddballs. In reality, it's been a mainstay of major historical figures, firmly believed in by monarchs and statesmen and scholars – something that continues to this day. The apocalypse is and always has been extremely mainstream.

A second point is that it hasn't been a passive background belief. Instead, it's something that's played an active role in conquests and colonialism, political power struggles and broad social movements. Whether the political players viewed it as an undeniable fact, or merely a convenient excuse, the looming end of days has been used to justify major decisions down the centuries that helped to form the world we live in now.

Bluntly, the apocalypse is an extremely powerful motivator.

The final point comes in the answer to the question: *why*

did a belief in the apocalypse spur Columbus to set sail for the Indies?

It's because he thought it was his duty to help bring it about.

This is one of the key things to realise about the end of the world: for many of the people throughout history who most fervently believed in it, it was not simply a terrifying event to be feared, but an ultimate triumph to be longed for and worked towards. At the end of days, Good would finally defeat Evil, all the woes of the material world would be swept away, and the true believers would be rewarded with the paradise of a new world.

For Columbus, Christ could not return to establish his blessed new kingdom until certain prophetic conditions had been met – among them that all the people of the earth had converted to His worship, and that the Holy Sepulchre in Jerusalem was restored to Christian rule. His goals were both to convert the world and to plunder it, the better to fund the conquest of the Holy Land.

Our common conception is that the apocalyptic mindset is one of fear, panic and despair. But in reality, at many times throughout history, it has been something that gave people *hope*. (Even if that hope was that they would finally be vindicated in the fiery destruction of their enemies.)

Aside from all this, the other noteworthy thing is the most obvious one: Columbus was wrong. Just like Jan Matthys and Dorothy Martin, Columbus's predictions entirely failed. Sitting here in the lofty vantage point of 2025, we know that the world's population is still not converted, control of the Holy Sepulchre remains bitterly contested, and the Second Coming has yet to announce itself. Despite all of Christopher Columbus's certainty, the world did not end.

Except, perhaps, for the indigenous population of the Americas. For them, it kind of did.

The word for the study of the apocalypse is 'eschatology'. But that's not all it means: eschatology isn't merely about the end of the world, but the end of *things*. The subject contains beliefs about world-ending cataclysms, but also deals with the structural (the end of the current order) and the personal (what happens to us when we die).

This isn't a coincidence. Throughout the history of how these ideas have developed, all these concepts have been deeply interwoven – ideas about the immortal soul inform conceptions of the Day of Judgement, and worldly concerns about the structure of society have fuelled apocalyptic movements for millennia. In the same way, the anxieties and hopes that drive apocalyptic beliefs are also foremost in those other topics – the difficulty of thinking about death, and the fear or hope that the world as we know it will not survive our lifetimes. The spiritual, the political and the personal merge together; our obsession with the Big Apocalypse is fuelled by our terror of all those Little Apocalypses.

All that might suggest that humans have an in-built compulsion to think about the end of the world. There's a temptation, when discussing ideas as long-lived and persistent as this, to suggest that they're somehow innate to us – that beliefs about the end of the world are 'hard-wired' into our brains.

This becomes all the more tempting when you start to spot the common features that occur in apocalyptic stories across times and cultures. It's easy to jump to the conclusion that there's something deep within us that yearns for precisely this narrative: some particular arrangement of neurons that lights up at tales of doomsday; an apocalypse-shaped hole in our souls that demands a story to fill it.

And yet that can't be the case, because while apocalypse stories are common, they're far from universal. Plenty of cultural traditions around the world have happily existed for millennia without ever really troubling themselves over questions of whether and when everything might come to an abrupt halt. The apocalypse is not there in Greek or Roman mythology; it's rare in traditional African spirituality; it's effectively absent from Japanese Shinto. Despite what you might have heard a bit over a decade ago, the ancient Maya emphatically did *not* believe that the world would end in 2012.

Apocalyptic narratives are undoubtedly very effective at tickling the euphoric-terror centres of our brain, but there's nothing hard-wired about them.

Instead, what history shows us is that the apocalypse idea is incredibly good at *spreading*. It may not spring fully formed from our subconscious, and it's not an eternal presence in human history, but ever since the first apocalypse story was told – around 3,000 years ago – it has proven adept at jumping from culture to culture, being adapted and recontextualised to fit the circumstances. Even in places with little tradition of doomsday tales, once the concept is introduced, it can quickly take root.

To put it another way: Columbus brought the apocalypse with him in more ways than one. There are many different ways for the world to end.

The first time Hong Xiuquan's world ended was in the 1830s, when he failed an exam.

It was an important exam, one on which he'd pinned his self-image and his hopes for a better life. His failure was a crushing blow. He retook the exam; he failed again. When he failed for a third time, his world shattered.

As he tried to put himself and his world back together, Hong struggled to make sense of unnerving dreams full of strange images he couldn't comprehend. He found his answers in unfamiliar texts that were being distributed in his home province of Guangdong by foreign travellers – people who had come for trade, but stayed to spread the word of their God.

The result was a heady stew of messianic, apocalyptic ideas that Hong created from a blend of Western Christianity, Chinese folk religion, and the more eschatological strands of Taoism and Buddhism. This new belief system placed Hong at its centre: no longer a repeatedly failing exam candidate, but the son of God, put on Earth to establish and rule over a new heavenly kingdom.

Hong began to preach his truth. To begin with, he attracted a few followers. Gradually, the number of followers grew to become a flock. The authorities started to get worried about this challenge to their power, but the followers kept coming. Eventually they were no longer a flock, but an army.

Twenty years later, somewhere around 30 million people were dead. Hong's visions of a world upturned – and the backlash against them from the forces of the current order – had brought about one of the bloodiest wars in human history.

This is shocking, but not surprising. Hong's uprising may be one of the more extreme examples, but throughout the ages, the apocalypse has been important fuel for rebellions, revolutions and uprisings of all sorts. Like Jan Matthys before him, Hong's vision of a new spiritual kingdom was a challenge to the existing order; it is almost inevitable that the two would violently clash. Throughout history, the powerful have often weaponised the apocalypse to advance their interests, but it has also been a profound source of hope for the powerless, the disenchanted, the outcasts. After all, if you can imagine the end of the world, then you can imagine a different world.

And that's the key to why doomsday has such a hold on us. Because when we talk about the end of the world, what we really mean is the end of *our* world.

Ultimately, our apocalypse obsession is about change – our anxiety about it, and our desire for it. Those who despondently prophesy imminent destruction are normally reacting to societal changes they disapprove of. Those who eagerly await the end of days are really yearning for the overturning of an order they deem insufferable.

And this is the core idea that's present in just about every tale in this book, one that permeates the entire history of the end of the world.

It's there in the Brazilian jungle, in a community of formerly enslaved people, where a dying man holds on to the last fragments of hope in the world he tried to build, as all around them government forces close in.

It's there in the lands of the Xhosa people, where a teenage girl has visions that tell her that soon the dead will arise and injustice will be overturned, but first the people must purify their land in appalling ways.

It's there in Montana, with a family of prophets pushing a cart down an underground track as they retreat to their purpose-built bunker, believing that tonight is the night that the long-foretold bombs will fall.

It's there at a gathering near the Sea of Galilee, where a man tells his followers that some of them will not taste death.

It's there in Tianjing, as Hong Xiuquan looks out over the destruction he has caused; it's there on the deck of the *Santa Maria* as Columbus looks to the horizon, a herald of destruction to come. It's there in the backyard of a suburban Chicago house, as Seekers huddle in the December chill, awaiting their alien saviours; and it's there by the gates of Münster, as Jan Matthys has the last glimpse of this world that he will ever see.

It's in our news, in our social media feeds, in our culture, and in our minds. The idea of doomsday has spread far and wide. It has spurred oppression and rebellion, given hope and brought terror. It has never, *ever* been right, not even once, and yet it has indeed changed the world, time and time again. This book is about how, and why.

It's an attempt to understand the end.

2.

Apocalypse Pop

Roland Emmerich has killed more people than almost anyone else in history.

Now, it's important – for both ethical and legal reasons – to clarify here that the German-born film director has not *actually murdered* anybody. Mr Emmerich's death toll resides purely in the fictional realm; in real life, he is an extremely non-murdery man, who should definitely not sue anybody.

But still, what a death toll it is.

Hailed as the 'master of disaster', Emmerich's none-more-apocalyptic films bestrode the box office across the nineties and noughties (with somewhat diminishing returns in recent years). Beyond their individual successes, though, they also helped to kickstart a frantic arms race for maximal cinematic destruction that – at the time of writing – shows very little sign of abating.

In his role as the conductor of cataclysm, Mr Emmerich

has brought our planet to the brink of annihilation in no fewer than five movies: 1996's *Independence Day* (alien invasion); 2004's *The Day After Tomorrow* (climate catastrophe); 2009's *2012* (full-spectrum Maya calendar-themed destruction); 2016's *Independence Day: Resurgence* (they're back!); and 2022's *Moonfall* (the moon . . . falls). We're not even counting 1998's *Godzilla*, as it merely lays waste to New York City, which – despite what some of its residents may believe – is not the whole world.

Establishing exactly *how* high Emmerich's cinematic kill-count runs turns out to be a tricky endeavour – one that, if I'm honest, I wasted several days of research trying in vain to pin down.

Only *Independence Day* has a canonical death toll, thanks to it being mentioned in the sequel. It's around 3 billion dead – most from disease and starvation in the aftermath of the alien invasion, rather than that many people all having had the misfortune to be standing by a famous landmark when it exploded. The sequel is even more destructive (a substantial portion of Asia appears to be . . . dropped on London?), so that's probably another few billion of the people who survived the first round.

In happier news, the climate cataclysms of *The Day After Tomorrow* seem worst in the USA (a brief clip shows American refugees fleeing to Mexico). Also, there's a bit where Jake Gyllenhaal outruns a cold front that's chasing him down a corridor and escapes by simply shutting the door. In other words, this thing . . . seems survivable? We can guess that the death toll during the movie is comparatively minor by Emmerichian standards – tens of millions, perhaps? – even if it's probably a safe assumption that global agriculture would be screwed in the following years.

The destruction in *2012*, by contrast, is almost total: the film suggests only one small bit of Africa and one ark-full of elites/plucky protagonists survive, so a reasonable mortality estimate is within handwaving territory of 7 billion.

This brings us to *Moonfall*. Like most of its audience, I don't have a firm grasp of what was going on in this film, but honestly, it seemed pretty bad! The moon's gravity starts lifting things like oceans and landscapes into the air, then lifting the air into space, all of which is probably not ideal. (Also – spoiler – it turns out the moon is an alien spaceship.) Let's play it safe and call it 3.5 billion, shall we? Cool.

The point here is that Emmerich's cumulative cinematic body count is plausibly in the 15 billion range – in other words, more than double *the actual population of the Earth*. The apocalypse itself is not big enough to contain his wrath.

But the thing that really gives you the flavour of our cultural moment is that, while Emmerich's commitment to unleashing havoc upon our planet is unusually dedicated, he doesn't even have the highest cultural kill-count. In the movie realm, that title probably goes to either the Russo brothers (if you count the snapping away of half the universe's population in *Avengers: Infinity War*, despite the fact that they were all brought back in the next film) or J. J. Abrams (who's enthusiastically embraced the George Lucas technique of demolishing entire planets for dramatic effect, doing so in both *Star Trek* and *Star Wars: The Force Awakens* – accounting for hundreds of billions of unnamed victims).

It's not quite the same, though, this casual obliteration of far-off fictional worlds. They're not *our* world; it doesn't register on the same emotional level. But that feels entirely in keeping with the weightless mass death of the modern blockbuster, which has taught us not to consider whether those falling buildings have people in them, or if those crashing cars have drivers.

And that's kind of the point – none of this orgy of destruction feels out of place in our doom-laden cultural landscape. The end times have spread through our entertainment landscape like a zombie infection through a holiday camp. If you have even a passing engagement with pop culture, you'll have beheld more apocalypses and near-apocalypses and post-apocalypses in recent decades than any single planet should be expected to take. If you take any message from it all, it's that the end – to quote the words sprayed on a church wall in *28 Days Later* – 'is extremely fucking nigh'.

We've seen our world brought to the brink of destruction by blight (*Interstellar*), by badly thought-out solutions to climate change (*Snowpiercer*), by fungus (*The Girl with All the Gifts*), by infertility (*Children of Men*), by garbage (*WALL-E*), by the rotation of the Earth's core abruptly stopping (*The Core*), by dragons (*Reign of Fire*), and even by Satan (*End of Days*), which I suppose represents a nice return to tradition.

Aliens have caused us problems many, many times (*Independence Day, The Matrix, Battle: Los Angeles, Oblivion, A Quiet Place*), possibly losing the 'Most Popular Apocalyptic Threat' contest only to the resurgence of zombies – which themselves have come in versions that are fast (*Dawn of the Dead, World War Z, Train to Busan*), slow (*The Walking Dead, Shaun of the Dead, Zombieland*) and not-technically-zombies-but-clearly-still-zombies (*28 Days Later, I am Legend*). Asteroids, comets and other forms of space stuff are also perennial favourites, of course.

If you're a gamer, you can shoot fungus-infected not-technically-zombies in the post-apocalyptic ruins of *The Last of Us*, or shoot irradiated mutants in the post-apocalyptic wasteland of *Fallout* – and when your fingers get tired, you can put down the controller and watch the prestigious live-action adaptations of both. If you're a fan of high-quality literature, you can read incredibly bleak post-apocalyptic tales (*The Road*) or quietly hopeful post-apocalyptic tales (*Station Eleven*). And when your book hand gets tired, they too have prestigious live-action adaptations.

Apocalyptic events have been the subject of everything from the biggest blockbusters imaginable (the *Avengers* diptych of *Infinity War* and *Endgame*) to small indie dramedies (*Last Night*), weird arthouse experiments (*Melancholia*), outright comedy (*This Is The End*) and rather heavy-handed satire (*Don't Look Up*). They've given us some of the most memorable works of recent decades (*Children of Men*, *Mad Max: Fury Road*) and – let's be honest – some of the worst (looking at you, *Geostorm*).

Now, the sheer variety of apocalypses on offer has not always made for completely distinctive entertainment. In the late nineties, you had the choice of watching Kevin Costner manfully surviving in a very wet post-apocalyptic landscape (*Waterworld*) or in a very dry post-apocalyptic landscape (*The Postman*). In the summer of 1998, if you went to see *Armageddon*, you could watch the East Coast of the USA get destroyed by meteorites before the world is saved from an asteroid by an astronaut with a nuclear bomb sacrificing himself. By contrast, if you bought a ticket for *Deep Impact*, you could watch the East Coast of the USA get destroyed by a comet fragment before the world is saved from a larger comet fragment by several astronauts with nuclear bombs sacrificing themselves.

Which all raises the very real possibility that we might be

on the verge of suffering from apocalypse fatigue. There are, surely, only so many times you can witness the end of the world before the novelty wears off. When Roland Emmerich's *Moonfall* hit cinemas, one Hollywood analytics firm reported that audiences had soured on the director's output – accusing him of 'hating Earth'.

Throughout history, depictions of the apocalypse have inspired fear, awe and hope in their audiences. What does it say about us that today our main reaction might be boredom?

Ours is far from the first age in which culture has turned its eyes towards doomsday. Disaster, as Susan Sontag wrote in 1965, 'is one of the oldest subjects of art'.

That's from her essay 'The Imagination of Disaster', which analysed the deeper meaning – or lack of it – in films that blow shit up good. And there was plenty of material for her to work with. Fuelled by the new anxieties of the nuclear age, the previous fifteen years had seen a glut of sci-fi films (of varying degrees of schlock) which featured wanton destruction and imminent planetary catastrophe. Her analysis of their formulaic nature ('often includes a rapid montage of news broadcasts in various languages'; 'an obligatory scene here of panicked crowds stampeding along a highway or a big bridge') still reads as incredibly familiar today.

But of course, culture had focused on matters apocalyptic long before the twentieth century – there's a history of artistic representations of the apocalypse that stretches back at least a thousand years. In fact, it almost certainly stretches back even further than that – but only small fragments of physical culture survive that long, so discussing it starts to involve a bit of educated guesswork. (Also, the stuff that does survive tends to be the bits that were made out of stone or owned by kings, which aren't always terribly representative.)

Now, for most of that time, the purpose of this cultural apocalypticism wasn't to make people go, 'Wow, look at all that stuff exploding – *awesome*.' Or rather, it was – but 'awesome' in the 'tremble before the fearsome power of God' sense, rather than the 'heh heh, cool' sense. If you walk into a medieval English church – or, more accurately, if you walk *out* of a medieval English church – there's a chance you'll get a glimpse of this in action. Many of them have 'Doom paintings' across the wall around the exit – massive, detailed, extremely visceral depictions of the Last Judgement. The world fractures, and Christ sits in his judging seat, dispatching the virtuous towards paradise and the wicked to an array of precisely rendered torments. The purpose is clear: to freak everyone out as they leave church, reminding them of the fate that awaits those who forget the sermon the second they're out the door.

The thing is, before the age of print or radio or streaming platforms, slapping something over the exit of a church was the closest thing to broadcast mass media there was. Outside of 'very catchy folk song' or 'compelling rumour', if you wanted a lot of people to absorb a message, then a massive painting on a church wall was one of your best bets.

The most famous Doom painting is also one of the most unusual: Michelangelo's vast and awesome *The Last Judgement* in the Sistine Chapel. This one isn't placed by the exit – it's on the wall right behind the altar. In contrast to the transcendent beauty of his ceiling efforts, Michelangelo's doomwork is designed to strike terror into the hearts of everyone forced to stare at it for the entirety of the service. And it marked a political shift: unlike the blissful scenes on the ceiling, painted decades earlier when the Church was confident in its status, the apocalypse scenes were commissioned during the explosion of Protestant thought, as Rome realised that it was in a knock-down scrap for religious dominance. The message? No more Mr Nice Church.

The feeling was mutual: an awful lot of England's Doom paintings were destroyed or painted over during the Reformation, as Henry VIII went to town on Catholicism and all its trappings.

But the apocalypse wasn't just a message pushed on the public during this time – it could also be a luxury good. For those who could afford them (which was very, very few people) illuminated manuscripts were becoming a must-have status symbol, and one of the more popular subjects was the end of days. Little showed off your elite status like owning your own personal depiction of Armageddon. The sixteenth-century Augsburg *Book of Miracles* is perhaps the pinnacle of this form, a sumptuous collection of depictions of disasters and bizarre events that ends in a sequence of glorious technicolour renditions of the coming last days. (More on this in Chapter 9.)

By the time the *Book of Miracles* was produced, though, the nature of culture was already shifting – one-off artworks were on their way to being supplanted by mass reproduction. The printing revolution also gave us some of our most popular and enduring apocalyptic imagery: Albrecht Dürer's *Apocalypse With Pictures*, the smash-hit woodcut sensation of 1498. Launched in a Europe hot with conflict, dizzy from rapid social change and trembling in the expectation of Judgement Day arriving in the near future, Dürer's *Apocalypse* presented the hallucinatory imagery of the Book of Revelation with an unprecedented realism – and cemented the Four Horsemen of the Apocalypse as a defining symbol of the looming End.

It wasn't just visual art that bore the mark of doomsday, though. As text itself became more widely available, people quickly took it up to talk about all things apocalyptic – and the results were often hugely popular. *The Day of Doom*, an extremely long poem by Michael Wigglesworth first published in 1662, became possibly the best-selling text in New England for the best part of a century – despite the fact that it's overwrought, grim doggerel.

Wigglesworth himself was a closeted Puritan clergyman, much tormented by homoerotic yearning and wet dreams, and described by one scholar as 'a morbid, humorless, selfish busybody'. The poem is a reflection of his outlook, in which a brief exciting segment of awesome spectacle ('The Mountains smoke, the Hills are shook / The Earth is rent and torn') quickly gives way to an interminable litany of judgement in which Wigglesworth explains why almost everyone is going to hell. That's a fate reserved not just for 'Witches, Inchanters, and Alehouse-haunters' and the like – the poem spends many stanzas justifying why babies who died in infancy, never even having had the chance to sin, are also hell-bound.

But not every religious text that considered the apocalypse was quite as dour and doctrinaire. Even before the age of print, one of the first-ever novels produced in the Arabic world offers a far more intriguing exploration of all things doomy.

Penned by the remarkable polymath Ibn al-Nafis some time around 1270, the *Theologus Autodidactus* ('The Self-Taught Theologian') is the story of a child who miraculously springs into existence on a deserted island, and goes about figuring out the world from first principles. As a plot, it's part theological exegesis, part coming-of-age tale, and mostly an opportunity for al-Nafis to drop in all his thoughts about life, the universe and everything. (Ibn al-Nafis was a pioneering physician – the first to accurately describe the circulation of blood between the heart and lungs – so it also features some lengthy digressions about anatomy.)

The part that concerns us comes, naturally, at the end: a detailed description of exactly what will happen in the final days. This section is, frankly, a banger – for the simple reason that al-Nafis has set himself the task of coming up with a plausible, logical, non-supernatural explanation for why all the things mentioned in prophecies of the end times should happen. At this point, the novel stops being a theological *Bildungsroman*. Instead, it becomes, effectively, a kind of early sci-fi.

You see, the plausible apocalypse al-Nafis comes up with is . . . climate change. Based on his (admittedly flawed) knowledge of astronomy, he predicts that the seasonal changes in the sun's path across the sky will eventually diminish to nothing – leaving the day length unchanging and the seasons static across the planet. The outcome, he says, is that 'the regions far from the equator will become exceedingly cold, and those near it intensely hot; this will make the climate unsuitable for the human temperament'.

The effects of this will be severe: 'there will be many fires', 'water will become very scarce', and 'there will be much smoke and this will produce unhealthy winds . . . and in consequence of this the soil will lose many of its earthy and watery parts'. Humanity will suffer: 'Their hearts will become weak, and they will often die suddenly', while 'fruit and crops will become very scarce . . . for this reason there will be many thefts', and 'crimes and troubles will become prevalent'. When the extremes of hot and cold eventually 'make health and life impossible', then 'the inhabitants of those two climates will be forced to emigrate . . . with their kings, armies and mounts'. The result will be war and, ultimately, complete destruction.

The finale envisioned by al-Nafis seems very familiar in our warming world – you can find equivalents of many of his predictions in modern environmental warnings. Not all of them, admittedly: he also forecasts that it will cause mass lesbianism. 'On account of the many wars many men will be killed, and women will be in the majority. Therefore they will become lustful and lecherous as they cannot find enough men to satisfy them, and there will be much female homosexuality.' Just as the prophecy foretold.

The work of al-Nafis is notable for taking the religious idea of the apocalypse and tackling it with a scientist's eye. In this, he was ahead of his time, because he was prefiguring one of the most notable ways that the apocalypse and culture would intersect – the rise of the secular apocalypse.

Throughout the nineteenth century, the twin forces of art and science worked in tandem to ponder a new possibility: that of apocalypse without divine intervention. As astronomers and geologists and medics examined new breakthroughs, the possibility of a global cataclysm that was distinct from religious prophecies became apparent. And at the same time, cultural pioneers were grappling with exactly the same idea.

If you want to put a date on it, the secular apocalypse entered culture in the same borderline-apocalyptic year that birthed the modern horror story. Which makes sense, because it was the same people who did it: Lord Byron, the Shelleys and their friends, who were sheltering from the eerie volcanic winter of the 'year without a summer' in the Villa Diodati and telling each other spooky stories. The same extended house party that saw the creation of Frankenstein's monster and the modern vampire also gave us a fresh new apocalypse.

Byron's poem 'Darkness', written that year, presents an apocalypse that alludes to scripture but stands apart from it, with a clear scientific influence: an Italian scientist had caused a sensation by predicting that the sun would be consumed by sunspots and go out on 16 July that year. (This did not happen.)

Mary Shelley, of *Frankenstein* fame, would also dip into the apocalyptic well a decade later with the publication of *The Last Man* in 1826, which imagines the sole survivor of a world devastated by a pandemic. Critics hated it; it's now considered a pioneering work.

Throughout the nineteenth century, scientific discovery and artistic imagination would cross-fertilise to develop ideas of the secular apocalypse. It wasn't just a question of each inspiring the other: scientists themselves would turn to fiction to explore their ideas. The celebrated French astronomer Camille Flammarion wrestled with these questions of how the world might end in his 1893 novel *La Fin du Monde*, in which a group of far-future scientists debate whether a passing comet will extinguish all life on Earth.

In our time, we take for granted that all these threats – comets, pandemics, geostorms – are a part of our cultural landscape. But that wasn't always the case. Our understanding of what the apocalypse will look like is deeply influenced by centuries of its depiction.

In 1910, when Halley's Comet made its return to Earth's celestial neighbourhood for the first time in seventy-five years, it sparked a wave of both excitement and fear.

The last time that cosmic wanderer had passed our way, back in 1835, the age of mass media was only just dawning. It was a time when newly launched newspapers with a populist mindset and a knock-down price were competing fiercely for public attention – but they were still early in the trial-and-error process of figuring out what grabbed readers and what didn't.

But by the time the comet swung back into town, a decade into the twentieth century, they'd got that down to a fine art.

Two examples – one scientific, one religious – from that time illustrate the impact the comet's arrival had on the apocalyptic imagination. In February, the *New York Times* reported on its front page the fears of none other than the famous French astronomer Camille Flammarion: that the Earth might pass through the comet's tail – recently discovered to contain the 'very deadly poison' cyanogen – with the result that it would 'impregnate the atmosphere and possibly snuff out all life on the planet'. This prediction blasted out across the media like a shockwave, propagated via wire services and reprints and follow-up stories – and before too long, the question of whether the comet would result in the 'wholesale extinction of life' was one that was preying on everyone's mind.

That question might have originated in science, but it made an impression on those of a less empirical mindset as well. 'Superstitious Driven to Suicide and Crime by Comet' ran the headline in the *Los Angeles Times* on 19 May, the morning after the comet's tail was said to have passed the Earth. Reports from across the country brought news of the frenzied emotional outpourings the night before: a wealthy rancher in New Mexico drank deadly poison, not wishing to witness the disaster unfolding; churches had been full, with the faithful praying all night for salvation; in Mexico, religious ceremonies held to drive the comet away transformed into fiestas as they realised the moment of crisis had passed. But most shocking were the events near the small town of Aline, Oklahoma.

Around forty members of a sect known as the Select Followers had attempted to conduct a human sacrifice – what the report described as a 'blood atonement', which their leader Henry Heinman had insisted was the only way to avert catastrophe. He had received a message from God that, without such a sacrifice, the 'heavens would be rolled up like a scroll following contact with the tail of the comet'.

The sacrifice was to be a local sixteen-year-old girl, Jane Warfield, whom they had clothed in ceremonial white robes. The horror was only averted at the last minute. The authorities had been tipped off about the planned slaughter, and, in the form of a posse led by Dewey County's Sheriff Hughes, they arrived just as Heinman was about the wield the knife. Jane was saved; Heinman was taken into custody.

These vignettes from the comet panic of 1910 are interesting for two reasons. Firstly, they illustrate a trend that would accelerate throughout the twentieth century, showing how scientific and religious concepts of the apocalypse had begun to merge and feed off each other in the culture – new scientific discoveries informing religious interpretation, and familiar religious narratives being used to discuss science.

Secondly, and perhaps more importantly . . . they're both complete bollocks.

Neither Flammarion's toxic prediction nor Heinman's blood sacrifice were real. Instead, they were inventions of the American press – apocalypse myths that have still been repeated over and over in the decades since.

These examples show how our cultural ideas about the apocalypse aren't just influenced by fiction – or at least, not just by fiction that *admits* it's fiction. The world of non-fiction also moulds itself into shapes that are often better at tickling our brain's narrative centres than they are at accurately representing reality. They help us see the two flip sides of our fascination with doomsday. We take our own apocalyptic speculations very seriously, and greedily feed them with overblown predictions of imminent catastrophe; at the same time, we also love stories about how everyone *else's* apocalyptic beliefs are batshit crazy.

In reality, Flammarion had never claimed that the comet's tail would poison the Earth. In fact he'd repeatedly said the exact opposite, insisting that even if the planet did pass through the comet's tail, our atmosphere would protect us. He hadn't just said that in response to Halley's Comet: it's even the conclusion of his apocalyptic novel *La Fin du Monde*. The press had simply quoted his description of the scenario he was debunking and ignored his conclusion.

By the time the *New York Times* ran its story in February 1910, Flammarion had actually been fighting a largely hopeless battle to get his true views out for months, having been initially misquoted the previous year. Rather than correcting themselves, the press instead gleefully went round asking other scientists what they thought of Flammarion's 'prediction', then running 'Boffins Slam Comet Weirdo'-style headlines when Flammarion's colleagues inevitably expressed scepticism about the predictions wrongly attributed to him.

But if Flammarion was the victim of twisted half-truths and missing context, the ritual sacrifice in Oklahoma was invented from whole cloth. There was no such person as

Henry Heinman, no Jane Warfield, and no chanting circle of Select Followers. Aline, Oklahoma, is a real place, at least, although it's not in Dewey County and the local sheriff wasn't called Hughes. Its local newspaper, the *Aline Chronoscope*, never mentioned the incident, which is odd given that there wasn't exactly a glut of news in the tiny town competing for column inches.

Indeed most Oklahoma newspapers passed on the story, which is a bit of a tell, given that it was printed in newspapers across the country after being sent out on the Associated Press wire service. Even more notably, one of the few local outlets that did run the AP copy – the *Cherokee Republican*, based in the same county as Aline – prefaced it with a sceptical paragraph noting that the tale sounded 'suspiciously like Ed Marchant'. He was the founder of the *Aline Chronoscope*, and had sold the paper a few years earlier. It's possible, we might speculate, that Mr Marchant was simply finding ways to amuse himself in his retirement.

These two trends in our non-fiction depiction of apocalypse – hyped-up warnings of imminent doom, and dubious reports of other people's apocalyptic lunacy – are far from limited to the 1910 comet mania. Once you start looking for them, you begin to see them all over the place.

The modern era of online journalism – with its collapsing business models and desperate hunger for clicks, any clicks – is bad in a lot of ways. But the Pavlovian feedback loop between eyeballs and content does at least give us some insight into what people are actually interested in. And we can deduce from the preponderance of overblown stories about imminent catastrophe that people are really, *really* into them. Everyone loves a doomscroll. The exact nature of the apocalyptic threat varies with the newspaper's political preferences (climate change, disease, multiculturalism, kids these days with their phones); the degree of sensationalism involved can range from 'slightly exaggerated' to 'completely made up'. But the message is broadly the same: EVERYBODY PANIC.

As an example, let us examine the longstanding love affair between the *Daily Express* and asteroids.

For many years now, the *Express* has been obsessively hyping up every rock in the sky as a potential planet-killer. (If you're not familiar with the *Express*, it's a low-rent British tabloid; think the *Daily Mail* but without the restraint and self-respect.) It doesn't especially matter if they're not actually going to hit us – which they never are – because close passes, wild hypotheticals, and occasionally the prophecies of Nostradamus will be deployed to talk up the doomsday potential.

'Apocalypse warning as "God of chaos" asteroid to pass "exceptionally close" to Earth' reads one recent headline (there was no apocalypse warning). 'Exact date deadly asteroid could hit Earth as scientists warn "we're not prepared"' reads another (there is no date; it's about a training exercise involving a fictional scenario). The wild-eyed tone of the stories has stayed the same over many years, although in fairness the frequency has calmed down a bit lately from its frantic peak in previous years. As the Futurism website noted in late 2019, the *Express* had published no fewer than eighty-seven killer asteroid stories in the previous month. 'It's rare for a day to go by,' they observed, 'without the newspaper warning, or heavily implying, that a deadly space rock is about to annihilate civilization.'

If we are hungry for tales of impending doom, we also love to mock those who believe a little bit too fervently. And for decades, the news media have obligingly played up to this, scouring the world for fringe tales of apocalyptic expectation – from eccentric preachers and oddball sects in the nineteenth century to the more organised preppers and doomsday cults of the late twentieth.

These aren't necessarily entirely fictional, like the tale of the Select Followers and their blood sacrifice – although they're often vague enough on the details that it's hard to be sure, and they frequently read as a little *too* good to be entirely unembellished. But there's a whiff of formula. The choice to elevate small, weird, local dramas to global attention, the focus on the most extreme or baroque details, the tone of wry amusement – they're stories that identify their subjects as the butt of a particularly long-running joke.

'Simple-Minded Canadian Farmers Expecting the End of the World Next Sunday' reads a headline in the *New York Times* from 15 June 1881. It reports that in Ontario, these addle-brained sons of the soil were abandoning their fields in the face of the world being imminently burned up. 'I says to a nabor friend o'mine a week agone, waal, if the world's to come to a hend on the 19th o'June, I beant agoin' to work no more,' the report quotes one farmer as saying. Did he actually say that? Did he say it in *that accent*? Who knows. Pressed on concerns that their produce would spoil as they neglected their duties, the unnamed farmer supposedly asserts that 'hif the hearth hends hon the 19th, we woant want no pertaters'.

Yeah, it turns out that the *Times'* fondness for condescending yokel safaris did not originate in the midwestern diners of the 2016 election.

Pertaters aside, the story is not alone – as a quick bimble through just the *NYT*'s archive shows. From December 1901: reports of a sect in Germany who – interpreting a stopped clock in their house as a sign of the Last Judgement – killed one of their members and then danced naked through the streets of their village. October 1902: the story of a new end-times cult in Russia that believed modern technology was the cause of an imminent 'universal calamity', proclaiming that 'in every gramophone sit several little devils and one large devil on top'. At times, there's the feeling of the media coverage eating itself: in September 1909, one member of a doomsday movement in Massachusetts is said to have taken his own life in advance of the final hour, dying with his pockets 'filled with newspaper clippings relating to predictions by members of the Church'.

Again, it's not that these stories are necessarily untrue, or the public's interest in them misplaced. (Look, I'm writing a book about this, and you're reading it: you'll be relieved to know that freaky apocalyptic beliefs are in fact a real and fascinating thing. The rest of the book would be extremely dull otherwise.) 'World to continue as before' is simply not as big a story as 'World to end'. 'Church holds raffle' doesn't quite match up to 'Church burns all their clothes in preparation for rapture'.

But like everything that our taste for sensation induces the media to hype up – gruesome crimes, inventively depraved scandals, hardscrabble underdogs triumphing against the odds – it's really the frequency with which they appear, relative to all the other stuff in the world, that can distort our understanding. The thirst for novelty elevates rare occurrences into defining ones, while the desire to fit events into familiar narratives flattens out all specificity.

And this bleeds over from the world of news into the world of fiction. We have expectations of what apocalypticism should look like, cherry-picked from reality, that are deeply embedded in our pop culture. The tousle-haired prophet who turns out to be right this time; the bunker-dwelling paranoiacs who were the only ones prepared for the cataclysm; the white-robed chanters waiting serenely for redemption as the world burns around them. These have reached the level of shorthand: the guy standing with a sign that reads 'The end of the world is nigh' is an almost universal symbol for 'nutter'.

This all leaves the question: why?

To an extent, the waves of apocalypticism in art are simply influenced by the technology of production and distribution. Every time we get better at depicting things, or at getting those depictions in front of larger audiences, someone has the bright idea of using this to show people what it would look like if the world exploded. As a subject, it's pretty high up the list of things we try to depict as soon as we have a new medium to play with, somewhere just after 'hot naked people'.

Dürer's woodcuts were a product of mastering innovative new techniques, and could reach audiences across Europe through the reproductive power of print. Without the growth of the printing press, Wigglesworth's judgemental doggerel could never have become a cultural phenomenon in seventeenth-century New England. And the feature film was only a few years old before someone made one about the apocalypse.

This was the hugely popular 1916 Danish film *Verdens Undergang* ('The End of the World'), in which – once again – a passing comet causes havoc. Its special effects were cutting edge for the time. Admittedly, they mostly consisted of collapsing sets and people throwing fireworks in front of the camera, but even the jaded modern viewer can see how it would have been impressive to contemporary audiences. The film was obviously influenced by the Halley's Comet panic of a few years earlier, but its scenes of destruction feel particularly resonant given it was produced while Europe was still deep in the grip of the Great War.

So in some ways, our late glut of doom is simply a product of technology – the moving image is our dominant cultural form, and around thirty years ago it suddenly got much better at depicting a wide range of catastrophes.

What changed in the nineties was that the same 'melting tanks, flying bodies, crashing walls, awesome craters and fissures in the earth' that Sontag wrote about in the sixties could now be rendered with gasp-inducing photorealistic fidelity. Filmmakers no longer needed to simulate the end of the world by chucking fireworks around, or by having a guy in an unconvincing rubber suit jump up and down on model buildings. If you could imagine it, and had a big enough budget, you could put it on screen.

(It was probably James Cameron's 1991 *Terminator 2: Judgement Day* that lit the fuse. Its most eye-catching special effect may have been a shape-shifting quicksilver CGI cyborg, but it was the brief, wildly expensive dream sequence of a nuclear weapon destroying Los Angeles – a combination of traditional model work and CGI – that most clearly sparked the imaginations of fellow filmmakers.)

Beyond technology, there's also the economics of entertainment. Business models demand blockbusters. And as screenwriter Damon Lindelof bluntly put it a decade ago, 'Once you spend more than $100 million on a movie, you have to save the world.' The profusion of pop apocalypses is down to an escalatory arms race of dramatic stakes.

There's an impulse to always make the threats bigger, to show the audience something they haven't seen before. To quote Craig Mazin, the screenwriter of *Chernobyl* and *The Last of Us*: 'We are currently in a state of stakesflation in Hollywood, where everything gets upped. It's not enough to destroy a planet, now you must destroy the galaxy. No, now you have to destroy multiple galaxies. Now you have to destroy half of everything that is alive . . .'

Of course, these stories also provide an outlet for us to exorcise the anxieties of our age. Just as the Year Without a Summer turned the minds of some romantic poets to destruction, and the bloody mess of World War I inspired early Danish filmmakers, so the nuclear paranoia of the post-Hiroshima age triggered the movies Susan Sontag was so unimpressed by. The apocalypses we imagine may not be exactly those that we fear in real life – comparatively few apocalyptic tales of recent times have featured climate change as much more than a background detail – but you suspect it's what we're really talking about.

This metaphorical weight is why poets have often followed Byron to the well of apocalyptic imagery. Yeats used it to express the aftermath of war in 'The Second Coming' ('Things fall apart; the centre cannot hold / Mere anarchy is loosed upon the world'); Robert Frost teased out the emotional tenor of different dooms in 'Fire and Ice' ('Some say the world will end in fire / Some say in ice').

In literature too, its evocative power sees it sneak into unexpected places. When Dickens conjures the chaos of the age in the opening passages of *A Tale of Two Cities,* he references two apocalyptic prophets, promising the imminent 'swallowing up of London'. In Dostoevsky's *Crime and Punishment*, Raskolnikov's name straightforwardly refers to a schism, but it summons up the Raskolniki – the self-destructive Russian schismatics who burned themselves alive in anticipation of doomsday.

And of course, the apocalypse really works as a dramatic device because it provides the most extreme form of several fundamentals of the narrative art. A classic story structure involves disrupting your protagonist's life and forcing them to go on a journey. In shorthand, the dramatist needs to burn down their hero's house. Demolishing their planet to (for example) force them to hitchhike around the galaxy is just taking that to its logical conclusion.

The apocalypse also provides a dramatic sandbox for deconstructing society. It strips away all the constraints and rules and obligations of everyday life, and lets you see humanity in a raw state – whether you think that will show us in a positive or, as tends to be the case, a negative light. In the apocalypse, nobody needs to put the bins out, or obey traffic rules, or save for their pension. You can reimagine the world as you wish. This dismantling of society, in fact, is the same attraction that the end of days has held for apocalyptic social movements throughout the ages.

But perhaps most importantly, the thing the end times give us is, well, an *ending*. And the ending is essential to understanding a story. Without the ending, a story is just a sequence of events; with an ending, it has resonance and import. As Frank Kermode wrote in *The Sense of an Ending*, we crave 'fictions of beginnings and fictions of ends, fictions which unite beginning and end and endow the interval between them with meaning'.

What is true of story is also true of our lives. When we die, we want to know it meant something, and the same is true of the world as a whole. Realistically, we know we don't live at the beginning of history; and it is very unlikely that we actually live during the climax of history. But in that case, how can we know what all this means? How can history be an unsatisfying tale without a conclusion, like a whodunnit with the final pages ripped out? And so we are people of the second act, imagining ourselves a finale.

Which leads us to perhaps the overriding reason we are so attracted to the apocalypse story: we are a species that is addicted to narrative. We desperately want our lives to have a satisfying dramatic arc; we want the world around us to be meaningful. It's the same reason we picture ourselves as the protagonists of our own lives; it's why we imagine shadowy conspiracies controlling the world around us; it's why we convince ourselves that we're about to hit a lucky streak at the roulette table. It's how politicians ask for our votes and how con artists relieve us of our savings.

The apocalypse isn't just a good story. It is, very literally, the ultimate story.

It's also a story that's been present in culture for many thousands of years; its form is as familiar to us as a comfy pair of narrative trousers. It hasn't just been a constant narrative presence, it's also shaped our expectations of what a story should even look like. This means that to properly understand the end, we need to start at the beginning.

It's time to meet the man who invented the apocalypse.

3.

The Beginning of the End

We don't know much about the man who invented the apocalypse. Not with any certainty, at least. We don't know when he lived, with different estimates that span a thousand years. We don't know where he lived – we've got the general region, but it's a pretty big region. We don't know what really inspired him to invent the apocalypse, or what the impact of his invention was in his lifetime. We can't even be entirely sure he was one single person at all. Also, in the interests of transparency, there remains a significant amount of debate about whether he did in fact invent the apocalypse.

History is fun like that.

But look, here's what we have: this man's name has come down to us as Zoroaster, sometimes written as Zarathustra. He lived somewhere in the greater Iranian world – most likely to the east, somewhere in the thousand-mile stretch between the Caspian Sea and the Hindu Kush, but possibly somewhere else. He lived somewhere between 3,500 and 2,500 years ago, ish. He apparently trained to be a priest of the ancient Iranian religion – a belief system that, like most religions of the time, featured a multitude of deities, each with its own domain.

Everything changed for Zoroaster, and ultimately the world, after he had a vision at the age of thirty that showed him the true form of existence. It was a grandiose vision: rather than the messy interpersonal dramas of a squabbling pantheon, the story of the world was that of an epic struggle between a singular force of Good and a mirrored force of Evil. That story would culminate in an ultimate battle between the opposing forces of light and darkness; when the light triumphed, as it surely would, then the world's tale would be done, and the chosen few would live on in a blissful eternity with their creator.

The idea of the apocalypse is such a pervasive one in our minds that it feels weird to think about someone coming up with it. It's like the first person to have the idea of heaven, or vampires, or shaking hands. Obviously *somebody* must have been the first ever; even if it didn't emerge fully formed, even if it adapted something that came before, there's got to be a point, somewhere, that you could theoretically look at and go 'Yep, that's a vampire', where before there never was a vampire. But what was that like? Did it feel meaningful in the moment? Did anybody even notice that the world had subtly shifted?

That feeling's only magnified by the fact that Zoroaster's cosmology doesn't just introduce the end of the world as a coherent concept, but also stands as one of the first clear expressions of dualism – the opposing forces of light and darkness, good and evil – in theological history. That's such a basic, central concept in both religion and storytelling as a whole that it's baffling to think of a world where it wasn't a fundamental, dominant narrative. I mean, it's *Star Wars*, for heaven's sake.

But as we've already said, these ideas are neither eternal nor universal, even today. While most major world religions now have some version of an apocalypse story – depending on how exactly you define 'religion', and indeed 'most' – this was not always the case. Many belief systems have toddled along perfectly happily without ever delving into these issues. The apocalypse – the event, but also the idea – is not inevitable.

And it was a *religious* idea. In our modern age, we're beset with secular apocalypses – while it's possible to interpret, say, impending nuclear Armageddon as the wrath of a vengeful God, the deity isn't necessary for the story. We're entirely capable of wiping ourselves out all on our own, thank you very much, with no supernatural intervention required. But the idea of the apocalypse is one that is rooted very firmly in religious history.

This shouldn't be a surprise, of course. For much of human history, there was no clear separation between what we'd now term Church and state. Religion was law was politics; both as a pragmatic matter, with great power residing in those who commanded the spiritual realm, but also as an intellectual issue. There was no way to disentangle religious questions from the messy daily business of power and governance and justice – they were effectively one and the same.

To talk about the apocalypse, therefore, we need to understand its religious aspect – because the history of the apocalypse idea is overwhelmingly a religious one, and even when the idea crossed over into the secular realm, its form and character were heavily informed by its religious origins. These chapters, therefore, are a whistle-stop tour of apocalyptic religion – what it says, where it came from, how it developed, and why it became so pervasive.

An apocalypse is a revelation. Literally. The word is from the ancient Greek *apokalypsis*, which means, you've guessed it, 'revelation'. The biblical Book of Revelation – which was written in Greek – is not just one of the more famous apocalypses in history, it lends its name to the whole genre.

That last word is kind of important. Throughout this book, we'll be using the word 'apocalypse' in the common way we use it today – as something that means an *event*, a synonym for any kind of civilisation-threatening catastrophe. But in the world of religious scholars, it's used quite differently. Apocalypse isn't a thing that happens, it's a *literary genre*. It's like 'romance', or 'thriller', or 'gay werewolf erotica'. So when we're talking about, say, *The Apocalypse of Pseudo-Methodius*, that doesn't mean 'the world-ending events envisaged by Pseudo-Methodius'. Instead, it's talking about what shelf it would have been put on in the Middle Ages equivalent of WHSmith.

And like any literary genre, apocalypses have tropes – all the little tics of topic and style and structure that let you file a work under a particular genre in the first place. They're the things that distinguish popular history books from epic fantasy novels, and cosy English village murder mysteries from . . . well, gay werewolf erotica.

The most obvious of these apocalypse tropes is where we came in: they're revelations. Some fundamental truths about the nature of the world have been revealed to the author. They are mystical, and they're prophetic, not just revealing the shape of the world as it is, but also what is to come. They are often concerned with the grand sweep of history, an inevitable progression from one age to the next. Their style is often allusive, marrying occasional specifics with wild and metaphorical imagery.

And quite a lot of the time, their authorship is ambiguous – with the text attributed to a great historical figure who may well have had nothing to do with it. (Hence *The Apocalypse of Pseudo-Methodius*, a late seventh-century text that was absolutely not written by the influential fourth-century bishop Methodius, to whom it was falsely attributed.)

The specific genre of apocalyptic literature is heavily focused in the Jewish and Christian traditions (with some of it later incorporated into Islam). But many of the tropes are echoed in texts from outside the Abrahamic faiths. Moreover, these tropes extend beyond authorial style and literary contexts into the kind of stories they tell. While there are important differences between them, there are nonetheless a series of themes and characters and plot points that recur time and again.

If you were to sketch out this sort of universal apocalypse story, what would it look like? Let's have a go:

> *It would tell us that history is divided into distinct ages, the progression of which is knowable and predictable. These ages differ in how happy human existence is, and – relatedly – in how closely the people of the age stick to the path of moral righteousness. Once (the story will usually go) there was a golden age, in which people were pure and the land was a place of peace and plenty.*
>
> *But the story of these ages has been a story of decline, as with each age humanity sinks ever deeper into corruption and wickedness. Our current age is either the final age, or perhaps*

the penultimate age. Either way, it marks a new low point in humanity's moral degradation, one in which licentiousness, cruelty and deceit flourish.

This is a failing of people, for sure, but there are also dark forces at work. There is some embodiment of evil, an Adversary, which in past times was held at bay by the force of good, but has since been insinuating its way into the world. It is now stronger than ever. A great conflict between the forces of good and the forces of evil is inevitable.

The coming of this conflagration will be marked by strange and fearful signs. Inexplicable and extreme weather will become general; the sun will change colour and the earth will shake; cataclysms and tragedies will abound. Strife will erupt – threats of invasion and conquest will loom on the horizon, while the bonds of civil life will fray, with neighbours pitted against one another, and brother shedding the blood of brother. The natural order of things will be inverted; the profane will sit in judgement of the righteous, and the weak will dominate the strong.

Amidst this upheaval, a great figure will arise. They will be a hero to lead the armies of goodness in the coming war; they will be a teacher who shows the way of truth and purity. They may well be the long-prophesied return of a great figure from the past, who for a long time was thought dead, or exiled, or gone beyond this world; they may be a new aspect of this legendary figure, changed and yet the same, or they may be a descendant of that figure.

But this hero will be opposed. They will have a dark mirror: a figure of great deceit and malignancy who will work against them; a trickster spreading lies and gathering together all those who oppose or stray from the path of righteousness into a coalition of chaos. Those who follow the true way will be outnumbered, and beset on all sides by calumny, temptation, injustice and oppression.

The time of woe before the final battle will be a profound trial for those who believe in the true way.

Nonetheless, these forces will eventually meet in the great battle that determines the fate of the world. And despite being outmatched, the forces of good will prevail. The dead shall arise, and the resurrected righteous of the past age will join forces with the living, and they shall celebrate their ultimate victory.

At the moment of triumph, all the living and the dead will be judged, and those who followed the true path will be joined together with the all-powerful force of light who guided them on their journey and assured their victory. Together they will enter the world beyond, and in that world there will be no strife, no pain, and no want, but a blissful existence of peace, harmony and plenty.

Not every apocalypse story fits this template; almost all differ from it in *some* respect. Maybe the dead are not resurrected at the final moment. Maybe the hero is not opposed by a single evil figure, but by many; maybe there is more than one hero. Maybe the ages are not a universal story of decline: sometimes humanity is becoming more pure with every age; sometimes the moral degradation happens only at the end of the age, and the new age signals a moral rebirth. Maybe the end is not the end, but simply the beginning of a new cycle, and the whole story will start once more.

Nonetheless, if you lay all the apocalypses on top of one another and squint at them, the blurry shape that emerges looks *something* like the story we've told here.

It's historical: dividing time into discrete categories, with each age having distinct characteristics. It explains where we are and how we got here, and places our small local concerns and troubles into an epic narrative.

But it's also prophetic, promising a road map to the future. It ties together suffering with hope in an emotionally thrilling way – an explanation of current tribulations, a prediction of worse to come, but with the promise of redemption for those courageous enough to stay on the path, and judgement for those who do not. It offers certainty, although a strange kind of certainty: in many tellings, the apocalypse is somehow both inevitable and contingent - it will assuredly happen, and yet we must work to bring it about. This is logically quirky, but again, emotionally resonant.

It's fundamentally a moral story: there is good and evil in the world, and the arc of its history is intimately connected with right and wrong ways to live. The progress of the ages is one of moral change; disaster and destruction are tied to the moral failings of people; everything will culminate in an all-encompassing judgement, and only the morally pure have something to hope for amidst the horrors.

It speaks of an end, but not an end. It's easy to assume that tales of the end of the world are about oblivion and finality – I mean, duh – but in fact almost all such narratives envisage *something* continuing after the end. We seem to struggle to imagine true non-existence; the apocalyptic almost always comes with a 'post-'. Religions with cyclical notions of time start the tale over again, but even those with linear timelines – one-and-done stories where the narrative wraps up tidily – still imagine some kind of epilogue, a world beyond that the righteous can inherit. The end of the world is the end of *our* world; these are stories about change. Change so profound it upends all we know and dissipates all current concerns, but change nonetheless.

And crucially, the tale is – to use the term that developed

in the Jewish tradition – messianic. It predicts a great saviour who will emerge, a hero who will lead the people into the new world. Of course, you could easily tell an apocalypse story without a messiah – some do – but this connection between the apocalypse tale and the personification of hope into a single charismatic individual would become a key reason why it spread. It made it easy to hang social or political hopes on to it; much of the history of the apocalypse is a history of those who claimed messiah status, or had it claimed for them.

And this is a story that, in many of its key moments, is largely present in the apocalypse that Zoroaster imagined.

Zoroastrianism – the religion Zoroaster founded – still exists today, with its largest communities in Iran and India. It's in the running for the oldest still-practised religion in the world (as we'll see, the question of dating its origins is a thorny one; aspects of Hinduism or Judaism may predate it.)

For all that it introduced a welter of new concepts into the religious world, Zoroaster did not create his dualist cosmology entirely from whole cloth. Ahura Mazda, the Lord of Wisdom and the supreme deity of Zoroastrianism, was probably a figure in the ancient Iranian pantheon that Zoroaster had turned away from. But in the new religion, he was promoted above all other deities, the creator of things who was not created himself. The other deities of the pantheon did not fade entirely, but remained as lesser spirits – other *ahuras* through whom Ahura Mazda worked; malign *daevas* seeking undeserved worship.

Ahura Mazda is supreme, but not all-powerful, and there is a rival force working against him – Angra Mainyu, the adversary, who spreads evil in the world.

There are four ages to the world, each three thousand years

long. In the first, before humanity existed, Ahura Mazda held Angra Mainyu in captivity, preventing his evil from spreading. But he escaped, and began to poison the world. They struck a bargain: Ahura Mazda would rule the second age, while Angra Mainyu would rule the third. It was under his rule in the second age that Ahura Mazda created people; in the third, Angra Mainyu afflicted creation with all manner of woes, and worked to tempt Ahura Mazda's creations from the righteous path.

It was at the end of this rotten third age that Zoroaster placed himself. He was the herald and prophet of the fourth age, in which – their truce ended – Ahura Mazda and Angra Mainyu would fight for the future of creation. This would be a dire age; Angra Mainyu would have the upper hand, and corruption and wickedness would be everywhere in the world. But once every thousand years, a new figure would arise: a descendant of Zoroaster himself, who would counter Angra Mainyu's deceits and prepare humanity for the final conflict that would mark the end of the fourth age. In this great and terrible battle, the dead would be resurrected, the mountains of the Earth levelled, and eventually fire would consume everything, destroying Angra Mainyu. The chapters of history would come to a close; the souls of the righteous would be joined with Ahura Mazda, and would live on joyously in eternity.

There are two things worth noting here. One is that the apocalypse of Zoroaster feels deeply familiar, even if you've never heard it before. It has the shape of a story we all know; you can see exactly why people think it may have been the origin of our universal apocalypse tale.

The other is that, if a rough dating of Zoroaster to around

three thousand years ago is accurate, then it's supposed to happen any day now.

That's a big 'if', of course.

One of the problems with the study of ancient religion is that there's a lot of piecing together tiny fragments of evidence with very little certainty about what they mean.

After all, these were primarily oral traditions – Zoroaster's words would have been learned and repeated, passed down the generations in the memories of priests. Most of what people thought never got written down; most of what got written down did not survive into our day; and what scraps did survive must be interpreted through our own assumptions and biases.

A particular problem is that by the time people did get round to writing things down, they were often living in a very different world to that in which in which the beliefs had originated. This makes it tricky to tell what's an accurate record of ancient beliefs, and what's been given a little polish by a later scribe trying to zhuzh it up a bit.

It gets worse. A lot of the time, the people writing stuff down weren't actually the ones who believed the thing itself, but outsiders. Indeed, they were often very keen to tell these new people they'd just met about their *own* beliefs, which were much better beliefs, the kind of beliefs that a sensible person who did not want to get burned alive might be wise to adopt. As such, it's hard to disentangle the truth from what the authors wanted to be true.

Religious ideas rarely develop in a bubble. They are influenced by other beliefs around them at the time; they get adjusted for reasons of cultural shifts and political expediency. Those spreading the word may tweak their sermons to appeal to new audiences; those who convert, whether by choice or force, may bring concepts over from their former religions. This is especially notable in apocalypticism, where new movements are often explicitly syncretic, merging worldviews from two or more belief systems – think of Hong Xiuquan from the first chapter, with his mishmash of Western and Eastern traditions.

Put together, this all means that the whole enterprise is riddled with ambiguity and assumptions. Put another way, you're about to get very bored of phrases like 'the earliest surviving texts we have date to the eleventh century, but the belief likely dates to much earlier'.

Was Zoroastrianism truly the origin of the apocalypse idea? The answer to that question really comes down to dates. The earliest surviving texts we have of Zoroastrianism date to the eleventh century. Placing the origin of the beliefs they describe at least 1,500 years earlier is possible for a couple of reasons – but the details get gnarly very quickly.

First, there are contemporaneous accounts of the religion from other, older sources. Notably, Plutarch – the Greek philosopher and historian writing in the first century CE – describes the Zoroastrian belief system and its apocalyptic themes in some detail. Plutarch himself is cribbing from an earlier Greek historian, Theopompus of Chios, who wrote in the fourth century BCE; not enough of Theopompus's work survives to be sure *exactly* what he said, but enough later Greek writers cite his work in consistent ways that we can be pretty confident he was describing Zoroastrianism, eschatology and all, as an established religion with firm traditions by the mid-300s BCE.

There's also archaeological evidence, carvings and

inscriptions that survive longer than stuff written on flimsier materials. The Iranian Achaemenid Empire, founded by Cyrus the Great in 550 BCE, certainly worshipped Ahura Mazda. This doesn't necessarily make them Zoroastrians – Ahura Mazda may have been part of the pre-existing Iranian pantheon, remember – but it's certainly suggestive.

And then there's the language in which many of the texts are written – Avestan, a tongue long since departed from the world. Much like the Latin Mass, the religion preserved a language for millennia after people stopped speaking it in their daily lives.

Taken together, this gives an absolute latest date for the development of Zoroastrianism somewhere around the fourth century BCE, when Theopompus was writing and Avestan was beginning to fade out of everyday speech. A more likely date is somewhere earlier in the Achaemenid era, possibly in the sixth century BCE. However, some linguistic analyses of the Avestan language used suggest an even earlier date, predating the Achaemenids – somewhere around 1000 BCE, or possibly even earlier.

This matters for the question of the apocalypse's origins, because Zoroastrianism was not the only religion with intriguing new ideas during these centuries. To the east in the urbanising Indian world, the old religions of the Indo-Aryan peoples were being synthesised into early Hinduism, which would speak of history divided into ages and cycles of destruction and rebirth. To the west in the Levant, polytheistic Yahwism was starting its transformation into monotheistic Judaism, with its interventionist God who would rain terror on wrongdoers.

And in that transformation, the seeds of doomsday were

also stirring. The Book of Amos, a prophetic Hebrew work from the eighth century BCE, speaks of the 'Day of the Lord', when Yahweh would join battle against Israel's enemies and judge the impure. This is not quite an apocalypse – it's a strictly local affair – but it's certainly got an apocalyptic vibe, and would influence later works.

The great formative event in early Judaism was the period of Babylonian exile, between the 580s and 539 BCE. The Judeans had been defeated by the latest and last Babylonian empire; their temple lay in ruins, and many of them were forced to live as captives in Babylon.

This time of deep trauma marked a turn towards the apocalyptic that would only grow in early Judaism over the following centuries. Their world would have felt like it had already ended; it's unsurprising that from it came both a sense of rolling crisis, and a yearning for enemies vanquished and a world remade. The Book of Ezekiel – ascribed to a priest living as a captive in Babylon, although (as usual) likely polished up by subsequent authors – stands as perhaps the first work in the Hebrew canon that has clearly apocalyptic elements, with its prophecies of dry bones brought back to life, mountains overturned, and fire and brimstone raining upon the enemies of Israel. Most of it was likely written during the exile itself; it's possible that the later verses, which contain the apocalyptic material, may have been added later.

The Jewish exile was only ended when an outside force defeated the Babylonians, liberated the Judeans and allowed them to return to their homelands. That force? The Achaemenid Empire of Cyrus the Great.

You can see immediately that there are two stories it's possible to tell from this. (Okay, three.) The first is: if you take the earlier dates for the origin of Zoroastrianism, and accept that Ezekiel's apocalyptic sections were later additions, then the Judeans may have been influenced by the beliefs of their liberators – integrating the structure of Zoroaster's dualistic end times into their burgeoning monotheism, a structure that both explained their suffering and promised eventual salvation. The second (if you take a later date for Zoroaster) is that perhaps the influence flowed the other way. Apocalypticism developed organically in Judaism, and maybe inspired a disillusioned priest of the old Iranian pantheon to see the world anew – a vision that rapidly became popular in a new and expanding empire, thanks to its ability to place the Achaemenids as righteous agents of a powerful god in the ultimate historical narrative.

The third option is that it's all a coincidence and they came up with roughly the same story independently, because it's a good tale that people enjoy.

I lean towards the first explanation, but there remain strong arguments for the other two. History is messy as hell, so whatever the truth is, it's unlikely to be anywhere near as neat as a brief summary like this could convey. Ideas flow easily, and influence in any age is rarely a single arrow pointing in one direction: instead it's a criss-crossing lattice of thoughts shared, borrowed and disputed, with everybody in it both influencing and being influenced.

But either way, what we can be sure of is that by around 2,400 years ago, the idea of the apocalypse was live in the world. And from there, it would blossom and spread, morphing into new forms and finding new places in diverse societies. The end had firmly begun.

4.

For Those About to Ragnarök, We Salute You

Nothing is ever entirely new, of course.

There are plenty of beliefs older than Zoroaster's apocalypse tale that, while they may not have quite the same narrative beats, do sound oddly familiar.

Many ancient religions included mythologies that resonate with the idea of the world's destruction. Most obviously, there's the Great Flood myth, present in many ancient belief systems – such as those in the Mesopotamian *Epic of Atrahasis* and *Epic of Gilgamesh*. (Basic plot: a god gets annoyed by humans and plans to destroy them; another god betrays the secret and tells one chosen human how to survive; the flood is really bad but our hero makes it through; humanity survives.)

There are also Great Battle myths, in which powerful supernatural forces clash and bring great destruction, but a righteous figure eventually triumphs.

The main thing that distinguishes these kinds of apocalyptic tales from the end-times stories we're familiar with is that they're intended as histories, not prophecies. They've already happened; there's not much suggestion that they're especially likely to happen again, even if the possibility can't be ruled out. The purpose of the stories is to emphasise continuity, not culmination. Indeed, many of them are effectively creation stories: this is how the world we know came to be, not how it will end.

Of course, there are also plenty of actual prophecies in ancient religions too. And plenty of them are prophesying really awful things that will, at some point, happen. For example, there are lots of ancient Egyptian texts that predict disasters – drought, plague, infertility, violence. There's a clear apocalyptic quality to such prophecies – and yet, none of them seem especially *ultimate* in nature. They're not the end of the world, they're just bad stuff you should watch out for.

There is one intriguing moment in ancient Egyptian lore that suggests a bit more than that. In one of the 'Coffin Texts' (as in, texts written on coffins), Atum, a primordial god who gave rise to the other deities in the pantheon, says that one day he will destroy his creation and that 'the earth shall return to the Abyss, to the surging flood, as in its original state'. Which is pretty straightforwardly apocalyptic! But as with the epic myths of historic destruction or battle, again the intention seems to be emphasising continuity (he's mostly explaining that Osiris will survive it). And more to the point, the ancient Egyptians don't seem to have made a particularly big deal of it. Ancient Egyptian religion was heavily focused on *personal* eschatology, with its emphasis on life after death and making sure you've got nice stuff to take with you, but cosmic eschatology of the kind we're interested in doesn't seem to have played a notable part.

One of the most famous apocalypses is the Norse Ragnarök, which has been kept alive in popular culture long after belief in it ebbed from the world, thanks to various operas, block-buster movies and videogames. Its origins are murky – the earliest surviving texts are from the tenth century (wahey!), with the most complete texts from the thirteenth, well after the Christianisation of the Nordic lands was underway.

Ragnarök's descriptions in these texts bear many of the hallmarks of a syncretic tale – a new story grafted on to an old one. It's possible that the idea of the end of the world was only introduced as Christianity spread, the narrative applied to the Norse pantheon to nudge the population towards the twilight of their old gods. But there's enough to suggest that the Ragnarök narrative is far older than that, and was an independent part of Norse lore long before a bunch of pesky missionaries showed up. There are even intriguing echoes with Iranian and Indian tales that raise the possibility of much earlier cross-continental influences.

Ragnarök certainly has plenty of similarities with the standard apocalypse tale (Loki in the role of the adversary, demonic forces being released into the world, social upheaval, destructive weather and supernatural battles, the world perishing in fire and flood). But narratively, it's altogether a messier affair. It doesn't have the clean symbolic resonance of other apocalypses; the vibe is more that of showrunners on a long-running series trying to wrap up everybody's plotline by the finale.

It also lacks the clear moral message of those other apocalypses: it may be the end of the world, but it isn't really a Day of Judgement. Virtually the only life lesson you can take from it is: 'You should cut your nails.' (The nails of the dead will be used to build the boat *Naglfar* on which the forces of destruction will travel during Ragnarök, you see, so obviously it makes sense to limit the nail supply in order to stave things off for as long as possible.)

One similarity that Ragnarök does have with other apocalypses, however, is that it is not truly the end of all things. Some gods endure past the cataclysm; there are human survivors who will repopulate the cleansed world. It may be part of a cyclical tradition, in which the world is unmade and remade over and over. Indeed, while the word Ragnarök is usually interpreted as meaning 'the Fate of the Gods' or 'the Twilight of the Gods', there's even an argument that it can be interpreted as 'the Renewal of the Gods' – the source word *røkk* meaning 'dawn' as well as 'dusk'.

If that is the case, and Ragnarök is just one moment in a cycle, then it certainly wouldn't be alone.

Separated by an ocean from the lands where the apocalyptic tales we're familiar with were brewing, the indigenous peoples of the Americas also had their own stories of worlds ending and beginning in turn.

Attempts to discern exactly what those tales were, however, are afflicted by the same thorny problem as the Norse tales – only massively magnified. Many texts describing Native American beliefs were only written after Europeans arrived. And Christopher Columbus was far from the only voyager to the New World who was seized with apocalyptic certainties and intent on forcefully spreading them to the people of this shiny new continent. What was introduced and what was already there can be difficult to untangle.

Still, if there's one thing that most people know about indigenous American apocalyptic beliefs, it's this: the Maya predicted that the world would end on 21 December 2012.

Initially stemming from an accidental archaeological discovery in the 1960s – an ancient monument carelessly bulldozed back into prominence during the construction of a cement factory – this notion became an obsession in the English-language media as the date drew ever closer.

It filled newspaper columns and television broadcasts, and over a thousand books were published on the subject, melding the Maya prophecies with Western religious interpretations, New Age beliefs, environmental concerns or conspiracy theories – sometimes all at once. As we've seen, there was even a blockbuster Hollywood movie pegged to the date from Roland Emmerich. Inventively titled *2012*, it was released in 2009, presumably to avoid missing out on several years of DVD sales before the end came. In short, as the supposed end approached, the 2012 prophecy became something of a mania.

As such, you'll be astonished to learn that the whole thing was nonsense.

Where did the idea come from? Let's start with the bit that has a kernel of truth: it's almost certainly true that the Mesoamerican 'Long Count' calendar once used by the Maya really did tick over into a new *b'aktun* on 21 December that year.

A *b'aktun*, for the uninitiated, was a roughly four-hundred-year-long period, one of the longer time divisions in the multilayered Long Count calendar. One day was a *k'in*; twenty *k'in* made a *winal*, eighteen *winal* made a *tun* (360 days, so effectively a year), twenty *tun* made a *k'atun*, and twenty *k'atun* made a *b'aktun*. It might sound complicated, but just try explaining how *our* calendar works.

Matching up days between calendars is tricky, but the scholarly consensus is that the basic claim is almost certainly right: somewhere overnight on 20 December 2012, the date 12.19.19.17.19 turned into 13.0.0.0.0, and the thirteenth *b'aktun* ended. Which certainly *feels* significant, much as the millennium did. Tonight we're going to party like it's 12.19.19.

But why assume that the end of the thirteenth *b'aktun* marked the end of all things? That brings us back to the carving discovered in the Mexican state of Tabasco when they were trying to build a cement factory. Now known as 'Monument 6', it had an inscription that referenced the thirteenth *b'aktun*. One way to translate it might go as follows: 'The thirteenth one will end on 4 Ahau, the third of Uniiw. There will occur blackness and the descent of the Bolon Yookte' god to the red.'

This can – if you're of a certain mind, and culturally predisposed to expect certain narrative shapes – be interpreted as an apocalyptic prophecy. Respectable academics speculated that it *might* have apocalyptic meanings; less respectable academics were certain that it did; non-specialists and enthusiastic amateurs bulldozed right through any remaining caveats and built a cement factory of assumptions on top of it all.

If you want to be generous, speculation was understandable in the sixties, when academic knowledge of Maya glyphs and their cultural meanings was in its infancy. If you're less generously inclined, you might side with one author who, writing about the 2012 phenomenon, simply notes that early Maya scholarship 'included many crackpots'.

So. Here's an alternative, probably more accurate, translation of the Monument 6 text: 'The thirteenth one will end on 4 Ahau, the third of Uniiw. There will occur a seeing, the display of the god Bolon Yookte' in a great investiture.'

Suddenly, it doesn't read as an apocalyptic prophecy at all. If anything, it has celebratory overtones. Not only is it not about the end of the world, it's about *longevity*: our culture will still be here in over a thousand years' time for the Bolon Yookte' festivities.

In reality, when you look at Maya cultures more broadly, it's quite clear that the end of the thirteenth *b'aktun* harboured no apocalyptic concerns, and that a cycle of the Long Count was never intended to encompass all time from the beginning to the end of existence. There are Maya texts that discuss dates long after 2012 – one talks of events that aren't due until 4772 CE – and others that describe events that took place before the Long Count's year zero. The Long Count has many longer time periods available after the *b'aktun*; an *alawtun*, for example, is roughly 63 million years, which seems unnecessary if the world is only supposed to exist for a little over five thousand of those years. And, perhaps most notably, the Maya themselves don't seem to have attached any great long-term importance to the Long Count – just one of many calendars employed over their history – given that they'd stopped using it of their own accord centuries before Columbus ever touched American shores.

The 2012 'prophecy' was entirely the creation of Western enthusiasts who read their own culture into the ambiguities of old Maya texts. Some may have thought they were being complimentary, attributing to the Maya ancient wisdom and great foresight. Actual Maya begged to differ: the leader of one indigenous group condemned the exploitation of the date as 'lies' and 'folklore-for-profit'.

But if the Maya apocalypse was a figment of overactive imaginations, that leaves the question of what they – and other indigenous Americans – really did believe.

If you're looking for threads of apocalypse in Native American beliefs, there's certainly material there for you. There is no single indigenous American belief system, nor even a single one within any particular American cultures; they have varied widely across both space and time, becoming deeply localised, with individual communities and city-states evolving their own deities and legends. But still, among the many belief systems of the many peoples of the continent, there is one motif common across several cultures that seems to chime with apocalyptic thoughts: namely, that the world has been made and destroyed multiple times already.

This reflected a process of trial and error on the part of the gods – they were trying to create a people capable of worshipping them appropriately. Previous attempts at the world had fallen short. They'd try making people out of wood, for example, but find that these woody creations were underwhelming worshippers. And so the world would be crumpled up like a weak first draft, and remade: great cataclysms of flood or storm would bring about an end to the old age, and usher in the new. This was not an easy process. Sometimes a god would sacrifice themselves to enable the new world to live. Sacrifice from their people would be expected in return.

For the Nahuas of Central America – the peoples we often call Aztecs, after the Mexica empire that ruled many of them in the pre-European period – the world we lived in was the fifth. For the Hopi to the north, we were in the fourth world; for the Maya to the south and east, the third or fourth.

There was no guarantee that the current world would be

a final, lasting one. Indeed, it was expected that the process would eventually occur again. The great twelve-foot-wide Calendar Stone of the Mexica, carved shortly before the Spanish conquest of their empire, anticipated that the fifth world would end, this time with earthquakes providing the destructive impetus.

This all feels pretty unambiguously apocalyptic, in the form we're familiar with. If you're looking for an apocalyptic tradition that's very clearly not connected to the ideas that emerged in the Iranian, Indic and Levantine worlds – if you want to find evidence of an innate, hard-wired apocalypse story that emerges naturally from the human mind – then this is your Exhibit A.

There's even an oft-repeated tale that adds weight to the notion that our apocalypse narratives match up in ways that predate any civilisational contact. This is the story that the conquest of the Aztec Empire by the Spanish was helped along because Moctezuma – the ruler in Tenochtitlan, the city-state at the heart of the vast Aztec empire – was fatally hesitant in opposing the small band of conquistadors because he believed that Hernan Cortes might have been the returning god Quetzalcoatl.

In this telling, Quetzalcoatl has the role of the 'long-prophesied return of a great figure from the past': the deity whose self-sacrifice had ushered in the fifth world, now come back at that world's end to usher in the next. Moctezuma – the story goes – credulously believed that Cortes was the Aztec equivalent of the Second Coming; as a result, anticipating the apocalypse, he ended up welcoming a very different kind of apocalypse with open arms.

The story isn't entirely implausible. But, ehhh. There's

reason to be sceptical: almost all the accounts of it are Spanish in origin. The earliest reports of the meeting simply portray Moctezuma greeting Cortes as a dignitary – and they weaponise that courteous welcome to paint their subsequent conquest as legitimate, even consensual. The idea of Cortes being seen not just as a noble but as a *deity* doesn't get introduced until decades later; Cortes himself never mentions it. The few Nahuatl-language accounts that also portray Moctezuma as effectively surrendering the empire likewise don't reference the Quetzalcoatl aspect, which you'd probably expect them to. (They're also from decades after the conquest, their production was overseen by Spanish clerics, and they were sourced from Nahua communities who had political reasons to oppose Moctezuma.)

In short, this all sounds like the 2012 phenomenon: people imposing a narrative shape that's familiar to them on to a story that doesn't really fit it.

Because while there certainly are common themes between our apocalypse tale and the destruction and recreation of the world in Native American beliefs, the *meaning* of these stories seems quite different. The American world cycles were meant to emphasise continuity over cataclysm. They give no timescale for how long our current world is supposed to exist. The relationship between people and their gods is not one of fearsome moral judgement, but reads as a more reciprocal one of mutual sacrifice (even if the provision of that sacrifice on the human side was a fairly gruesome bit of business). It's a worldview that turns disasters into something expected and manageable rather than omens of terror. And it was probably politically useful to the powerful, in portraying elites as trustworthy stewards who could guide the people through times of change.

Where the apocalypses of the Eurasian world are often terminal, terrifying and morally urgent, the apocalypses of the Americas are as much about renewal as destruction, an expected and accepted part of life.

Any religion that has a cyclical view of history, almost by definition, probably has *some* kind of apocalypse baked in. Even if the fundamental point of the tale is that the world will be reborn, you can't entirely ignore the '. . . after it's been wiped clean' aspect. The notion of the world ending, or at least fundamentally changing, is inherent.

So it is with many of the major religions of Asia, several of which were also forming in the latter half of the first millennium BCE. As was the case to the west, these religions did not develop in closed-off bubbles, but grew up in a network of mutual influence, borrowed concepts and shared inspiration.

(It's worth noting that Asia is also the birthplace of the two most notable major religions to have largely avoided apocalypticism. Sikhism has no major apocalyptic component, and has generally avoided prophecy, too – the few works in the Sikh tradition that include prophetic or eschatological components tend to be controversial, and are often considered what might be termed 'non-canonical' literary works. Japanese Shinto, meanwhile, is so unconcerned with eschatology – either personal or cosmic – that most of its death rituals are borrowed from Buddhism, with the result that there's a saying: 'Born Shinto; die Buddhist'.)

In Hinduism – which grew from a synthesis of older beliefs that may stretch back to the ancient Indus Valley civilisation – history is divided into four ages, or *yugas*, which repeat in a vast cycle. With each of the four ages, humanity descends further into wickedness and greater troubles plague the world. We live in the final *yuga* of the four, Kali Yuga, a time of great corruption and suffering.

Kali Yuga will end when Kalki, the tenth and final avatar of the god Vishnu, appears on earth to lead an army of the few remaining true believers in a battle against the forces of darkness. With their victory, the earth will be cleansed in a great rain, and Krita Yuga – the purest and happiest of the *yugas* – will start up once more.

This obviously has the structure of the classic apocalypse story. But it is not the ultimate apocalypse; rather, it's merely a sort of interstitial mini-apocalypse. One thousand of these *yuga* cycles must occur to make up a *kalpa*, one single day in the existence of Brahma the creator. At the end of each *kalpa*, heaven and earth are truly destroyed, and existence sleeps in oblivion until the next *kalpa* dawns and the grand cycle begins once again. There are cycles within cycles, with echoes of the grand structure of birth, death and rebirth in each.

For Buddhism, too, history is divided into recurring *kalpas* that contain predictable cycles of destruction and renewal. There's no single practice of Buddhism, and as such there is no single eschatology. Some Buddhist practices place a lot of emphasis on these cycles of destruction and renewal; others, less so.

Still, there's a familiar shape to be found. On the cosmic scale, there is a grand cycle, in which the world is born, endures and finally dies in a cataclysm of fire or water, followed by a rebirth. Within that grand cycle, there are smaller cycles of decline and renewal in human affairs. Where lots of religions imagine themselves as underdogs – a small and dwindling band of believers standing against a corrupted world – Buddhism is unusual in that it goes way further: at the lowest point of the cycle, it predicts its teachings will have effectively vanished from the world entirely.

This period ends with a catastrophic war; the few who are left after this will gradually relearn the righteous path. This will culminate in the arrival of Maitreya, the next Buddha, who will lead humanity into a new age of enlightenment, before eventually the decay begins once more, because nothing good lasts forever.

Maitreya plays a sort of messianic saviour role – and like any messianic figure, history is littered with individuals who have claimed to be Maitreya – but it's not quite the same. They don't show up to lead a force of good in the great battle, but emerge on the opposite side of the cycle, when people have already started figuring things out for themselves. (In some Buddhist traditions a different figure, Prince Moonlight, plays the role of the great leader at the time of strife, but they're more of a stop-gap solution that delays the bad stuff a bit.)

Buddhism's eschatological parts probably cross-pollinated with Taoism, the blend of religion and philosophy that developed in China. Taoism's origins stretch back to the *Tao Te Ching* of the great philosopher Laozi, the earliest text of which is from the fourth century BCE. (In classic style, Laozi may or may not have existed, and parts of the *Tao Te Ching* may or may not have been added at a later date.)

Taoism too sees the world in terms of grand cycles of death and rebirth, with shorter cycles of moral decay, destruction and renewal within them. Plenty of Taoist literature is very specific on exactly how, at the point of maximum immorality, really horrible things will happen to wipe the earth clean of evil and leave only a few select individuals behind. (One says that 'floods will reach up to the heavens and, of human and beast, only one in 10,000 will be spared'.)

It also has a saviour figure in the form of Li Hong, a great leader who is prophesied to appear in the aftermath of these cataclysms. Throughout history, there have been an awful lot of people claiming to be Li Hong, or acting on his behalf. It's not surprising that the apocalyptic strands of both Taoism and Chinese Buddhism developed in the early centuries CE, when China was plagued by natural disasters and dynastic drama, and everyone would have been looking for a saviour – or keen to claim the mantle of saviour for themselves.

Eschatology has played a major role in Taoism throughout much of its history, but has a less significant role in Hinduism and most strands of Buddhism. Why? All the components would seem to be there: a prediction of cataclysm and decline, a messianic figure who will arise, destruction and rebirth to follow.

One answer is fairly simple: timing. The apocalypses of these religions will undoubtedly be significant – they're just not due to happen for ages.

The grand Buddhist cycles are predicted to last unimaginably long amounts of time; even the shorter ones between Buddhas take thousands of years. Each *kalpa* is supposed to have 1,000 Buddhas, and we're only on the fourth one of the current *kalpa*. And while there have been plenty of pseudo-Maitreyas, most traditions agree that the actual coming of Maitreya probably isn't expected for several millennia.

In Hinduism, meanwhile, the Kali Yuga in which we live is certainly the last age of the cycle – but it's due to last over four hundred thousand years. Given that we're only about five thousand years into it, this places the next mini apocalypse somewhere around the year 428,899 CE. It isn't something we need to immediately trouble ourselves over.

Taoism, too, often set its apocalyptic predictions on massive timescales – one text suggests a period of 999,999 years before the destruction of heaven and earth, while another suggests a relatively paltry 280,000 years – but its apocalyptic predictions remained relevant due to the fact that it was never specified exactly *when* those periods were supposed to have started, so it could always be due tomorrow.

Of course, none of this means that apocalyptic movements are unknown in Buddhism or Hinduism. It's always possible to reinterpret texts if you're really motivated, and Chinese Buddhism in particular has had some fairly apocalyptic eras. But in terms of relevance to everyday life, the end times are generally way down their theological pecking order. Where Native American beliefs didn't put a timescale on the length of the world at all, these religions tend to give it a specific timescale that renders it mostly irrelevant to the lives of people here and now.

For apocalypticism to become a central and active component of a religion, in other words, it helps to have just the right combination of specificity and vagueness.

If this brief tour of the world's ideas about the end of the world makes one thing clear, it's that simply imagining the world ending – or rather, *our* world ending – doesn't necessarily bring with it all the stuff we tend to associate with doomsday. We can picture our world being washed away without making that the driving force of our worldviews; the meaning of the end can vary. It may be an expected part of life, or a far distant event. We can picture an apocalypse without getting all apocalyptic about it.

But of course, some religious traditions insist the apocalypse should be very apocalyptic indeed. They give the end times a starring role in faith, making the end of the world central to understanding the world.

If the idea of the apocalypse maybe originated with Zoroaster, the literary genre of apocalypse was developed, experimented with and refined in the Jewish world. During the Second Temple period – between the return from Babylon in 539 BCE and the destruction of said temple in 70 CE – apocalypse became ever more central to some strands of Judaism. Sections of the Book of Enoch dating to the third century BCE contain apocalyptic passages, while the visionary Book of Daniel – the only fully fledged apocalypse in the Hebrew Bible and the template for much of what was to follow – was written in the second century BCE. (In classic literary apocalypse style, it was backdated to a prophet from the Babylonian exile.)

Some of these early apocalypses lacked one crucial element: messianism. The Hebrew word *māšīyaḥ* literally means one who has been anointed with oil, often signifying a king or a high priest. The earliest Jewish apocalypses don't have a messiah figure; other texts discuss messiahs without any apocalypse being attached. It's only from the second century BCE that the two get linked up, and apocalypses and messiahs start to go hand in hand.

This early Jewish apocalypticism was deeply influenced by real-world events. After the euphoric return from Babylon, things were – how to put this? – not always easy for the Jewish people. They came under the rule of multiple empires, and saw their culture modified and sometimes suppressed, to say nothing of internal disputes. Conquest from without and schism from within created an environment in which hopes of salvation and desire for a great leader to birth a golden age were ever present. Not all Jewish traditions at this time were into apocalypticism – some sects ignored the whole business, not believing that there was an immortal soul that could be judged – but it was a driving force for others.

The Jewish apocalypses of the Second Temple period set the template for the other faiths that would emerge in turn from the same tradition. The portents, the coming of a messiah, the Day of Judgement, the resurrection of the dead – they're all present in Christianity and Islam as well. Christianity, of course, believes the messiah has already arrived, and will return before the end times in the Second Coming, being opposed by an Antichrist. Islam, too, believes that the Prophet Jesus will return before the Last Hour, although his role is secondary to the Mahdi, the messianic descendant of Muhammad who will defeat the adversary, the Dajjal.

But if the Abrahamic faiths all share versions of the same apocalypse, then the emphasis they place on it is different. Mainstream Judaism largely turned away from messianic apocalypticism after the Second Temple period, the hopes it offered having been repeatedly crushed. The Day of Judgement is a central pillar of Islam, but the possibility of its imminent arrival is played down in most branches of the faith. Both religions include apocalyptic works in their holy books, but they're just one aspect among many.

The same can't really be said for Christianity.

Of all the religions, it is Christianity that places Judgement Day in the most exalted position. The Christian Bible contains the most apocalyptic sections of any holy book, with the Revelation of John of Patmos taking up the coveted closing slot. It's Christianity that has most consistently obsessed over the question of when the end times would come – and that has most consistently come up with the answer 'really soon'.

This should not be surprising, because it's been there from the start. Christianity began as an apocalyptic sect; its messiah preached imminent judgement and salvation. 'I say to you, there are some standing here who shall not taste death till they see the Son of Man coming in His kingdom,' Jesus tells his followers in Matthew 16:28. The end of the world and the beginning of the new were supposed to happen within a lifetime. It's not for nothing that one scholar has described apocalypticism as 'the mother of Christianity'.

This remains controversial to some; it's been the subject of much scholarly debate down the years. If most experts would now view Jesus as a messianic claimant and a preacher of the imminent judgement, there are still plenty who'll say that this is being over-literal: the correct reading is symbolic and metaphorical, with the promises of everlasting life being a strictly spiritual affair.

The counterpoint to this is a complex, interdisciplinary, deeply researched academic case that I'm going to sum up with the phrase: 'Ah, come on now.' The basic argument boils down to 'this thing is exactly what it looks like,' and attempts to retcon away the apocalypticism of Christ's message are dubious. A messianic new religion that promises imminent and immense change in the world and eternal life for its adherents? Which has a strongly dualistic worldview in which an interventionist God directs the course of history? Which explicitly tells its early followers that they will not see death, and asserts that 'the kingdom of God is at hand'? *Ah, come on now.*

Backing this up, we have not just the religious texts of

Christianity itself, but a bunch of suggestive contextual evidence about the vibes of the time. The Qumran manuscripts – commonly known as the Dead Sea Scrolls – are not early Christian texts (as was sometimes suggested), but rather come from a different Jewish sect of the time, probably the Essenes. They reveal a community in which apocalypticism was a central force, which expected to see a climactic battle in their lifetime, in which the outnumbered forces of good would defeat the massed ranks of evil, and the only survivors would inherit a utopian world.

And the Qumran community were hardly alone: as the region's Roman overlords imposed stricter and more direct rule, the age was littered with messianic claimants and upstart sects that channelled the desire for a message that God and history were truly on their side. The Jewish-Roman historian Josephus writes of numerous potential messiahs in this period: Jesus of Nazareth was but one of many.

This was the context in which the historical Jesus existed. A new messianic Jewish sect of the time being deeply apocalyptic is no weirder than a modern blockbuster having a big action set piece in its third act: it's more surprising if it's not there.

And whatever Christ himself may have said, the early Christian followers who came after him most definitely *thought* their religion was apocalyptic. The first few centuries of Christianity as a distinct religion are overwhelmingly apocalyptic in character, with the *apokalypsis* of John and its eventual place as the culmination of the Bible being just the most obvious example.

You can still argue that Jesus himself was something other than the leader of a doomsday cult. The Gospels were written retrospectively; you can make the case that Christianity's apocalyptic elements were simply post-Christ additions, a PR job by overenthusiastic advocates hopping on to the hot messianic trend of the time. Look, it wouldn't be the first time that apocalyptic extras were inserted into religious texts to suit the mood of the age.

This feels like a bit of a stretch – but it also doesn't really *matter.* At least, not for our purposes in this book. Did the historical Christ personally tell his flock that the end was near? Probably! But what's important is that over the next centuries the people who turned his religion into a history-shaping force with few equals most certainly believed that he had.

But how exactly did that force shape history? How does the end of the world drive people to radically change the world as it is? Enough of the theology: it's time to look at the politics of the apocalypse.

5.

Worldly Ends

'All men should be lawfully armed spiritually and bodily to fight against antichrist and his upholders.' So says a tract published in 1588, a commentary on the Book of Revelation that is unambiguous in its apocalyptic message. The harbinger of the final battle is already at work in the world, it says – and that battle will not be a purely spiritual one, but a fight of steel and flesh. The enemy is identified in equally blunt terms: 'The pope is antichrist,' it says, 'and popery is the loosing of Satan.'

The author of this warlike tract was not a fringe figure – no ranting street preacher or eccentric theologian. It was the twenty-two-year-old King James VI of Scotland.

A monarch since he was an infant, he'd only recently come into full control of a kingdom that was riven by religious schism, and found itself in a precarious dance of allegiance with the great powers of Europe. It was a time that called for a delicate hand on the tiller of state – and yet here was the young king urging his subjects to take up arms in preparation for Armageddon. 'That wintar,' the Presbyterian diarist James Melville wrote of that turbulent year, 'the King was occupied in commenting of the Apocalypse.' His tone suggests that he thinks the King might have been better served paying attention to more immediate matters.

Which prompts the question: why was the King so keen on doomsday? The end of the world, at first glance, doesn't seem like a *great* fit with the petty power struggles of simple mortals on this earth.

After all, if the lights are going off any day now, then does it really matter who's in charge? If anything, the game of thrones is a distraction from the existential crises facing humanity. Matters of dynasty or legacy would seem to have no relevance to an imminently departing world; those who imagine themselves immortalised by future historians have little to play for when there will shortly be neither historians nor future. Court gossip about who's up and who's down seems spectacularly irrelevant when we're all about to find out whether we are – in a very terminal sense – up or down.

But the idea that the apocalypse is disconnected from our worldly concerns is not really how things have played out.

Instead, for millennia, apocalyptic beliefs have frequently played a central role in the pragmatic, prosaic and political sphere of fights over power and influence.

They've been used to demonise or deify pretenders to the throne, and to rationalise crusades and colonialism. They have stoked repression, reform and revolt in equal measure. The end times have fuelled endeavours that fundamentally reshaped the world, and their predictions and prophecies were co-opted to justify and legitimise choices large and small whose effects we still live with today. The thunderclap of doomsday echoes loudly in a future that was never supposed to arrive.

Apocalyptic eschatology played a central role in power struggles between emperors and popes for centuries of European history. In sixteenth-century China, the interpretation of signs of the coming doom was a crucial component of power in the court. For the Aztec Empire, the ability to manage the transition to the next world – whenever it might arrive – was a central message in projecting imperial power. The English Civil War upended the constitutional order on the back of a wave of apocalyptic expectation. And the original texts of many apocalyptic traditions, from the Jewish Book of Daniel to the Christian Book of Revelation, were intimately concerned with contemporary politics and the fundamental questions of who ruled, and who should rule.

Still, the question remains. Why? What is it about this idea, which would seem to render considerations of worldly power irrelevant, that's allowed it to have these kinds of effects?

One explanation is simply that whenever politics and religion are intertwined (most of history, in other words), the apocalypse is just one part of the rhetorical toolkit that power players have at their disposal.

After all, history is littered with examples of profoundly impactful events that seemingly hinged on some relatively minor doctrinal dispute. And while there's little doubt that the protagonists genuinely cared about questions like 'Who can dispense indulgences?' or 'Lads, is it cool if the King gets divorced?', with the benefit of hindsight, we can be fairly confident that these arguments were also proxies for the more fundamental question: 'Who's in charge around here?'

There's no reason to expect the apocalypse to be any different.

But beyond this, apocalypticism has a few features that make it stand out in the religious proxy argument toolkit. The first is that, as we saw in the last chapters, it's a theory of history. If you want to convince people that your petty power struggle *isn't* just a petty power struggle, then there's not much better than a doctrine that can paint it as a pivotal moment in the history of humanity.

Tied to this is the quality that makes it such a potent recruiting tool for new religious movements: urgency. The imminence of Judgement Day makes questions of what's right or wrong acutely important. An apocalypse scheduled for tomorrow may render today's political manoeuvrings irrelevant – but one scheduled for the next decade or two renders them desperately relevant.

The usefulness of apocalyptic ideas in political struggles doesn't end there. The simple dualism that helped make Zoroaster's ideas a hit in the first place is a vital component. (Good vs Evil is, as every election consultant knows, the easiest framing in which to situate any political dispute.) The messianic element of apocalyptic thought allows you to paint leaders not simply as leaders, but as saviours, divinely anointed to usher in the righteous world. And the presence of an adversary – an Antichrist – in the tale allows you to paint your enemies in, well, just about the least flattering light possible.

You can see all of this at work in James VI's apocalyptic commentary. The Catholic Church is identified as the embodiment of evil, with the pope cast in the role of the Antichrist;

the climactic battle of history has already begun, and it is an urgent priority for men of true faith to take up arms.

But if you look beyond the text itself, the importance of the end times in political manoeuvring becomes even more clear – because James's tract is completely at odds with most of what we know about him.

Granted, James could be forgiven for feeling like the end was drawing near, given that the looming threat of a very personal apocalypse was never far away. His childhood had involved his mother Mary being imprisoned, his father murdered (possibly with the blessing of his mother), a succession of regents who ruled in his stead also being murdered, and at one point him being kidnapped and held hostage for almost a year. The threat of his own potential assassination was ever present. Less than a year before he began work on his apocalyptic commentary, Mary had finally been executed – an event that left him either deeply traumatised or oddly chipper, depending on which account you give the most credence.

But James VI was no holy warrior. Raised in strict Protestantism after his Catholic mother's imprisonment, he spent his whole life trying to strike a balance between the many battling religious factions who laid claim to his kingdoms and his person. Many Catholics viewed him as a traitor – some would, of course, try to blow up him and his parliament a few decades later – while many Protestants feared that he still held worryingly Catholic sympathies.

James's approach throughout his reign was to remind everybody that he was in charge, while trying not to annoy any particular faction too much – a little light repression of Catholics here, a bit of stamping his authority on the

Protestant churches there. He couldn't be further from the image his apocalyptic commentary paints of a warlike king yearning for a terminal showdown between the forces that claimed Christendom as rightfully theirs. Instead, he spent most of his time trying to avoid exactly that. Could everybody please chill, was the general message, and just let me have a nice time being king and persecuting witches.

And that's what his apocalyptic tract was all about. Just a few years previously, he'd imposed the 'Black Acts', which asserted the crown's authority over the Kirk, the Scottish Presbyterian Church. This infuriated the ministers, and suspicion remained about his possible Catholic sympathies. With his mother's death, his eye had already turned south to England, and his desire to succeed the childless Elizabeth I. James urgently needed to make nice with Protestantism; a religious tract that honoured the centrality of their belief in imminent apocalypse and railed against the evils of Catholicism would do just the job.

In other words, for James, it was a political tool, one that worked to bring him closer to his goals of establishing absolute power and uniting the crowns of Scotland and England. He would use the apocalypse when it was convenient, just as he would later write against the validity of prophecy when it seemed like it could challenge his authority, and then later again pick up apocalypse once more.

And honestly, it *kind of* worked. James VI of Scotland – and I of England and Ireland, as he would indeed become – lived out his reign firmly unassassinated, and with the cracks in his realm's religious fabric successfully papered over. He used every tool in his possession, including the apocalypse, to stave off the end of *his* world.

But the end of the world was too powerful a force to be contained for long.

There is, perhaps, no better illustration of the role that apocalyptic expectation played in the grubby world of politics and power than the grand, smack-down fight between the Holy Roman Emperor Frederick II and a succession of popes: a fight that convulsed much of Europe in the thirteenth century.

The Holy Roman Empire may now be inescapably linked with Voltaire's quip that it was 'neither holy, nor Roman, nor an empire'. But Voltaire was quipping in its diminished latter days – at a time when it was arguable that the Secular German Principality Association might be a more apt title. Over five centuries earlier, however, Frederick had reigned over a dominion that considered itself extremely holy, was intimately concerned with the affairs of Rome, and was pretty damn certain that it was an empire – one with ambitions to rapidly grow.

It had been formed originally in an attempt to reclaim the legacy of the dissipated Western Roman Empire in medieval Europe. You can date its origins to Charlemagne in 800 CE (the first to get the title 'Emperor' in centuries), or to Otto I in 962 CE, when the political settlement the Empire involved became solidified. That settlement was, effectively, a bargain: the Church granted the emperor legitimacy, while the emperor's power upheld the dominant position of the Church. The pope conferred the title upon the emperor, and with it both the spiritual weight of the Church and the claim to be a continuation of ancient Rome. Meanwhile, the secular and military might of this emperor solidified the political potency of the Church, acting as a buttress against both squabbling nobles and the influence of the Byzantine world, Rome's other offspring-empire in the east.

Unfortunately – if somewhat predictably – this bargain turned out to be an unstable one. Its creative ambiguity around who was ultimately in charge became a near-constant source of tension. Once you tell someone they're the emperor, after all, they tend to want to do emperor things. So it wasn't long before the Empire was embroiled in a series of rolling power struggles between its spiritual and secular rulers that would last for centuries.

This turmoil coincided with a revival of apocalyptic thought in Western Christianity – a revival that the political conflict both fed on and contributed to. Central to this was the struggle with the Muslim world for control of Jerusalem; this was easy to interpret as a harbinger of apocalypse, the great battle of the end times, and apocalyptic beliefs played a notable role in fuelling the Crusades (alongside more prosaic motives, like good old-fashioned plunder).

This increasingly became the vibe of the age; in the emperor-vs-pope power struggles, accusations from both sides that the other represented the Antichrist were common. Some of this may have been little more than mere invective, but there was also profound belief at work as well: as just one example, Hildegard von Bingen, the visionary German nun, explicitly identified the fight between Emperor Henry IV and Pope Gregory VII in the eleventh century as a sign of the beginning of the end.

This reached its peak with Frederick II. His early biography is oddly similar to that of James VI: a ruler in name since he was a young child, whose regency period was an extended, violent succession crisis as warring parties fought for control of the young prince, who was kidnapped and held for several years shortly before coming of age. Where he differed from James was that, even before he was born, he had been the subject of eschatological prophecies, inherited from his grandfather Frederick Barbarossa: he would be an Emperor of the Last Days, who would reclaim the Holy Sepulchre in Jerusalem and initiate the Second Coming.

In the real world, what he inherited was a mess of factional battles: he was King of Sicily and of Germany, but not of Italy, and he couldn't be Holy Roman Emperor yet because that was Otto IV – who, following tradition, was busy going to war with the pope.

Unsurprisingly, this all led Frederick to focus his efforts on consolidating his rule at home in the 1210s. Initially, this seemed to signal hope for improved emperor/pope relations, as he joined forces with Pope Innocent III to resolve the Otto issue. But this presented a problem: Frederick had repeatedly pledged to join the Crusades, and yet, repeatedly, he didn't show up. Despite promises that he'd get round to it any day now, honest, he didn't; his failure to turn up to the Fifth Crusade was widely blamed for its ending in humiliating defeat in 1221. When an attempt to give Crusading one more go in 1227 was abruptly halted on the grounds that Frederick got ill, Pope Gregory IX – feeling that the quid pro quo was not being upheld, and suspicious of Frederick's ambitions at home – went for the nuclear option, and excommunicated Frederick.

Thus began a war of apocalyptic words that would last for decades, and whose influence would be felt even longer. Gregory's allies condemned Frederick in eschatological terms: he was the 'Forerunner of Antichrist', the 'Beast of the

Apocalypse'. One furious papal encyclical began with references to the imagery of Revelation: 'Out of the sea rises up the Beast, full of the names of blasphemy who . . . opens its mouth to blaspheme the Holy Name and ceases not to hurl its spears against the tabernacle of God and against the saints who dwell in heaven.' Gregory's successor, Innocent IV, excommunicated Frederick again in 1245, the first excommunication having not quite stuck, and announced him deposed as emperor.

Frederick did not take any of this lying down. He and his allies fired back with, effectively, 'No, *you* are.' The pope was the heretic, the pope was the Antichrist; more than one person could quote and interpret the visions of Revelation. 'He, who is the Pope in name alone, has said that we are the Beast who rises from the sea . . . we maintain that he is the monster whereof it is written: another horse rose from the sea, a red horse, and he who sat thereon stole peace from the earth, so that the living slaughtered one another.'

Not only did Frederick condemn his papal enemies as antichrists, but he cultivated for himself a messianic image. This was helped by the fact that, when he finally did get round to going to Jerusalem in 1229, he successfully retook the city through the power of diplomacy and negotiation, rather than conquest. Being crowned the King of Jerusalem painted him as a Christlike figure – a comparison that he deliberately played up – and seemed to fulfil the Last Emperor prophecies that had been laid on him since before his birth.

This was obviously propaganda, but it wasn't merely propaganda: the reality of the imminent apocalypse does seem to have weighed on the protagonists. The upcoming year of 1260 had been identified by the influential theologian Joachim of Fiore as the likely date when the world would enter its new age; both Frederick and Gregory seemed to take the possibility seriously. In 1227, Frederick wrote '*Forte nos sumus, ad quos devenerunt seculorum fines*' – 'Perhaps we are the ones to whom the ends of the ages have come.' Six years later in 1233, Gregory IX echoed almost exactly the same words in a letter: '*Cum simus . . . in quos fines seculorum secundum apostolum devenerunt.*'

Frederick died in 1250, ultimately leading to a lengthy interregnum in the leadership of the Holy Roman Empire, which would never again cover as much territory as it had under his rule. And – more importantly for our purposes – his inconvenient demise presented a problem for those who had expected he'd be around in 1260 to fulfil his role in the end times. But it turned out that even death didn't stop him being the centre of apocalyptic expectations.

While in life he had been assailed as the Antichrist, in death it was his messianic image that took over. The Church was widely seen as corrupt, greedy, its wealth and status decidedly un-Christlike; in opposing the papacy, Frederick (an actual emperor, lest we forget) became transmuted into a champion of the poor and oppressed. Tales were told that he was not dead, or that he would come back to life. He had been seen riding to the slopes of Mount Etna with five thousand knights – beneath the mountain he would rest, only to return as a saviour at the time of greatest need. Just as with previous monarchs of both history and myth – Charlemagne, King Arthur, Fionn mac Cumhaill and many more – Frederick entered folklore as the king who sleeps beneath the mountain.

The legends of Frederick's Second Coming would echo for centuries, with many claimants insisting over the years that they were indeed the returned Frederick. The first was an imposter who gained a following on the slopes of Mount Etna in 1260, exactly when Frederick might be expected to return. Even after that fateful year passed with little in the way of apocalypse, new Fredericks kept popping up.

Some of these people may have been deliberate charlatans; some may have been delusional. Some may simply have been perfectly ordinary hermits who were surprised to discover that, after somebody impressed by their poverty and aura of holiness shouted, 'He is Frederick returned!', everybody suddenly started being extremely nice to them. Hard to blame them if they decided to simply go along with it.

The mania for Frederickian resurrection was so great that at least one of these pseudo-Fredericks had Second Coming myths – or rather, Third Coming myths – spring up around them in turn. This Frederick impressed people so much that he was able to establish a court in the Rhine town of Neuss in 1284, whereupon he marched his followers towards Frankfurt, where he planned to be crowned King of Germany. The *actual* King of Germany had some issues with this plan, and the pseudo-Frederick was eventually captured by his army and burned at the stake. But myths soon emerged that said this supposedly once-resurrected Frederick would soon be resurrected in turn, raising the possibility of relentlessly recurring resurrections, sustained by a succession of suspect messiahs.

But regardless of the disappointment that a succession of non-Fredericks might be expected to produce, the messianic role of Frederick endured. Into the fifteenth and sixteenth centuries, Frederick became a central figure in many German apocalyptic texts.

And the prophecy of the Last Emperor was not applied to Frederick alone; many figures took on, or were given, that mantle.

Charlemagne had already played a similar role in France; in the sixteenth century, Francis I being identified as the Last Emperor would underpin his claims to the French throne. That was also true of Holy Roman Emperor Charles V in the same century, while after 1453, Constantine XI – genuinely the last emperor of the Eastern Roman Empire – would become the centre of enduring resurrection legends, the Last Emperor who would return to sort everything out.

The same was true of Sebastian, King of Portugal, who vanished during battle in 1578, his body never discovered. Pseudo-Sebastians cropped up repeatedly in the following years; his prophesied resurrection became incorporated into interpretations of the Book of Daniel and the Book of Revelation, both in Portugal and in Brazil, where many would await his triumphant return that would herald the end of days.

And the expectation of resurrection could work the other way as well: for centuries in the early Christian period, many believers fearfully expected that at the end of days, their great persecutor, Nero, would return as (or in league with) the Antichrist, for one final bout of oppression.

Ultimately, the dual roles of saviour and adversary, so central to apocalyptic narratives, are ideally suited to being adapted and grafted on to the prospects of powerful individuals.

The hope for a leader who will make everything right is a powerful one; the desire to identify an enemy who is the embodiment of everything we despise equally so. The power of a leader can rest as much in symbolism as in pragmatic force – their ability to represent a nation, an idea, a story. And what greater symbolic power could there be than that of the central figure in the ultimate narrative of history?

* * *

But the power of the apocalypse to influence the world of politics does not rest solely in its usefulness for painting the powerful as either heroes or villains. In giving a shape to history – and in placing contemporaneous events at the ultimate moment of that history – it's both a powerful way to frame battles of ideas, and an urgent call to action. Often, to bloody, bodily action.

Take the English Civil War.

If James VI and I had been adept at balancing the demands of opposing factions and preserving his grip on power in a fracturing nation, his son Charles I was . . . not. But for all his failings as a monarch, perhaps there was little he could ultimately have done to keep the schisms in his kingdom from breaking through. James's efforts to diplomatically play both sides, while asserting the absolute power of the monarchy, did not help. And in his embrace of apocalyptic speculation, he had encouraged a tendency that – by the middle of the 1600s – had become dominant in the intellectual life of the country.

The belief that the last days were fast approaching became commonplace in Protestant Britain. The Church of Rome was still identified as the Satanic Babylon of the end times, although different people placed different estimates of how far its corruption spread. John Napier – the Scottish mathematician and enthusiastic eschatologist, who predicted that Judgement Day would occur between 1688 and 1700 – identified the pope as 'that only antichrist prophesied of in particular'. Joseph Mede, the thinker who solidified apocalyptic expectation as being a fundamental element of British thought, painted the whole Catholic hierarchy as the enemy, writing: 'The two horned beast or false prophet is the bishop of Rome with his clergy.' The anonymous author of *Sacrae heptades, or seaven problems concerning Antichrist* went even further: 'Every papist is an antichrist,' they asserted.

But if James had believed the apocalypse could be wielded as a simple rhetorical weapon against a fixed target – something to be picked up and put down as it suited you – then the dissolution of the kingdom he left after his death would prove him wrong. The thing about the imminent Day of Judgement is that it is a totalising philosophy; it dominates everything, and it offers no room for compromise. It forces polarisation. Not only will the evildoers be judged, but so will all those who aided them, or who simply did not oppose them firmly enough.

And so the search for adversaries did not stop at Catholicism. It turned inwards: while the Reformation in England had been a step in the right direction, the trumpet blast that signalled the beginning of the Antichrist's downfall, it had not gone far enough. Corrupt and greedy bishops still held sway. The Church of England was not yet truly one of the people. Also, the new king had taken a papist bride, which was *extremely* concerning behaviour.

Those who saw the Antichrist everywhere were not necessarily a united front: they lined up along a spectrum of militancy, on which even those who shared many of their beliefs could be suspect if they sat on a slightly different part of the spectrum.

The influential Thomas Brightman wrote of a Church that was 'neither cold, nor yet hot'. This lukewarm Church required, he said, 'a full and due reformation'. The more militant Alexander Leighton fulminated in more colourful language: 'These bishops be the knobs and wens and bunchy popish flesh which beareth down, deformeth, and deadeth the body of the church that there is no cure (as we conceive) but cutting off.' That cutting-off was no metaphor: he insisted that while 'spiritual warfare' was an important duty for Christians, 'so next unto it, in my judgment, is the bodily war'.

That the stage was being set for a prolonged and bloody conflagration was in little doubt. And the importance of this fight was no mere sectarian matter, because many of the apocalyptic believers who provided the impetus for war were convinced that this was not merely a fight over who ruled, or how. Instead, they believed that the country itself had been chosen for a starring role in the ultimate drama. Brightman and those who came after him believed that England could be the 'elect nation' – the place where the final battle would take place, and where the new kingdom of the saints would be formed in the post-apocalyptic age. He wrote: '[T]he glory of this kingdom is so much greater, because it should be eternal.'

And so, war. But even when the war was won, and the opportunity to build Christ's kingdom on earth presented itself, the battles did not stop. Cromwell had become ruler, and was quite happy with that, but there were still those who wanted him to go further. The Fifth Monarchy Men – named for the belief, derived from the Book of Daniel, that four great evil kings of history would be followed by a final just and divine rule of the people – rebelled against Cromwell's rebellion.

Their demands offer an insight into just how closely entangled the spiritual and apocalyptic was with the pragmatics of daily politics. They asked for reforms to the tax system, a fairer legal system and the introduction of civil marriage. These are not exactly demands that easily align with the sheer drama of the apocalypse – 'the end of the world is nigh, let's reform the planning system and amend child tax credits' – but they show that this was no mere abstract theological argument.

Anyway, Cromwell eventually had a bunch of them executed.

But the push and pull of the English Civil War period shows why apocalyptic thought, as tempting as it might be for the powerful to wield, rarely results in quite the outcome you might expect. The very thing that makes apocalyptic expectation such a potent political force is also the thing that makes it unstable. Bluntly: no matter how apocalyptic you are, there is always someone more apocalyptic than you.

Those who seek power by riding the back of the apocalypse tiger very often end up consumed by it.

'God made me the messenger of the new heaven and the new earth, of which He spoke in the Apocalypse by St. John,' wrote Christopher Columbus in the year 1500. And furthermore, he adds, 'He showed me the spot where to find it.'

Columbus was heavily influenced by the philosophy of Joachim of Fiore (the thinker who had first predicted the end of the world in 1260), as well as the theological and prophetic works that had followed in Joachim's tradition. In particular, Columbus got much of his information from the writings of Pierre d'Ailly, a French theologian and astrologer. It was d'Ailly whose calculations gave Columbus his date for the end of the world, 155 years hence.

(It is one of those gnarly little historical ironies that d'Ailly is also the source he relied on for his inaccurate estimate of the Earth's circumference – an error without which he'd probably have never set sail on his impossible journey to Asia.)

As we saw in Chapter 1, the prophecies said that Christ would not return to earth to establish his blessed new world until all the people of the earth had converted to his worship, and the Holy Sepulchre in Jerusalem was restored to Christian rule.

Columbus's first voyage was meant to bring both these goals to fruition. When he initially set out for Asia, his explicit goal was to speed the conversion of its peoples to Catholicism.

When it turned out that instead of making it to China or Japan he'd actually stumbled on a *whole new continent* – one full of people who'd never even had the chance to hear the word of the Lord – it only reinforced his belief that the Second Coming could never have occurred without him. He immediately began musing in his diary how easy it would be to convert the indigenous peoples of these new lands to Catholicism. (He also began musing about how easy it would be to enslave them; as well as being an apocalyptic zealot, he was also just horrible.)

This self-image as the man who would spread the word of the Lord to new lands only grew with time. A few years later, Columbus had taken to signing his letters with an inscrutable symbolic collection of letters that culminated in '*Xpo-ferens*' – 'Christ bearer' – indicating that he believed he had taken on the role of his namesake St Christopher in carrying Christ across the waters.

And, as his comment about God showing him 'where to find' the new heaven and new earth shows, Columbus did not limit his ambitions merely to proselytising. He believed that the lands themselves would be central to the establishment of Christ's kingdom. Indeed, he proposed that the Americas should be forcibly kept as the sole preserve of those who would be favoured on Judgement Day, writing: 'Your Highness ought not to consent that any foreigner do business or set foot here, except Christian Catholics, since this was the end and the beginning of the enterprise . . .'

When it came to the restoration of the Holy Sepulchre to Christian rule, Columbus's reasoning was even more straightforward.

Put bluntly, he wanted to take vast riches from these bountiful lands to fund a new crusade.

The day after celebrating the first-ever Christmas in the Americas, Columbus wrote in his diary of his hope that his voyage would hasten 'the time of gold and the spices', recalling how he had urged the Spanish monarchs, Ferdinand and Isabella, that 'all the gain of this my Enterprise should be spent in the conquest of Jerusalem'.

This was a point he was very, *very* insistent upon, and would continually press the monarchy to fulfil. On his return from the New World in March 1493, he wrote to the King and Queen that he hoped his plunder would, within a few years, be significant enough to buy 'five thousand cavalry and fifty thousand foot soldiers for the war' to retake the Holy Sepulchre.

In his vision of an aggressive push to create the universally Christian world that would usher in the Second Coming, Columbus was hardly alone.

Rather, it was very much the flavour of the age. The marriage of Ferdinand and Isabella had unified the crowns of Aragon and Castile into a single Catholic monarchy; one of their earliest acts had been the establishment of the Spanish Inquisition. Just three days before the *Nina*, *Pinta* and *Santa Maria* set sail, an edict had gone into force expelling from Spain all Jews who would not convert. Six months prior to that, the defeat of the Nasrid dynasty in Granada had wiped out the last Islamic rule in Spanish lands; within a few years, Muslims would also be faced with the choice of conversion, exile or slavery.

Given all that, it's hardly surprising that Columbus believed the armies of the Lord were on the march, and viewed himself as a vital soldier in that advance. And many of those who followed his path to the Americas had the same beliefs – that the end was near, and that these untouched lands would be the place where Christ would establish his kingdom. The New World would truly be the place where the new world would come into being.

And as we'll see, they would bring the apocalypse with them in more ways than one.

In a sense, the apocalypse was always political.

The formative apocalypses of the Judeo-Christian canon were intimately concerned with issues of power and the direction of society. The Hebrew Book of Daniel was ascribed to a visionary who had lived during the formative Babylonian exile, but was likely compiled and reworked during another era of political turmoil for the Jewish people. Greek rule of their lands – and the sense of cultural crisis that came with the increasingly Hellenised outlook of many Jewish elites – sparked the Maccabean uprising. Crafted in the same period, and with similar concerns, the apocalypse of Daniel is a political work, calling back to an age when one imperial oppressor was overthrown to suggest hope for the same thing happening again.

The Book of Revelation, likewise, is deeply political. Written by a self-described exile at a time when the early Christian sects were hardly flavour of the month with their Roman overlords, its hallucinatory images of beasts and horsemen and trumpets and seals are open to a wide variety of interpretations. But one seems, well, significantly less ambiguous than others. The beast has seven heads; and these heads are the seven hills upon which the Whore of Babylon sits. And what city, you might ask, is notable for sitting on seven hills?

(Rome. The Whore of Babylon is Rome. Granted, Rome later expanded to include more hills. But still: it's Rome.)

This all became a bit of a problem a few centuries later, from an apocalyptic interpretation perspective. The Roman Empire's abrupt Christianising about-face under Constantine had disrupted all the old certainties. What had been a fervently apocalyptic outsider sect, its followers yearning for divine retribution against their enemies, suddenly found itself sitting pretty as the official religion of the imperial machine. What do you do when you unexpectedly end up in a committed long-term relationship with the Whore of Babylon?

This was the political context faced by Augustine of Hippo, who was – and this is important – not a hippo. A man with a good claim to being the most important figure in the history of Western Christianity, excluding those who actually wrote or appeared in the Bible, Augustine's influence stretches across vast tranches of theology. Original sin! Free will! The compatibility of a loving God with the existence of suffering! Lad got everywhere.

But from our perspective, Augustine's most important contribution is that he put off the apocalypse for a very long time.

Augustine pushed back hard against the forces within early Christianity that were still attached to their expectations of an imminent millennium. There were plenty of these about – violent groups that fought against imperial rule, fundamentalists insisting that only the absolutely pure would be saved.

Augustine's response was to divide existence into the worldly and the spiritual realms. In the spiritual realm, perfection was possible, as was knowledge of the grand plan for the end times. But we do not live in that spiritual realm: we're in the impure, messy and confusing physical world, with only the promise of entering the heavenly city in the future. The term Augustine used for the state we live in was *saeculum*; it's where we get the word 'secular' from.

The upshot of this was to put the kibosh on apocalyptic expectation, and the use of it as a political cudgel. Augustine insisted that from our secular vantage point, we simply couldn't know when the end would arrive – and no amount of interpreting portents or reading the runes of history would get us closer to that unknowable date. And by insisting that perfection was impossible in the *saeculum* – that we all contain both good and evil – he tamped down the tendency to identify worldly actors with particular spiritual roles in the apocalyptic drama. Rome was not the Whore of Babylon, nor was it the Kingdom of Heaven. Rome was just a big city that was in charge of stuff.

Augustine's approach spread gradually throughout much of the Church, and over time became the standard interpretation in Western Christianity. It fitted well in a Church that was consolidating power, was ambitious in expanding into new territories, and found its old yearning for the world to be overturned didn't sit well with a world that was actually treating it pretty well. Also, people couldn't help noticing that the world still hadn't actually ended, which as time passed did seem to add some weight to Augustine's perspective.

The result was that for many centuries, the Church in Rome promulgated a fairly relaxed attitude towards the end of days. Yes, the Last Judgement would eventually come; yes, you should live according to the Church's law, lest you end up going in the wrong direction when your final hour arrives; but no, we're not particularly expecting it any time soon, and we're not going to devote much energy to anticipating it. Keep calm and carry on.

Naturally, this didn't last forever. The lure of the apocalyptic is too strong.

Over time, the belief that prophecies of the last days told us something important about the political situation around us crept back in. In the seventh century, it was our old friend *The Apocalypse of Pseudo-Methodius* that popularised the concept of the Last Emperor, that glorious figure who would arise to lead the righteous in the final battles. You can see why this idea might have been appealing to its author: it was written in modern-day Syria, in response to the sudden rise of Islam and that religion's rapid conquests of territory. The end times must have felt uncomfortably near; the hope of a strong leader tempting.

Then, in the twelfth century, Joachim of Fiore – the theologian whose influence we've already seen several times in this chapter – brought the apocalypse roaring back into the mainstream. His prophecies were a direct rebuke of Augustine's admonition against attempting to predict the date of the apocalypse by matching current events to biblical texts. Instead of not doing that, Joachim suggested, how about we . . . do it? As you might be able to tell from the fact that he influenced everybody from emperors to popes to Christopher Columbus, everybody was *extremely* excited about this possibility.

Joachim's prophecies built and expanded on the Last Emperor mythology, assigning all manner of eschatological roles to world actors, tying current events closely to the onrushing millennium, and sticking a tentative date on it all.

Joachim himself, despite living a traditional, extremely isolated monkish life on a Calabrian mountaintop, was a savvy political operator – multiple popes called on him for advice, and Richard the Lionheart stopped on his way to the Third Crusade to ask if he had any useful prophecies. As part of this political nous, Joachim never explicitly identified any of his contemporaries as prophetic figures, and took pains to not overtly take sides in the pope-vs-emperor scraps of his time. Of course, this absolutely did not stop everybody else from taking his work and matching it up to every ambitious noble or despised opponent they could think of, frequently with people on both sides of a conflict deploying Joachim to bolster their arguments. Politics will always pick up and use whatever tools are lying around.

What this all illustrates is that there is an inherent push and pull when the apocalypse and political power meet.

The polarising promise of an imminent apocalypse can be a potent rhetorical weapon, great for building a movement, demonising your enemies and demanding adherence from your supporters.

The trouble comes if you win. Because once you're in charge, it's rarely your friend. Apocalypticism is inherently chaotic and unstable. It rejects the possibility of detente or diplomacy. There will always be someone more extreme than you who can seize upon the fervour you've created. It's a fire that will burn brightly, but cannot be sustained indefinitely.

If nothing else, people will eventually start to get suspicious when the promised day keeps failing to arrive.

The result is that the use of apocalypticism by worldly forces tends to ebb and flow – embraced in times of strife and conflict, backed away from when stability is craved, then picked up in turn by new challengers.

Winning power is a matter for today. But if you want to *keep* power, you have to think about tomorrow as well.

Of course, the problem is that in accumulating power for yourself, you might just be creating groups of powerless people for whom the apocalypse suddenly looks like a very attractive option.

6.

Little Apocalypses Everywhere

The summer of 1562 saw the apocalypse come to the Maya of the Yucatán Peninsula.

The Franciscan friars who had flocked to the New World had a clear mission: to speed the Second Coming by converting the entire population of this new land. The same prophecies that had driven Columbus now drove the many who followed in his wake.

They'd built churches, they'd preached the word of the Lord, they'd persuaded early converts to write religious texts in local languages. And they'd had success. Part of that was due to coercion, of course. But it's also understandable that some indigenous people may have been genuinely interested in the tales the Spanish told. After all, these interlopers who spoke of their all-powerful God had conquered the lands with relative ease; maybe their God really was worth worshipping? For many Maya, whose worldview already involved a pantheon of deities who rose and fell, lived and died, as one world transitioned to the next, this may not have required a huge leap of faith.

What emerged, as it usually does when one religion attempts to supplant another, was a syncretic blend of traditions. The God of the Bible was integrated into the Maya pantheon; old legends were reworked to fit a Christian framework. But many of the old Maya ways hung on – and this was beyond the pale for the Franciscans. They weren't satisfied with their God merely being *accepted* by the Maya; the old religion had to be purged entirely.

So when in 1562 a collection of Maya religious artefacts were discovered hidden in a cave, the Spanish decided to crack down. They started an Inquisition, one that was as brutal as its counterparts in Europe and indiscriminate in its targets. Thousands of Maya were arrested and interrogated; many hundreds were viciously tortured, leaving at least two hundred dead and a lot more permanently injured. Vast troves of Maya sculptures and documents were seized and burned on huge pyres.

As the historians Matthew Restall and Amara Solari write: '1562 was an end-of-world date, the long summer a harrowing series of Judgment Days.'

But the outcome of this event and others like it during the colonisation of the Americas is a somewhat perverse one: it did indeed speed up the adoption of Christian ideas by the indigenous population. And not just as an act of submission, but also as one of resistance. This period saw the production of many of the Maya language works with apocalyptic overtones that would be misinterpreted by later scholars as evidence of pre-contact apocalyptic beliefs. Because the conquistadors hadn't just brought about the end of the Maya world; they'd given its people a framework for understanding what was happening to them. The Maya and the other colonised peoples of the continent began to adopt the apocalypse not just because they were forced to, but because it *made sense.*

That's the theme of this chapter. It's an obvious one, perhaps so obvious that it almost feels silly to bother writing it down. But still, it's worth exploring, because it's a theme that echoes down the history of the last days. The idea is this:

People believe in the end of the world when it feels like their world is ending.

Wherever you look in the history of apocalyptic movements, it's hard to not notice that they often seem to coincide with some kind of horrible catastrophe.

'Again and again,' Norman Cohn writes in *The Pursuit of the Millennium*, his hugely influential study of millenarian movements in medieval Europe, surges of apocalyptic fervour 'took place against a background of disaster'. He goes on to list a litany of examples.

Famines had preceded the earliest Crusades, a series of flagellant movements, and an outbreak of resurrected-king mania focused on Baldwin IX (a short-lived Emperor of Constantinople who was supposedly back for more). Jan Matthys's apocalyptic takeover of Münster, meanwhile, had followed in the wake of a catastrophic rise in the price of everyday goods. Devastating outbreaks of disease had presaged doomsday movements in 1260, 1348, 1391 and 1400, while the greatest and most sustained burst of apocalyptic expectation in the entire period 'was precipitated by the most universal natural disaster of the Middle Ages, the Black Death'.

This pattern repeats itself outside of the eschatological hothouse of medieval Europe. The Guangdong region of China from which Hong Xiuquan would fight his messianic war (see Chapter 8) was one in which famines were effectively endemic, and was plagued by pirates and bandits, while the country as a whole had long been destabilised by the political troubles of the Qing Dynasty. Hong's Taiping Rebellion was not even the first apocalyptic revolt to shake China in that period: in the late eighteenth century, the White Lotus Rebellion saw the uprising of a messianic Buddhist movement that expected the imminent catastrophic end of the *kalpa*, sparking a war that lasted for eight bloody years.

War, or the threat of war, was a huge spur for apocalyptic thinking – as well as being stimulated by it in turn. The virtually non-stop local wars between rival nobles provided a steady trickle of death and displacement that ensured the pervasive sense of destruction was never far away. And from afar, the threat of invasion and conquest reliably saw surges in doomsday discourse: the rise and expansion of the Muslim world, the seemingly unstoppable push of the Mongol Empire into Europe, the final overthrow of the last Roman Emperor by the Ottomans. Each of these in turn sparked an explosion of apocalyptic predictions – and that's something that carried on into the nuclear anxiety of the Cold War era.

It's not surprising to us that these would give rise to thoughts of doomsday. After all, pop culture has taught us calamities in general are usually accompanied by wild-eyed prophets of doom. We just assume that any crisis will make at least *some* people think that it's time to put on robes and chant.

But that these particular afflictions – death, starvation, disease and war – would be especially common triggers is also not surprising if you know your apocalyptic iconography. After all, there is perhaps no more enduring symbol of the end days in the Christian tradition than the Four Horsemen of the Apocalypse. You probably know them in their most familiar roles, which map very precisely on to these categories: Death, War, Famine and Pestilence.

But actually, the horsepersons' roles in Revelation are not quite what the popular depictions would have you believe. For one thing, they're not really central figures in the great drama of Judgement Day, more sidekicks in Revelation's phantasmagorical imagery. And what the horsemen are understood to represent has changed over time – indeed, for many centuries, one of the most popular interpretations was that the rider of the white horse was actually Jesus. If you're forced to assign them jobs, it might be more accurate to the text to say that their areas of responsibility are Death, Inflation, War, and War Again.

The rider of the pale green horse, Death, is fairly unambiguous, in that the text says their name is Death. Helpful; thanks, John of Patmos. The black horse rider normally interpreted as Famine can certainly be seen that way, but it's more ambiguous – the text talks about how expensive food is now, with a cup of wheat costing a day's wages, but it also throws in what sounds like a satirical jab about how the more luxurious goods of oil and wine must be protected. So possibly Famine, but definitely Cost of Living Crisis.

The rider of the red horse will 'take peace from Earth' and cause men to slay one another, which is why they're commonly and fairly reasonably described as War. But the rider of the white horse, the one previously interpreted as Jesus and whom we currently assume to be Pestilence, is thornier. Realistically, there's not much about pestilence in there: the white horse rider has a bow, is given a crown, and goes out 'conquering and to conquer'. The most parsimonious conclusion is that the author of Revelation is drawing a distinction between two types of war: wars from within, the civil strife that leads men to slay one another, and wars from without, those of invasion and conquest.

This isn't just a quirky little diversion. The varying ways that the horsepersons have been interpreted over time highlights the ways in which apocalyptic thinking is shaped by the crises of the age.

The author of Revelation was writing before humanity had truly entered the age of pandemics. Disease was common – extremely common, given the lack of modern medicine – but the kind of civilisation-shaking exponential outbreaks that would become increasingly common in the Middle Ages were still pretty rare. They only really picked up steam in the age of trans-continental trade and densifying urban centres. There were some destructive epidemics, to be sure – but when Revelation was being written, the Plague of Athens, which helped swing the Peloponnesian War in favour of Sparta, was centuries in the past, while the Antonine Plague, which would grip the Roman Empire, remained decades in the future. Fear of plagues was a distant, largely theoretical worry; fear of conquest was a live societal threat.

But flash-forward a millennium or two, and for those living at the end of the cholera-swept nineteenth century, the imagery of a rider who would go forth and conquer all before them much more easily suggested a pestilential interpretation.

If you're in an area prone to occasional catastrophic rainfall, then your apocalyptic imaginings are likely to include a great rain. Flood and drought are central to the doomsday scenarios of agrarian societies, just as ancient Egyptian prophecies of boom and doom focused heavily on what the Nile would be up to. Earthquakes are a central aspect of the last day in Islamic depictions, just as they would usher in the fifth world of the Aztecs. The Scandinavian Ragnarök is preceded by the great killing cold of the *fimbulwinter.* In China – regularly riven by violent conflict – fears of disease play little apocalyptic role, but fear of invasion was significant.

Our image of doomsday, in other words, is heavily shaped by all the little apocalypses that lurk in our cultural memory.

Nongqawuse was a shy girl of around fifteen when she first saw the new people, the ones who told her what must be done to bring about the renewal of the Xhosa lands.

She was an orphan, her parents possibly killed by the British in the vicious war that had raged around the Cape Colony – at the tip of what would become South Africa – some years previously. She was awkward, as teenage girls sometimes are, and dishevelled and distracted, as prophets sometimes are. One witness would record the unflattering observation that she had 'a silly look and appeared to me as if she was not right in her mind'.

The strangers who began speaking to Nongqawuse – and to nobody else – in April 1856 told her that they had an important message. Xhosaland, they said, was contaminated and sick. But they had a promise, of a kind familiar from other apocalyptic tales: soon the dead would return to life, the sick would become well, the old would become young. All would live in a land of plenty, free from troubles, and they would 'eat the same as English people eat'.

But in order to bring this about, the Xhosa would need to purge their land of the sickness, and make space for the bounty that was to come. They must stop using witchcraft. They must give up planting their crops, and allow the land to lie fallow. And they must kill all their cattle.

Nongqawuse's reports of the strangers' message initially fell on deaf ears, but she found a sympathetic audience in her uncle and guardian, Mhlakaza. He would become her first and loudest advocate, and the primary interpreter of what she was told.

Mhlakaza was an unusual figure: the first Xhosa ever to have received Anglican Communion, and the first to have been confirmed in the church. Coming into the service of the Archdeacon of Grahamstown following a traumatic life – his father murdered his mother – he experienced a profound spiritual upwelling, and the happiest months of his life seem to have been spent walking the countryside with the English minister, discussing his newfound faith with a man he viewed as a trusted companion on his spiritual journey.

Unfortunately, he discovered that he was not viewed the same way. He was and would remain a servant, no more. His devotion to his faith, the Archdeacon's family felt, was interfering with his duties. 'Too lazy to work,' was the Archdeacon's conclusion. Mhlakaza was summarily fired. Devastated, he returned to his sister's home, disillusioned with his adopted faith – a man filled to the brim with belief, desperate to find a vessel to pour it into. The message that Nongqawuse's strangers sent, with its blend of Christian apocalypticism and traditional Xhosa beliefs, could have been crafted for him.

Mhlakaza was not the only one with an incentive to believe. British colonisation had produced large numbers of

Xhosa refugees, displaced people who found themselves hungry and homeless in overpopulated towns. The War of Mlanjeni, an attempted Xhosa uprising against the British led by a prophet who said that his followers would be impervious to the colonisers' bullets, had been a profoundly vicious affair, the worst of the eight wars between the Xhosa and the British Empire in the previous seven decades. And right after the war had subsided, a Dutch ship brought an unwelcome new gift: lungsickness, which spread through the cattle of the region like wildfire. When Nongqawuse's visitors told her the land was sick, it resonated.

The king of the independent Gcaleka Xhosa lands in which Nongqawuse lived, bordering the recently established British colony of British Kaffraria, was one of her earliest believers. He too had reason to buy in to a promise of salvation and redemption: his father had been imprisoned and shot dead by the British after they had promised him safe harbour, he had lost many sons to sickness, and he was haunted by having failed to prevent the killing of his closest adviser during internal political strife a few years earlier. He could no more cure the lungsickness than anyone else could. And so he believed.

With a king on side, belief in Nongqawuse's words began to spread. Not everybody was convinced: when guests arrived asking to see the strangers, they would often fail to show up. Some people noticed that they only seemed to appear on misty or stormy days, when Nongqawuse would go and converse with them a great distance from any visiting dignitaries, who strained to make out indistinct shapes but sometimes thought they'd seen something. But still: the message spread across the land. Many Xhosa would do what they had been instructed. They would abandon witchcraft, they would plant no new crops, they would slaughter all the remaining cattle that had survived the lungsickness. And they would wait for the dead to arise, and the new world to come upon them.

The results were devastating for the Xhosa people. The appointed day did not come. Mhlakaza said that this was because not everybody had followed the instructions fully; they had kept some cattle back, just in case. Those remaining cattle must be killed also. Still, the dead remained dead. Many more soon joined them.

Somewhere between 35,000 and 50,000 Xhosa probably died of starvation in the famine brought on by the lack of cattle and crops. Many more were forced to flee to other areas; the Xhosa population of British Kaffraria dropped from 100,000 to just 25,000 in the space of two years. And the loss was not just counted in lives: with the lands not already colonised depopulated and desperate, the British claimed vast swathes of territory, around 600,000 acres in total, reducing independent Xhosa lands to the tiniest rump. The survivors, desperate for food, were expected to submit to forced labour in return for belated British charity. A belief in the renewal of their world had brought about its end.

Today, when it is remembered at all outside of South Africa, Nongqawuse's failed prophecy is usually presented as an episode of mass delusion. In his book on the topic, historian J. B. Peires suggests a different interpretation: as self-defeating and destructive as it was, to understand the motives of the Xhosa who believed in its promise, you also have to look at it as an act of resistance. It was, he suggests, something very much like a culture-wide hunger strike, by a people pushed to the edge by the slow erosion of their world.

* * *

The story of Nongqawuse illustrates the other side of the connection between real-life disaster and imagined apocalypse. It's true that great catastrophes can prompt a mass turning to apocalyptic visions. It's also true that, all too often, it becomes a horribly self-fulfilling prophecy.

The very act of committing wholeheartedly to apocalyptic certainty can bring disaster down upon yourself.

Sometimes this is for the simple reason that believing the end is nigh does not encourage a huge amount of forward planning. When you believe that tomorrow will never happen, tomorrow arriving will often catch you catastrophically short. As a Canadian farmer may or may not have said in the nineteenth century: 'Hif the hearth hends, we woant want no pertaters.'

The trope of farmers abandoning their fields in the face of an expected end is one that recurs throughout news coverage of apocalyptic movements – so much so that you suspect that at some point it did become just a trope, a little rural legend that always crops up regardless. But there's a core of truth to it.

Apocalyptic history is filled with groups that burn bright one day, before sputtering out in the face of tomorrow's stubborn insistence upon arriving. In Italy in 1304, followers of the radical apocalyptic preacher Fra Dolcino retreated up into the mountains north of Milan to await the end, which was due the following year. This didn't happen – and the thing about waiting in the mountains for an apocalypse that doesn't arrive is that you rapidly run out of food. Before too long they were reduced to raiding nearby farms and villages for sustenance.

(For some groups, this lack of planning for the future manifests on a longer timescale. The Shakers, a notable sect in the nineteenth century, have today almost entirely vanished thanks to the absolute vow of chastity required of all members. Intended to speed the Second Coming, this left them unable to create new followers through the traditional method, and there weren't enough adult converts or fostered orphans to keep the numbers up. At the time of writing, there are two living Shakers left.)

The promise of all the petty concerns of the world being imminently swept away can make the primal needs of human life – food, shelter, safety – seem to recede in importance, at least until those needs abruptly catch up to you. But it's not always as simple as just a reckless lack of foresight that makes such movements bring crisis upon themselves – even if that's usually in the mix.

A profound lack of concern about worldly necessities also fits well with the ideological and emotional tenor of many apocalyptic movements. In the Middle Ages, prophets of doom (like all those fake resurrected Fredericks) could pick up followers with overt displays of poverty. 'Give me a meal and I'll tell you about the end of the world' was roughly the deal; the performance of destitution seemed deeply Christlike in comparison to the ugly wealth of the Church.

This shedding of needful things isn't just a question of passive neglect, but active choice. Before Dorothy Martin's group in Chicago gathered to eagerly await their UFO saviours, many members had sold or given away their possessions in anticipation of their rescue from Earth. After the spaceships failed to arrive, they were kinda screwed.

There's a rich history of this: in Massachusetts in 1909, many members of the Triune Immersionists had 'disposed of all their worldly goods' and sold off their businesses in anticipation of the Earth's crust peeling away. Perhaps most famously, many of the 100,000-plus who gathered in 1844 for the apocalypse predicted by the preacher William Miller had also sold or simply given away all their possessions. It's hardly surprising that the subsequent failure of the world to end became known as the Great Disappointment.

For the followers who join such movements, the shedding of worldly goods and cares can be a powerful symbolic act – one that resonates with the broader hope that the world will crumble away. Divest yourself of the trappings of the world as was, and maybe you can usher in the world to be. (Of course, this kind of thing also fits perfectly with a cult's desire to have its members cut off contact with the outside world. I'm sure that's just a coincidence, though.)

You can't dismiss all those who bring themselves trouble through their apocalyptic belief as simply lacking foresight. When the members of the Church Universal and Triumphant went underground in the spring of 1991, heading down into their purpose-built shelters to ride out the nuclear war that was due to start in the next few hours, there were plenty of things you could accuse them of – but a lack of preparedness wasn't one of them. Yes, many of them had sold their possessions – up to and including their houses. They'd walked away from jobs and drained their bank accounts dry, all in the expectation that doomsday was coming, and they were left high and dry by its failure to arrive. But their problem was one of over-preparedness – millions of dollars ploughed into building and supplying the bunkers with years' worth of food, radiation suits and guns. Like many groups of that era, the apocalypse they expected wouldn't see them all magicked off to a higher plane – it was something they needed to survive.

Failing to plan for tomorrow can bring down disaster upon apocalyptic groups, in other words, but so can planning for the wrong tomorrow.

The world failing to end wasn't the only way that these preparations caused problems for the Church Universal and Triumphant. The guns they'd stocked up on also attracted the attention of the authorities, as that kind of thing often tends to. Criminal charges were brought; when the group headed down into the bunkers, they did so under the watchful eye of agents from the Bureau of Alcohol, Tobacco, and Firearms.

Despite the centuries between them, this was something they had in common with the followers of Fra Dolcino, up in their Italian mountain fortress in 1305. The authorities weren't happy about the Dulcinian heresy, but they might have got away with that if they hadn't also been raiding every village in the area. They needed food, and the people of the villages were obviously impure because, well, they weren't part of their group, so they were fair game. So they stole and killed and burned their way through the region – and in response, the authorities hunted them down as bandits.

And that's the other way that apocalyptic movements, fuelled by current disaster and predicting future disaster, can bring disaster upon themselves. These movements are by their very nature disruptive to authorities who govern on the assumption that we'll all still be here this time next year. A backlash is almost inevitable.

These themes all come together in the tale of Antônio Conselheiro – Anthony the Counsellor – who tried to craft a utopia from the shattered pieces of great trauma. His was an apocalyptic vision unambiguously born of crisis. A Brazilian preacher who spoke loudly against slavery and ministered to the poor in the rural region of Bahia – travelling from village to village with his followers and performing small, vital acts of aid – he had grown more and more convinced of an imminent end. To say this resonated with people would be an understatement. The region was devastated by Brazil's worst-ever famine in the late 1870s, the Grande Seca, which killed hundreds of thousands and forced hundreds of thousands more to flee their homelands. The end felt truly close.

Antônio had his own spin on Christianity, one that stood apart from Church orthodoxy and blended airy mysticism with strict conservatism. Like many such preachers, he targeted his ire at the perceived corruption and licentiousness of the contemporary priesthood. Over time, his followers would come to see the Conselheiro as a messianic figure – his ministry to the poor during the famine, in sharp contrast to the profound lack of interest shown by any authority figures, made him seem positively Christlike. (He also had extremely Jesusy hair-and-beard stylings, which probably helped.)

Politically, he was also an interesting combo: a monarchist liberationist. In the space of eighteen months in 1888 and 1889, his greatest hopes and worst fears came true: first the Emperor abolished slavery, then shortly after that, the Emperor got couped and the First Brazilian Republic was established. (Well, it was *called* a republic; 'military oligarchy' might be a more accurate term for what it settled into.) Antônio was a big fan of the first, and saw the second as the coming of the Antichrist. Leaning into messianic hopes, he began to prophesy the return of King Sebastian of Portugal (whom you may recall was last seen in 1578, disappearing off into battle). It was the classic apocalyptic formula: God would defeat the

Antichrist of the republic, Sebastian would return from the dead for a utopian reign, and then the world would end.

And like so many other movements, Antônio decided to try to build the first beachhead of the new world amidst the corruption of the current world. The place he chose was Canudos: a small farming settlement in Bahia, rural and remote. The community he created reflected his ideals: wealth was redistributed, sinful behaviour punished. What began with the Conselheiro and a small band of followers soon swelled as people flocked to promises of milk and honey.

Tens of thousands came. Once again, many sold all their property, paying into the communal coffers to gain entry. The wealthy and the destitute alike were represented, but the majority came from the underclasses: they were recently emancipated enslaved people, the landless poor, displaced indigenous people. People who had had next to nothing finally felt like, maybe, they might have *something*.

There was always going to be a backlash.

The landowners in the surrounding region were, to put it mildly, not best pleased about their new neighbours. Canudos was pretty peaceful, largely concerning itself with farming crops and trading leather. Didn't matter. Their new neighbours urged the authorities to crack down on them; when the authorities, distracted by the general chaos of the post-coup country, proved reluctant, they manufactured a *casus belli*. A judge in a neighbouring town blocked the delivery of some wood to Canudos; when a group of the townspeople, reasonably enough, set out to ask 'Can we have the wood we paid for, please?', this was painted as an invasion. Local troops were dispatched to suppress the Canudenses. They met them on the road between towns, and after a bloody skirmish, the troops were defeated.

This probably seemed like a victory to the inhabitants of Canudos. Instead, it brought down destruction upon them.

The national government of the tenuous new republic could not let this stand. Canudos was a hotbed of violent monarchists, went the narrative, respecting no authority and determined to see the republic fall. They were undesirables. They had to be defeated. The national army was dispatched.

It took two years for the army to crush Canudos. Three times they were beaten back, and every defeat made it all the more imperative that the settlement not be allowed to exist. In 1896, eight thousand troops mustered for the fourth and final assault against a starving community, and this time they won. Prisoners were massacred en masse; the town itself was razed to the ground. Antônio Conselheiro died of disease as the assault was beginning. The victorious troops cut off his corpse's head.

Those who hope for the world to pass away will often find that the world is brutal in its desire to keep existing.

As this book was being written, in early 2023, authorities in southern Kenya, acting on a tip, discovered a body buried in a shallow grave on land controlled by a pastor named Paul Mackenzie.

Then they discovered another. And another.

The full horror of what had unfolded in Shakahola Forest became apparent slowly, and then rapidly. Hundreds of Pastor Mackenzie's followers had starved themselves to death on his instructions, in the hope of hastening their admission to heaven.

For anybody familiar with the history of apocalyptic movements, this all felt horribly familiar. Even before knowing the precise details of what Mackenzie preached, you could make a solid guess that it involved an imminent apocalypse. And so it proved: Mackenzie was apocalyptic through and through.

He had a YouTube channel called 'End Times Breaking', filled with videos pumping out a toxic stew of eschatological panic and conspiracy theories. Talk of the New World Order and anti-vaccination screeds sat side by side with proclamations of doomsday prophecies fulfilled and one segment called 'End Time Kids', in which children delivered messages to camera. Mackenzie – who drew much of his theology from the radical American televangelist and faith healer William Branham – demanded his followers cut off all contact with the outside world, making them quit their jobs, insisting education was satanic and that children must be withdrawn from schools, and proclaiming that doctors were evil and should not be consulted. Eventually, he told them to fast until they met Jesus.

One of the most enduring cultural images of apocalyptic movements is that of the 'suicide cult'. It can seem, in some twisted way, to be the logical conclusion of all apocalyptic beliefs – the bitter endpoint of what happens when you stop believing in tomorrow and view all existence as a crisis. A spate of high-profile incidents in the twentieth century embedded it as a trope, a little mental shortcut many people have when they think about apocalypticism. There are plenty of cases to draw on: from the Raskolniki in seventeenth-century Russia, the schismatic Old Believers who burned themselves alive in their own churches, to the Heaven's Gate cult in 1997, who took their own lives in the belief this would allow them to ascend to heaven in a UFO hiding in the tail of the passing Hale–Bopp comet.

It is, perhaps, worth reconsidering some of these assumptions – because further investigation has often shown that some of the most infamous cases were more likely mass murder, not mass suicide.

Probably the most well-known is the Jonestown Massacre, the infamous death by cyanide poisoning of over nine hundred members of Jim Jones's People's Temple at their remote Guyanese compound. This has lived long in the cultural memory, immortalised in everything from indie band names to the phrase 'drinking the Kool-Aid' (no doubt to the chagrin of Kool-Aid, as the cyanide-laced drink was actually a cheaper knock-off). Jones was another follower of William Branham – appearing alongside him, and winning his endorsement for his first ministry – but took his beliefs in a different direction, advocating socialism and racial equality. The settlement in Guyana was intended as a location where they could survive the expected nuclear war.

Once again, the residents of Jonestown helped bring themselves to their crisis point: they too attracted the attention of the authorities, and the final crisis was precipitated by the inexplicable decision to murder everybody in a congressional delegation checking up on the compound. The massacre was originally reported as a mass suicide – that's certainly how the group's leaders wanted it to be understood in the audio recordings they left to spin the event – but subsequent investigation revealed that many of the dead had not drunk the poison, instead being injected against their will, while guards were ordered to kill anybody attempting to flee.

The deaths of members of the Order of the Solar Temple in multiple incidents across the nineties were a mixture of murders and suicides; the deaths of hundreds of members of the Movement for the Restoration of the Ten Commandments of God in Uganda in 2000 remain controversial, with official investigations determining they were murdered, while some scholars argue it was truly suicide.

And so it is with Pastor Mackenzie's followers in Shakahola Forest: it emerged that he had hired thugs to kill all those who tried to leave, or who simply weren't starving to death fast enough.

Ultimately, this distinction may matter little. The line between murder and suicide coerced by someone exerting psychological control is fuzzy to the point of non-existence. This is as much about the psychology of cult leaders as it is about cult followers: the desire for absolute control, expressed in the ultimate act of control, the ending of life.

What it tells us about apocalyptic thought is that one of its fundamental components is often the wholesale rejection of the world. That sense of irresolvable crisis, of disconnect from any kind of mutually imagined future, is what allows believers to be both blasé about their own lives and utterly callous about the lives of others. 'We are rejected by the whole world . . . We also reject this planet,' wrote Joseph Di Mambro, the habitual conman who founded the Knights Templar/UFO cult that was the Order of the Solar Temple, and would oversee his followers' extended murder–suicide sprees. 'Life for me is intolerable, intolerable.'

People believe in the end of the world when it feels like their world is ending – or when they can no longer conceive of any reason why it should continue. This is the apocalyptic cycle: when a sense of crisis pushes those who believe it into creating their own self-sustaining crisis.

* * *

There's a caveat here. Of course there is!

While crisis commonly acts as a spur for apocalyptic expectation, it's not *quite* as simple as that might suggest. Individual disasters will commonly trigger at least some people to predict the imminent end of all things, and a rolling state of crisis – like that seen in medieval Europe – can sustain long-lasting apocalyptic movements. But when you zoom out in history, it's not a perfect correlation. Even if you could precisely quantify such things, you couldn't draw a graph where the amount of apocalyptic fervour goes up neatly alongside the amount of crisis occurring.

Many periods of great strife coincide with surges of doomsday belief. But many others don't, even when it feels like they probably *should*.

For example: the years around 540 CE were a surpassingly awful time for the residents of the eastern Mediterranean. A series of eruptions in 536 had brought about a terrible volcanic winter, a Little Ice Age; further eruptions in 539 and possibly 547 made it even worse. In the middle of this, disease struck: the Plague of Justinian, the first recorded appearance of bubonic plague in Europe, and an event that's often referred to as the first modern pandemic. Exactly how severe it was is disputed, but some estimates suggest that a quarter of the population may have died. The one-two punch of climate crisis and pandemic led the historian Michael McCormick to describe it as 'one of the worst periods to be alive'.

And yet, all these extremely apocalyptic goings-on don't seem to have stimulated a rise in the importance of apocalyptic thought. In Western Christianity, the influence of Augustine and his rejection of apocalyptic expectation mostly held sway; in the Byzantine world, where the epidemic was centred,

Augustine was less influential, but there was still little interest in apocalypticism as an active practice. The most notable theologian of the age, Gregory of Tours, spent most of his time insisting that the end was very much not nigh (about two centuries away, he reckoned). Even when he did allow himself to ponder whether some of these events might be signs of something dramatic happening imminently, he didn't seem to peg the apocalypse as the most likely answer.

Indeed, Augustine himself had been writing around the time of the sack of Rome in 410 – an event that in our modern imagination has become almost synonymous with apocalyptic imagery. 'The fall of Rome' is used as a metaphor for civilisational collapse, 'the last days of Rome' as a stand-in for oblivious hedonism in the face of impending doom. And while it certainly did prompt apocalyptic speculation – Augustine's contemporary Jerome pondered if it might be a harbinger of an imminent Judgement Day – the main theological outcome of it was Augustine putting the apocalypse back in its box for many centuries. It would only be with the rise of Islam several centuries later, and the threat to Christendom it implied, that apocalyptic expectation would start its return to the forefront of everybody's minds.

In fact, you could even point out that Revelation itself – a work deeply concerned with the oppression of Christians by Rome – was most likely written during decades when this oppression was relatively mild, compared with what had gone before and what would follow. Its apocalyptic concerns were written at a time when the drivers of those concerns were on the wane.

These aren't the only examples. As we saw in the last chapter, the period leading up to the English Civil War was filled with apocalyptic predictions. Many dates for the end were proposed; one of the most common was the year 1666 (on the fairly simple grounds that it included the number of the beast, and was thus scary).

When 1666 rolled around, it had the distinction of actually including a number of pretty apocalyptic events: the Great Plague that had started the year before continued to sweep the country; war with the Dutch raged on the seas; the Great Fire of London destroyed swathes of the capital; perhaps the worst tornado in English history struck Lincolnshire and Nottinghamshire.

This must have seemed an awful lot like a bunch of prophecies were being fulfilled – and yet England did not see a great resurgence of apocalyptic belief. There was speculation, of course: booksellers started reselling *An Interpretation of the Number 666*, a 1642 work that had predicted the end in 1666; news of one Sabbatai Zevi, a claimed Jewish messiah in the Ottoman Empire, spread widely; a sense of gloom overtook many.

But the mood remained one of uncertainty: in February that year, Samuel Pepys, having picked up a copy of *An Interpretation of the Number 666*, wrote in his diary that 'certainly this year of 1666 will be a year of great action; but what the consequences of it will be, God knows!' People had *questions*, undoubtedly, but apocalyptic certainty was a spent force by this point. The wars were over, the nations of Britain unified, a king sat once more on the throne. Everybody was very tired. The hopes of those most fondly anticipating the Second Coming had been crushed by the failure of Cromwell's regime to fulfil its eschatological role, and the subsequent restoration of the monarchy. In the end, the overwhelming feeling that emerged from that apocalyptic date was one of relief: despite all the woes to befall the land, the following year, John Dryden would commemorate it in verse not as a year of doom, but as an 'Annus Mirabilis'.

There are three conclusions you could draw from all this.

One is simply that humans aren't always great at perspective. We don't have the luxury of seeing the troubles afflicting us today through the wide lens of historical context; for us, the current crisis is *always* the greatest crisis. Pointing out that, technically, it *could* be worse does nothing; it's roughly as effective as any time an older person tells a younger person: 'Kids today don't know they're born. In my day we didn't even have shoes. We had to eat soil and we never complained.' The response is the same: you just don't *understand*. It's no surprise that the strength of apocalyptic belief over time doesn't neatly correlate with how bad things really are – because our own assessment of how bad things are also doesn't correlate with how bad things actually are.

The second is that, while apocalyptic beliefs are often driven by crisis – a way of contextualising them and giving them narrative shape – not all crises are equal. Natural disasters may be seen as omens or harbingers of the ultimate catastrophe – but they're much more likely to spark thoughts of doomsday when they're accompanied by a political or cultural crisis.

The third is that, maybe, when things get *really* bad, people are too busy just trying to survive to think about the bigger picture. Dramatising your woes, placing them into a compelling narrative, and debating what all this *means* may be a luxury in which the truly desperate rarely get the chance to indulge. 'There are no atheists in foxholes,' runs the old canard. Maybe we might more accurately say, there are no preachers in an earthquake.

But – as we'll see in the next chapter – whenever unhappy people *do* have the time to ponder the idea of a world suddenly unmade, the consequences can be explosive.

7.

Revelation and Revolution

The Holy Spirit first spoke to Nat in the fields of rural Virginia, while he was praying beside the plough that his owner made him work the soil with.

'Seek ye the kingdom of Heaven and all things shall be added unto you,' the Spirit told Nat, quoting a passage from the Gospel of Luke that had long intrigued him.

For Nat, an enslaved man in the year 1822, the question of how he might 'seek the kingdom of Heaven' was a difficult one. What kingdom would open its gates to him? Or, put differently: how might those gates be forced open? But Nat had a mind and a status well-suited to answering such questions. Growing up a preternaturally gifted child, his rapid grasp of reading and writing and his charismatic air – not to mention his seeming knowledge of events that predated his birth – had seen him labelled a prophet long before the Spirit ever touched his life.

In the following years, further visions revealed the shape

of an answer. 'I saw white spirits and black spirits engaged in battle,' he would tell his captors shortly before he was put to death, 'and the sun was darkened – and thunder rolled in the Heavens, and blood flowed in streams.' His visions told him that 'the Serpent was loosened', and that his great purpose was to take up the yoke that Christ had laid down – to 'fight against the Serpent, for the time was fast approaching when the first should be last and the last should be first'.

Nat Turner had seen the apocalypse of Revelation, and he understood what it meant.

On 13 August 1831, the sky above Virginia turned green, and he knew it was a sign that he must act. A week later, under cover of night, he and six followers stole into the house of his enslavers and killed them all with axes. None was spared, not even a sleeping baby.

From house to house his little band went over the following day, their numbers swelling as word spread and both the free and the enslaved joined their ranks. In every wealthy house they entered, they would kill the white inhabitants – at least fifty-five souls, all told. (They spared the houses of the white poor, because Nat perceived that their circumstances were of a kind with his own.) Eventually, with his band of followers grown to around sixty, now mounted on horseback and well-armed with guns and swords liberated from the houses they'd passed through, Nat's army marched upon Jerusalem – the county seat of Virginia's Southampton County, whose inhabitants in that moment may have been questioning the wisdom of the naming choice.

They never made it. A force from Jerusalem met and crushed the revolt. Most of Nat's followers were killed; some escaped. He managed to hide for several weeks before he was captured, tried and executed. It was during his short captivity that he told the tale of his divine revelations to his lawyer.

Nat Turner's rebellion was one of very few organised rebellions by enslaved people in the history of the continental United States that ever made it past the planning stage. It was a small, grim affair of blood and desperation – an abortive shock-and-awe campaign that never gained enough of a foothold to answer the question of what came next. Nonetheless, for a few febrile, sweat-drenched August days, it had *succeeded.* Briefly, brutally, the world saw itself turned upside down.

It sent shockwaves across the country. The slaveholding states had, for decades, vibrated with a hum of background paranoia, terrified that a Haiti-style rebellion could happen to them. This was awful confirmation of their fears. Emergency laws were passed: Black people could not meet in groups, could not preach the gospel to one another. A conspiracist mindset became commonplace, one that saw foreign agents fomenting slave uprisings in every shadow. Nat Turner became a kind of folk devil for the white population of the south – who suddenly found themselves looking at familiar faces, and for the first time wondering if murder lurked behind their downturned eyes. One resident of Jerusalem lamented that the townsfolk could 'never again feel safe, never again be happy'.

Our purpose here is not to break out the nanoviolins for Southampton County's anxiety-ridden slavers. It is to note that their panic was not unusual; nor was it misplaced. It was a panic that was often felt by the representatives of the established order when confronted with apocalyptic inspiration.

Because while the apocalypse can be weaponised by the powerful for their own ends, it also tells the powerless that the world that treats them cruelly is not eternal. It is not just a response to crisis, but an answer to it. It tells the downtrodden that they are righteous, and that a great battle will come in which their oppressors will face justice.

And this has meant that for much of history, apocalyptic movements have presented a fearsome challenge to established hierarchies. These movements have focused discontent, spurred resistance, and prompted mass uprisings. They've acted as both a precursor to and an inspiration for many of the most radical and consequential political movements of the modern age.

The apocalypse promises a world overthrown. It promises that earthly powers will crumble, and that the order of all things will be inverted. It promises a day when *the first will be last*, and *the last will be first*.

In short: it promises revolution.

That panic felt in Southampton County had also been felt across a large chunk of Northern Europe in 1534. Fear of insurrection that would 'spring up like fire' gripped the elite: one academic letter-writer from Antwerp spoke of the pervasive paranoia that sedition lurked everywhere, saying, 'There is, I think, scarcely a village or town where the torch is not glowing in secret.'

The immediate cause of this worry was our old friend Jan Matthys, and the apocalyptic overthrow of Münster's authorities that he and his fellow Anabaptists had launched earlier that year. But the thing that caused such 'wretched anxiety' to this scholar in Antwerp – almost 150 miles distant from Münster – was not simply the disturbance to the civil order. It was that in Münster, the Anabaptists seemed to be attempting something like a radical political experiment.

'They preach community of goods,' he writes, 'with the result that all those who have nothing come flocking.'

That 'community of goods' was, in effect, a sort of communism-before-communism. Inspired by the belief that God had provided sufficient riches for all – that a true Christian community would share equally, while the hoarding of wealth was a bastardisation of God's plan – it envisioned an end to private property, and a return to what they saw as a more authentic biblical existence. As the radical German printer Hans Hergot put it in 1527 (the same year that he would be executed for rebellion), under the community of goods 'the people will all work in common, each according to his talents and his capacities. And all things will be used in common, so that no one is better off than another.'

In Münster, this was put into uncompromising practice. The Anabaptists initially took control in the town by exploiting its tolerance for religious dissent (with the obvious result that 'tolerance' subsequently saw a sharp drop in its popularity as a concept). They were already a sizeable minority in the majority-Lutheran community, and they rapidly grew their numbers as their fellow believers – including Matthys himself – flocked to what they hoped might be the New Jerusalem, to the point where they were able to legitimately win a majority on the town council.

Driven by an apocalyptic absolutism, Matthys quickly demanded that the town be purged of unbelievers. He favoured simply executing the Lutherans and the Catholics and anybody else who refused to be rebaptised into their faith; he was persuaded to take the more moderate approach of merely violently driving them all out of town during a blizzard, even the sick and infirm. Matthys and his followers then set about establishing the community of goods, at the point of a sword if necessary. The wealth of those who had already been forced out was quickly expropriated. Among those who remained, the private ownership of money was forbidden – those who held out were preached to about their Christian duty, and if that didn't work, threatened with execution. Food was shared and meals were to be taken in communal dining halls; private accommodation was gradually phased out, and the people were instructed that their doors should always be open to house the multitude who had come to seek this new paradise.

In part, some of this was simply a practical response to the fact that the town was now under siege by the massed forces of the extremely pissed-off religious and civil establishment. But their revolutionary intent is made clear in the letters they sent out to try and draw even more of the downtrodden to their New Jerusalem – the same people who 'have nothing' that so disturbed the scholar of Antwerp. The Münster authorities boasted: 'The poorest amongst us, who used to be despised as beggars, now go about dressed as finely as the highest and most distinguished.'

You can see why it was a popular idea.

That the imminent end of days should inspire the overthrow of the established order is not surprising. Almost from its first existence, the idea of the apocalypse has gone hand in hand with insurrection.

As noted in Chapter 5, the upsurge in Jewish apocalypticism in the second century BCE that produced the Book of Daniel was fuelled by the same sense of cultural and political crisis that spawned the Maccabean Revolt against Greek rule.

What began as a small band of insurgents – outraged at an ill-advised crackdown on Jewish religious practices and launching isolated guerrilla attacks from remote rural strongholds – would swell over time into an army capable of directly confronting an empire in battle. An apocalyptic prophecy that explicitly cast back to previous salvation from oppression in Babylon, and promised a world remade by divine intervention and retribution, was potent fuel for such an uprising. Revolutions run on hope, even when the world seems hopeless.

The early centuries of Christianity also showed the revolutionary potential of eschatological belief. Not just in its first years as a *cri de coeur* against Roman rule, but also at the point when Rome became Christianised – at which point the more extremist elements immediately turned on mainstream Christian leaders as lackeys and sell-outs. And what revolutionary movement would be complete without endless schisms and an overwhelming desire to beat up your own side?

'Beat up', in this case, is not a figure of speech. The most notable such movement in the fourth century were the Donatists of North Africa, and their paramilitary wing, the Circumcellions – who took a very blunt-force approach to resolving their issues.

As is often the case, this revolved around a theological dispute that served as a proxy for a far broader cultural grievance. It stemmed from the suppression of Christianity under the Emperor Diocletian, who (among other things, like cutting out peoples' tongues or boiling them alive) demanded that Christian ministers surrender their copies of the scripture. The Donatist movement insisted that any clergy who had obeyed and turned in their holy books were illegitimate, having abandoned their faith. Not only were the ministers false, but anybody *baptised* by those ministers was likewise not a true member of the faith. Like so many later movements, the Donatists drew strict, purist lines around the group of true believers who would be saved when the Big Day came. Those left outside that small club were their enemies, and so was anybody who hadn't opposed their enemies with sufficient vigour.

The mainline Donatists mostly focused their efforts on rebaptising people into the *true* true Church, just as the Anabaptists of Münster would over a millennium later. But the Circumcellions took a far more aggressive approach – namely beating the shit out of people. Carrying heavy clubs (they refused to carry swords) they would attack churches and clergy, and ambush travellers with demands that they prove they had been baptised by the right flavour of priest. With an eschatological fervour, the Circumcellions believed that the highest virtue of Christianity was to die a martyr; it's widely thought that one purpose of their attacks was to provoke their victims into granting them the gift of martyrdom, a sort of apocalyptic fourth-century version of suicide-by-cop.

All this behaviour led the new Emperor Constantine (on the verge of his own conversion to Christianity) to send troops to North Africa to crush the disruptive Donatists. Naturally, this fresh dose of martyrdom did absolutely nothing to reduce their apocalyptic certainties – all it did was give them another adversary they could paint as an omen of the end times. 'Ironically,' notes the historian Frederick Baumgartner, 'the first Christian emperor became the first Christian ruler to be identified by some Christians as Antichrist.'

The Circumcellions were among the earliest to put into practice a key element of many apocalyptic beliefs – an element that helps it fuel opposition to the established order. 'Antinomianism' is the technical term, but it's a pretty simple concept: the law simply doesn't apply to you. If this world is shortly going to be swept away, then obeying its petty rules seems like an unnecessary hassle. And that's especially the case if the law is unjust, or if it represents the rule of the very unbelievers who are about to get a nasty shock – in which case breaking the law isn't just a fun treat, but a duty. Obeying the wrong kind of law might just see you excluded from the elect who'll be saved when the big moment arrives.

The Donatist and Circumcellion revolt against authority was only partial: they objected to the specific authority of Rome, and of priests whom they saw as impure, but they didn't object to the notion of authority itself. They just wanted to claim it for themselves, in the most absolutist way possible. But many later apocalyptic movements would go further – questioning the right of elites to have authority over the masses at all.

In part, this was a response to the corruption and venality of both the Church and the aristocracy. In particular, the worldly riches of the Church were repeatedly held up as a sign of having fallen from the ideals of Christ; priestly corruption was commonly identified with the Antichrist. In the early 1400s, a scandal in Bohemia inspired a wave of apocalyptic uprisings across the region, carried out in the name of the Czech theologian Jan Hus.

This would probably have come as a surprise to Hus, by accounts a mild-mannered and thoughtful man who had simply refused to play along with the Pope's habit of selling 'indulgences' (effectively Get Out Of Sin Free cards) to the highest bidder. This unforgivable break with a lucrative papal side hustle was enough to get Hus executed in 1415; his perceived martyrdom would fuel a revolt in a region where the Church's wealth – it owned around half of all land in an area with widespread poverty – was bordering on the obscene.

An attempt in 1419 to suppress the Hussite movement in Prague by King Wenceslas (not the good one) backfired horribly, with the people rising up and seizing control of part of the city. For good measure, they also threw some of Wenceslas's hand-picked councillors from the windows of the town hall. Property was expropriated and redistributed; full Communion would be offered to all, rather than the previous approach of saving the good bits (i.e. the wine) for the wealthy. Even the language of faith would be democratised: no more keeping Church business in Latin. They would speak their own Czech language, so that all could understand.

The apocalypticism of the movement intensified rapidly. The sudden burst of unprecedented egalitarianism – combined with the inevitable backlash and attempted repression that swiftly followed – only increased the sense among the faithful that a new world was on the verge of being born. Just as they would in Münster just over a century later, the poor flocked to the region. They gathered in Hussite towns, and on a mountain where it was said that Christ would manifest his Second Coming. They were told to prepare for battle with the forces of the Antichrist, in which they would be 'washing their hands in the blood of sinners'. The faithful were told the apocalypse would come on Valentine's Day 1420, when all but the few settlements of the true faith would be consumed in terrible fire.

That world-destroying conflagration didn't happen, obviously. The battle – and the washing of hands in the blood – most certainly did.

The resulting war lasted almost two decades, complete with the inevitable splitting of the Hussite movement into numerous moderate and extremist factions, and eventually . . . a kind of settlement? The more extremist factions were defeated in battle, while the leaders of the moderate wings – because, obviously, even egalitarian and anti-hierarchy movements will have *leaders* – found that they could make accommodations with the existing power structures that would allow them to stay in charge. So it goes; once again, the apocalypse was postponed for another day.

And all told, it wasn't a bad compromise for everyone involved. For the established powers of the Holy Roman Empire, the breakaway religion would at least be kept in check; for the upstart Hussites, the breakaway religion would at least be kept in Czech. As uprisings go, it was one of the more successful ones – the inheritors of the Hussite movement would retain spiritual and civil authority in Bohemian lands for centuries to come.

This was a time when the old settlement of the medieval world was coming apart, which brought with it both unprecedented freedom and fear. As Norman Cohn argues in *The Pursuit of the Millennium*, the old order had been both a prison and a safety net – in a feudal village, peasants could never rise to any great height, but there was also a floor to how far they would be allowed to fall. The swelling population of Europe flocked into growing cities, where there was suddenly opportunity for riches – but also the risk of profound destitution.

It was among this mass of people suddenly unmoored from the oppressive stability of the old order, Cohn suggests, that apocalyptic uprisings found their greatest support. In the Hussite movement, both sides of the equation had found common cause: it was started by members of the rising burgher class, the skilled artisans who were now economically independent but still shut out of political power; meanwhile, the bulk of its supporters came from the impoverished urban underclasses. Elsewhere, there were insurgencies of the poor that, while they weren't inherently apocalyptic at their core, still had end-times preachers who played major roles: John Ball in the English Peasants' Revolt of 1381; Thomas Münzer in the German Peasants' War of 1524.

This revolutionary impulse is everywhere in the fringe groups that sprang up around the English Civil War – the ones who saw the overthrow of one established order as merely an *amuse-bouche* for the ultimate remaking of the world that was soon to arrive.

Gerard Winstanley saw this radical possibility. He wrote of 'the present state of the old World that is running up like parchment in the fire, and wearing away'. Winstanley was an apocalyptic preacher who led the True Levellers (better known, pejoratively, as the Diggers), who became infamous for asserting their right to farm the common land that had been appropriated by enclosure – and were driven from place to place by furious landholders as a result. Much like their predecessors in Münster, they sought to 'make the Earth a Common Treasury', to return the world to that biblical utopia in which all was shared.

Their vision was one with the potential to upend all of society, because they viewed even the act of labouring for a wage as corruption of the world. They called for, in effect, a permanent general strike among all the workers of the land – 'for by their labours, they have lifted up Tyrants and Tyranny; and by denying to labor for Hire, they shall pull them down again'.

Even more radical – if significantly less organised – were the Ranters, the gleefully anarchic self-proclaimed 'Mad Crew', who saw the imminent coming of a new dawn as an opportunity to unleash furious and piss-taking invective against the power structures of a sick world.

'To All the Inhabitants of the Earth; specially to the rich ones,' begins the second part of the Ranter pamphleteer Abiezer Coppe's *A Fiery Flying Roll*. Its full-throated declaration of apocalyptic class vengeance is hard to miss: 'Howle, rich men, for the miseries that are (just now) coming upon you, the rust of your silver is rising up in judgement against you, burning your flesh like fire.'

There's a line that gets trotted out quite often: 'It is easier to imagine the end of the world than the end of capitalism.' (It's variously attributed to Mark Fisher, Slavoj Žižek or sundry others; nobody seems entirely sure who said it first.) It gets to the heart of why the apocalyptic imagination has so often fuelled revolt. The structures of the existing world surround us and smother us; every day we drown slowly in the status quo. The concept of changing these structures through the normal tools of human agency can seem almost comically overwhelming, like relocating an ocean one cup at a time. But what if it could all burn? What if it could, in a moment, be swept away in its entirety?

The historical irony, of course, is that you can also flip the line around. For the European populace in the twilight of the Middle Ages, as old feudal certainties began to crumble, the potent combination of crisis and possibility fuelled wave after wave of apocalyptic expectation, as they sought to understand and shape the changes that were unfolding around them. The old world was dying; the birth of the new was troubled as all hell. For many who were caught in these upheavals, it was easier to imagine the end of the world than the *beginning* of capitalism.

How deep does the link between apocalypticism and revolution go?

Many later revolutionary movements drew inspiration from their spiritual predecessors. In the uprisings of the European Middle Ages, you can definitely see something new brewing – revolts that aren't simply responses to isolated crises, but envisage completely different ways to organise society.

But there are plenty of people who'd say that the relationship goes further than mere influence – that apocalyptic uprisings and political revolutions are fundamentally the same phenomenon.

Marxism is the example most commonly picked. You can see why: it ticks lots of the boxes of our universal apocalypse story. It divides history into ages. It foretells a crisis point being reached, when the moral failings of the age become unsustainable. It predicts a great struggle between the forces who wish to see a new world and those who oppose it – one that is both inevitable, but also must be diligently worked towards. It promises a utopia at the end.

It's not surprising, then, that some explicitly label it as such. 'The Marxist view of history can be seen as a secularized form of Judeo-Christian Messianism' is how one historian describes this view. Another author calls Marx's work 'an extraordinarily powerful version of the apocalypse meme for a secular age'.

It's not just modern authors who've drawn that connection: writing a decade before the Russian revolutions, the Bolshevik author Anatoly Lunacharsky made exactly the same parallel, drawing a connection between 'the suffering of the proletariat and the passion of Christ, the socialist revolution and the Day of Judgment, and socialism and Christ's millennial reign on earth'. And many have suggested that Russia's long history of apocalyptic movements, from the self-immolating Raskolniki onwards, helped seed the ground for what Communism offered.

It's possible to take this comparison too far, though. To state the obvious, one important difference between the religious revolutions and Marxist ones is that they are . . . well, *religious*. (This was certainly an important point of distinction for the Bolsheviks themselves, who expelled Lunacharsky for bringing religion into their business.) The line between religion, philosophy and ideology can be fuzzy, for sure. But the issue of whether you literally believe that a supernatural force is going to determine the outcome of events remains a hefty one.

This is especially the case because it tells you whether the new world is something that needs to be built, or something that will just pop into existence. As the Marxist historian Eric Hobsbawm put it: '[M]illenarian movements share a fundamental vagueness about the actual way in which the new society will be brought about . . . They expect it to make itself, by divine revelation, by an announcement from on high, by a miracle – they expect it to happen *somehow*.'

Political revolutionaries have many flaws, but vagueness is usually not one of them. For every airy pronouncement about how all problems will vanish under the new regime, there are usually a hundred incredibly pedantic planning documents and philosophical tracts and endless bloody meetings about *precisely* how things are supposed to work once triumphant victory is achieved. Their plans may be a touch optimistic, but they are definitely plans.

The political revolutionaries who followed in the wake of those earlier uprisings certainly shared an apocalyptic yearning for the old world to be swept away, but they rarely expected the new world to 'make itself'.

The revolutionary potential of the apocalypse wasn't confined to those trying to make sense of economic upheaval or to fight against oppressive rulers. In its focus on radical change, on the destruction of the old world, it's a natural bedfellow for any cultural currents that challenge authority and social structures more broadly. It's not just a material revolution, but a revolution of thought.

Back in medieval Europe, this was the other side of the movement against the perceived corruption and wealth of the Church. It was not merely resentment of a Church that had turned its back on the ideals of Christ, but a far broader denial of its right to dictate the lives of the people. This slow-burn revolution rejected the idea that the hierarchies of the Church had a monopoly on scriptural interpretation or moral authority. Instead, it sought to cut out the theological middle-man between believers and their God; it would return religion to the people. These democratising impulses were at the heart of the Protestant Reformation and similar movements (like the Hussites), but weren't limited to it. They drew on older traditions, and found expression in a vast blossoming of sects and communities and individuals, all with their own unique take on what this religion business was all about.

Some of the earliest stirrings of this revolt came in the form of the Brethren of the Free Spirit – less an organisation than a loosely connected bundle of heretical thoughts which had spread across much of Europe from the thirteenth century onwards. The Free Spirit was not an especially apocalyptic movement, nor did it draw its members from the downtrodden of society – it spread largely among the educated and the well-to-do. But it set the stage for much of what was to follow.

The adherents of the Free Spirit picked up the antinomianism of earlier movements, but where groups like the Circumcellions had used this sense of lawlessness to legitimise violence, the Free Spirits rode it in the direction of free thought and, in at least some cases, free love. They taught of a deeply personal, individual relationship with the divine, one that sprang from within and could attain perfection – not by following the strictures of ecclesiastical authority, but by direct communication with God. The Free Spirits were gleeful in breaking free from the norms of the time, often speaking of their holy journey in erotic terms. This was, apparently, not restricted to being a literary device: many adherents viewed sex not as a shameful or base act, but as a spiritual act on a par with prayer, in which men and women equally could return to a state of Edenic paradise by getting their Adam and Eve on. (It is, perhaps, not surprising that the movement attracted followers.)

Centuries later, the Ranters followed in this tradition; Abiezer Coppe wrote gleefully of breaking social taboos to expose the hypocrisy of society, of 'choosing base things to confound the things that are' – to *épater les aristocrates*. Alongside his tirades against nobles and priests, he revelled in defying social and sexual mores, writing of how he scandalously consorted with gypsies, and 'hug'd and kiss'd them, putting my hand in their bosomes, loving the she-Gipsies dearly'.

But the democratisation of religion and morality was not confined to those with a libertine bent. In the Puritan world of the recently established Massachusetts Bay Colony in the 1600s, another apocalyptically flavoured break with the rules of the established order caused scandal and discord. That it followed in the antinomian tradition is given away somewhat by the fact it's called the Antinomian Controversy. At its heart was Anne Hutchinson, an Englishwoman who in 1633 had followed her favourite preacher, John Cotton, to the New World. Hutchinson was a midwife, and in her conversations with the expectant mothers of the colony, she discovered a desire for spiritual discussion that was not served by the male hierarchy of the local church. So she started holding Bible studies in her home.

This quickly began to rile the authorities, especially as what Hutchinson taught was not *quite* in line with the teachings of the officially sanctioned ministers. They may have fled England to get away from the oppressive rules of the established Church, but hey, that wasn't going to stop them imposing their own rules in turn. Hutchinson, however, had the very free-spirited idea that the Holy Spirit resided within her, and that the blessings of the Church were not needed for a person to attain heaven. The backlash to Hutchinson's teachings was so strong that the Governor of the Massachusetts colony, John Winthrop, ended up putting her on trial. Hutchinson claimed that divine revelation had informed her that the colony would be destroyed in a great disaster. Her apocalyptic warnings didn't exactly turn the case in her favour – she was exiled from the state.

Hutchinson's case illustrates another way in which apocalypticism had the potential to upturn the old order: the role it often afforded women. It might be unexpected (and it certainly isn't universal), but apocalyptic movements often gave women a far greater role than they could find elsewhere – and women were often at the vanguard of support for these movements.

Partly this was due to the very antinomianist, anti-establishment vibe of so much eschatological expectation. If all the structures of the old world were set to crumble, why should the sexual hierarchy be any different? It can be easier to imagine the end of the world than the end of the patriarchy.

Sometimes it may also have been due to their view of sexual activity: apocalyptic movements were often wildly divergent from established norms when it came to that most heavily regulated of activities. Sometimes that went in the pro-sex direction, revelling in a carnal unshackling; sometimes it went to the opposite extreme, calling for near-total or complete abstinence. You can see why both may have been attractive to women, compared to the status quo: both freedom to pursue pleasure and freedom from the duty to provide pleasure could be liberating.

And a third component may be the specific role of prophecy in apocalypticism. In many places and many times, the doors of the ecclesiastical life were closed to women: they could not preach, they could not write, and for centuries in much of the Christian world, women were specifically banned from the act of interpreting scripture. But prophecy and divine revelation provided a way in: if they could convince others that they truly were a channel for the word of God, then their voices could be heard. Revelation was a path to participation.

You can see this path being followed by Hildegard von Bingen, the twelfth-century visionary nun and polymath, or Margery Kempe, the fourteenth-century mystic, both of whom became extremely influential despite the barriers placed in their way. In later centuries, women would even found and lead apocalyptic movements – such as Mother Ann Lee, the founder of the ecstatic Shakers in the late 1700s, whose profound distaste for sex led her to preach that a regime of total abstinence could hasten the imminent Second Coming.

Indeed, the breaking down of gender barriers in apocalyptic movements sometimes went even further than allowing prominent roles for women. Nowhere was this more apparent than in the case of the Public Universal Friend – a genderless preacher from Rhode Island who, after a near-death experience in 1776, announced that they were neither male nor female and instructed followers not to use gendered pronouns. As one kind of revolution already gripped their country, the Friend preached that the Day of Judgement would arrive in April 1780. While that didn't happen, they continued to grow their following, and ended up founding a town called Jerusalem in upstate New York. (There are a lot of Jerusalems in the USA.)

The role of a prophet was not an easy one for those who upset the gendered apple cart, and especially not ones who preached imminent judgement. The backlash that apocalyptic movements so often attract was felt by both Ann Lee and the Public Universal Friend, who were subject to both violence and legal attacks. The same is true for Eleanor Davies, one of history's most committed would-be prophets, who devoted much of her life around the time of the English Civil War to getting her words out into the world – despite a lot of people being very determined that she shouldn't.

Eleanor Davies was not from a humble background: she was a prominent member of the aristocracy, and at times in her life mixed with royalty. Things changed when she began experiencing visions, and became determined to warn the nation of the imminent Day of Judgement, which she pegged to around 1645. Her first pamphlets on the subject were met with a sort of bemused indifference, but they rapidly became more incendiary – in more ways than one. In a fit of 'Darling, please don't make a scene', her first husband went so far as to burn her manuscripts to stop her publishing them. After he died, she remarried, only to find that her second husband burned her papers as well. Eleanor was not deterred, at one point smuggling her writings out of the country while pretending to go on holiday so that she could get them published by a nonconformist printer in Amsterdam, then smuggling the books back into the country.

Her husbands, to be fair, might have had a point when it came to the trouble that Eleanor's doomsday prophecies would land her in. She ended up spending a large part of her life in and out of prison or Bedlam on various charges. She was not exactly a class warrior in the mode of many other apocalyptic preachers of the age, but she shared with the Ranters an impulse to shock, provoke and disrupt the norm. This culminated in her bursting into Lichfield Cathedral with a couple of friends and committing what a court would describe as 'insufferable profanations' – namely, pouring tar over the altar, sitting on the bishops' throne, and informing the congregation that she was in charge now. (This was the act that got her committed to Bedlam.)

In an extremely 'nice posh lady' move, she also made common cause with Gerard Winstanley's Diggers in 1650, offering to employ them on her estate when they were forced off their land. The Diggers, you might remember, viewed any waged labour as sinful, which made the offer a little less helpful than it might have seemed. Winstanley grabbed it anyway, taking up a job as Davies's estate manager, which attracted quite a bit of 'Sorry, what was that you said about jobs?' from the more sceptical among his comrades. Davies sacked him after a year because he was rubbish at it.

The prominent role played by women in apocalyptic movements was the case in Münster as well – although there, too, the hope for a more equal society would prove short-lived.

Women were some of the most enthusiastic early followers of Matthys and co. Anabaptists already had a reputation for the inclusion of women, and were on board with the same reformist traditions of opening up and democratising religion. To begin with, this promise was fulfilled. Women had an equal voice in public meetings, they were partners with rather than servants of their husbands. When the city came under siege, they were honoured for defending the walls alongside the men.

This . . . would not last.

After Jan Matthys was chopped into pieces by the prince-bishop's soldiers, the leadership vacuum was quickly filled by Matthys's acolyte, a Dutch apprentice tailor named Johan Beukelszoon – better known to history as John of Leiden.

Beukelszoon had what you might call a flair for the dramatic. His first act after Matthys was killed was to run naked through the streets before falling into a silent three-day trance. His charismatic ways and claims of divine visions – not to mention political cunning, in offering positions of power to various influential men – saw him rapidly adopted as the new leader of the Münster community. And just as quickly, things began to change. Any hope that the preaching of equality would lead to a less hierarchical society faded; absolute power became concentrated among a select few, all of them men, and before long Beukelszoon began dressing himself in regal attire. By September of 1534, he had proclaimed himself the King of New Jerusalem.

And what's more, in July of that year, he had issued a proclamation that there was one more important resource the people of Münster would be required to redistribute: women.

Both the attraction of Anabaptism for women and the expulsion of many of Münster's former inhabitants – many of them men – had left the city with a pronounced gender imbalance, with around three women to every man. And so Beukelszoon legalised polygamy. But more than that, he decreed that all women should be married – and that they couldn't say no to any proposal of marriage, but were obliged to accept the first proposal they received. This set off a mad scramble among the men to acquire as many wives as possible; Beukelszoon is said to have claimed sixteen wives for himself, one of whom was Matthys's widow. The histories of the Münster uprising rapidly descend from high-minded social reform into tales of, at best, quasi-spiritual orgies and, at worst, mass forced marriage.

There is a caveat to all this: most of those histories are fairly one-sided affairs. One thing about apocalyptic believers is that they're often not *super*-focused on documenting their actions for posterity – on the fairly obvious grounds that they don't think there's going to be any posterity. History, contrary to popular belief, is not written exclusively by the winners – but it *does* tend to be written by people who at least think there'll be a future to have history in.

This means that many doomsday movements are remembered mostly in records produced by their (often numerous) enemies. So it was in Münster. Virtually all the historical descriptions of it are sourced to those who considered the Münsterites dangerous heretics. Accusing your enemies of sexual immorality – the more outré and scandalous the better – has been a pretty standard propaganda technique for a very long time, and was especially potent in the sixteenth century. Anabaptists had been on the receiving end of spurious accusations of polygamy before.

But still, the historical consensus is that, yeah, this really is pretty much how events in Münster played out. Not only are the details agreed on by most sources, but it also has a grimy ring of truth about it. That what began as a movement promising egalitarian dreams would end up with people claimed as property by a self-crowned king; that a project which started with the violent expulsion of outsiders would then turn its oppression inwards . . . nobody is shocked-*shocked* by this. As is perhaps too often the case, the line between 'truly liberatory environment' and 'hideously exploitative sex cult' can be a surprisingly thin and porous one.

And that's a lesson that also applies to our last stop on this tour of the revolutionary nature of the apocalypse.

Robert Matthews was a fucking loser.

He isn't really the point of this story, but none of the events in it would have happened without this basic truth, so it's worth emphasising: Robert Matthews was a barn fire of a human being. Pathetic and dangerous in equal measure, he was one of those men who devote their lives to ensuring that their personal failings ripple outwards in concentric circles of misery.

Matthews was born – and soon orphaned – in a stricter-than-strict religious community of Scots settlers in upstate New York, near the border with Vermont. A sickly child ill-suited to the farming life, he became a carpenter and moved to New York City in 1808, where he proceeded to infuriate his hard-drinking workmates with his incessant preaching. But his surface piety was in tension with demons churning inside him: he returned to his childhood hometown after being convicted of an unprovoked assault on a woman.

For the next few decades, his life fluctuated between success and failure, contentment and tragedy. He married and had children; many of his children died. He built two businesses, only to see them ruined – one through his own errors, one through the intangible forces of financial crisis. His remaining family were left mired in poverty and forced to move house repeatedly. During the days, Matthews would work odd jobs and visit churches, seeking another shot of the powerful religious certainties he remembered from his childhood. In the evenings, he would beat his wife.

Like Hong Xiuquan and his failed exams, Matthews' break from reality and turn towards the apocalypse came when the contradictions between his self-image and his actual situation became too much to bear. He thought he had finally found the right church to restore his religious inspiration – that of Edward Kirk, the revivalist preacher who was part of the Second Great Awakening that was sweeping the nation. Matthews begged to join Kirk's congregation. In no uncertain terms, they turned him away – his reputation as 'a lazy, thriftless, dishonest fellow' had preceded him. They did, however, invite his long-suffering wife and children to join them. And with the church community to sustain her, Margaret

Matthews finally found the strength and support she needed to stand up to her husband.

Like many men before and after him, Robert Matthews proved unable to distinguish between the break-up of his family and the end of the world.

His behaviour became even more erratic; he stopped shaving, he would fall into trances and he had visions of a great flood that would soon consume upstate New York. One evening in 1830, after Margaret rebuffed his menacing attempts to baptise her into his own religion so that she might be saved from the imminent floodwaters, he went to the local church and ranted about the coming Day of Judgement until they turned out the lights on him. Then he returned home and kidnapped his sons. Search parties were sent out, but it didn't prove hard to find and rescue them – because a few days later, Matthews burst into another service a few towns over to once again shout at the congregants about the end times.

Matthews subsequently abandoned his family, and decided to devote himself to his mission – he would travel the land and preach the truth as it had been revealed to him. He understood now that he was not Robert Matthews, but the Prophet Matthias; his name, he realised, was the key, linking him to that apocalyptic prophet of a former age, Jan Matthys.

But Matthias was no Matthys. He would foment no uprisings, overthrow no worldly order. This story, remember, isn't *about* him. What success he had as a prophet was on a smaller, grubbier, griftier scale: along with another outsider preacher, Elijah Pierson, he leveraged his wild appearance and a measure of charisma into convincing a few rich people that he was the living incarnation of God, and that they should sign over their fancy houses to him so that he could establish his kingdom on Earth.

And so it was that he moved into the country estate of Benjamin and Ann Folger, about thirty miles north of New York City in the riverside village of Sing Sing. Matthias the Prophet did not have many followers: the Folgers, another wealthy merchant named Sylvester Mills, Elijah Pierson, and some servants – including Pierson's maid, a formerly enslaved woman currently named Isabella Van Wagenen (she had taken the surname of the farmer who had purchased her freedom). It was hardly a parliament of the elect, but it would do – especially given that it came with a country pile and a Manhattan townhouse. Matthias grandiosely renamed the estate Mount Zion, and settled into his rule as he awaited the destruction of the impure world outside its borders.

It was a cult, even if it was a really small one. But what it lacked in size, it made up for in a wild amount of unhinged interpersonal messiness. Most notably, Matthias quickly started a sexual relationship with Ann Folger. For her part, Ann initially seemed quite cheerful about this situation; her husband Benjamin was somewhat less so, especially after Matthias married Ann in a ceremony that he said was fine because he was the prophet.

In retaliation, Benjamin promptly seduced Matthias's married daughter. When he found out, Matthias beat his daughter, then abruptly decided that she and Benjamin should be married also – a state of matrimony that lasted for a few days until her real husband showed up, at which point Matthias insisted that Benjamin should marry the widow of one of Sylvester Mills's servants instead.

Unsurprisingly, all this reality-TV nonsense produced a

degree of unease in the community surrounding Mount Zion – not to mention among the relatives of those who were trapped in the cult. For a while, the local hostility to Matthias's heavenly kingdom and the attempted interventions from desperate relatives only served to strengthen his grip on his followers, as he insisted that any voices from outside the kingdom were deceivers who should be shunned. But things rapidly came to a head when Elijah Pierson suddenly died.

There's no evidence that the death of Pierson, an elderly man who had been in bad health for years, was anything other than natural. But the Folgers – who had begun, slowly and haltingly, to realise that they'd made a terrible mistake in giving this man control of their lives – seized the opportunity, and accused Matthias of his murder.

As the trial approached, however, the Folgers began to get cold feet. They knew just how much reputational damage Matthias could do to them on the stand if he decided to tell the *whole* truth about the weird sexual web that had been spun at Mount Zion. Both parties realised that there was a mutually beneficial way out: they would all blame the maid Isabella Van Wagenen, the only Black woman in the room. She was a perfect scapegoat, one that would allow everything else to be swept shamefacedly under the carpet.

But Isabella was no pushover. What's more, she was no stranger to the courts – she'd previously claimed an historic legal first when she won the return of her son, who had been abducted and returned to slavery after she gained her freedom. Able to provide plentiful testimony as to her good character, Isabella beat the murder charge. Matthias, meanwhile, was convicted on the lesser count of beating his daughter. The newspapers of New York – the scandal-hungry penny press at the dawn of the mass-media age – had an absolute field day.

Upon his release from prison, Matthias would continue to wander the land, trying to get someone to take him seriously as a prophet. He had little success: the closest he came was a meeting with Joseph Smith, the founder of the Mormon Church. His followers from the days of Mount Zion abandoned him. Isabella Van Wagenen, despite everything, was the last to leave.

She's the one this story is about.

She'd invested her belief in Robert Matthews, just as she had in Elijah Pierson before him, and before that a Christian perfectionist named James Latourette. Her belief was powerful, and the realisation that she had been let down caused her profound soul-searching. She would spend years thinking on the events of Mount Zion, and on the injustices that the world had thrown at her. She would look for answers. She would believe in the apocalypse one more time, in the 1840s, when she would become a charismatic figure in the vast Millerite movement that predicted the end of the world in 1844. She would be let down once again.

She would not be bowed by this great disappointment.

Instead, she found the answer within herself. Isabella did not need a prophet to mark the path for her, because God had his own plan for her – even if the path she would tread showed that an echo of Matthias still lingered. She decided that, like that disappointing prophet, she too would travel the land, and that wherever she went, she too would speak honestly about the world as she saw it. And in doing so, Isabella would once again take a new name – a name entirely of her own choosing this time, a name that she felt reflected this calling. It was under this name that, in the coming years, she would become famous as a voice for the liberation both of Black people and of women; a voice that still resonates today.

Sojourner Truth had been promised the end of the world. Like so many other such promises, it was an end that never arrived. But in imagining that her world could be ended, she was also able to imagine that her world could be *different*.

And sometimes, that's the most important thing there is.

8.

War to End All Wars

The origin of one enduring apocalyptic tale has more to do with the twin forces of economics and geography than it does with anything spiritual. Things usually do.

Let's explain.

Ever since the Bronze Age, the great trade route snaked its way up the Mediterranean coast of the Levant. Today it's sometimes known as the Via Maris: Latin for 'Way of the Sea'. Nobody at the time called it that, though, for a variety of reasons – chief among them that nobody would even speak Latin for another seven centuries. But whatever name those merchants 3,500 years ago gave it, it arced across the great civilisational cauldron of the Fertile Crescent, connecting the bounty of the Nile Delta to the rising cities of the Syrian plain, and the empires of Mesopotamia beyond.

It wouldn't have been much to look at. In places, it was little more than a dusty trail in the dry months, a path of churned mud in the wet. But still, it was a *route*; knowable, predictable, safe-ish. From Egypt, it wound up the coast of the lands that would birth religions, stopping at ports all along the shore, before suddenly cutting inland. This is where it crossed one of the major barriers to anybody who wanted to travel in this part of the ancient world – the daunting, almost impassable peaks of the Carmel mountain range.

Key word there: *almost* impassable. There were a few ways through: one pass miles to the north, and another further to the south. But the quickest, the one the Via Maris followed, was through the narrow valley of the Wadi Ara and the Musmus Pass, where steep slopes of rock rose on either side.

And near the mouth of the wadi, where the traveller would emerge from among the hills on to the bountiful lands of the Jezreel Valley, was a city named Megiddo.

It was a jewel of the region, ancient and wealthy, with great walls and advanced architecture. Here the weary traveller could stop for hospitality and rest, but this was not the city's only purpose. It was both waypoint and chokepoint – strategically perfect to guard the mouth of the pass, control the trade route, and command a vast swathe of the rich agricultural land beyond. If – to pick a random example – the Egyptian Empire wanted to march northwards to remind some uppity Canaanites who was in charge, then this was one of the most likely routes they'd take.

Except, of course, that would be very silly. It was a well-guarded pass. Marching your troops through a narrow valley controlled by the enemy would be madness – they'd be sitting ducks, vulnerable to attack on three sides and with no room to manoeuvre or bring up reinforcements. *Unless . . .*

Unless, reasoned Pharaoh Thutmose III – whose Egyptian

Empire was in the process of marching north to remind some uppity Canaanites who was in charge – unless marching through the pass was *such* an obviously hare-brained move that Canaan's forces would assume nobody could be that daft. Maybe then they might leave the wadi only lightly guarded. Maybe a rapid advance would catch them with their pants down.

Nothing ventured, nothing gained. Thutmose III decided to do his thutmost, and test this theory out.

The Battle of Megiddo in the fifteenth century BCE is one of the most notable in military history – primarily because it's kind of the *beginning* of military history. It's the first battle for which we actually have a written record of what happened. It's an incomplete, one-sided record, to be sure. It's very much written by the winners, Egypt, who after a swift ass-kicking and a lengthy siege consolidated their rule over the kingdoms of Canaan for the next few centuries. But still, the record gives us some idea of the forces deployed and the tactics used. It tells us that it marked the debut of new weapons technology, in the form of composite bows. It tells us what spoils of war were captured. It gives us history's first-ever body count.

This battle may be the first we have the details of – but archaeological evidence suggests it was not the first in the valley. And it most definitely was not the last.

According to one scholar, the Jezreel Valley has been the setting for no fewer than thirty-four significant battles throughout history. This blood-soaked legacy stems from a few fundamental causes: the economic importance of the trade that ran through it and control over the valley's fertile land; its location, slap-bang in the spot where the pointy ends of numerous empires would meet down the centuries; and its basic geography, a plain surrounded by barriers with limited exits and entrances, a true theatre of war. As a result, the valley is one of the most consistently fought-over patches of land anywhere on the planet, or – in the words of Lord Kitchener – 'the greatest battlefield in the world'.

The Judean King Josiah was killed in the second Battle of Megiddo in 609 BCE, as the empires of Egypt, Assyria and Babylon struggled for dominance. On the eastern side of the valley, the Romans fought Jewish rebels, and the future emperor Vespasian captured Yosef ben Matityahu, who would become the historian Josephus. Saladin skirmished with the Crusaders here in the 1180s; in 1260, the Mongols were denied conquest for the first time in their empire's history, as the Mamluks defeated them at the Battle of Ain Jalut. In 1799, mere months before he would seize power in France, Napoleon routed the Ottomans at the foot of Mount Tabor. And in World War I, General Edmund Allenby repeated Thutmose III's gamble, sending his allied cavalry on a danger run through the Musmus Pass to defeat the Ottoman forces in yet another Battle of Megiddo.

All of which is to say, it is perhaps unsurprising that when John of Patmos wrote his prophecy of where the great battle between the forces of good and evil would occur in the last days, this is where he placed it. At the time John was writing, many of those conflicts lay in the future, while Megiddo itself had already lain abandoned for several centuries. But its cultural memory must have lingered. Stories of past battles – the routing of Canaan, the death of Josiah – became memorialised, and the ruins of the old city became legend, a once and future Camelot where great and terrible deeds had taken place, and would again. And in any case, the twin forces of economics and geography still held sway – the slopes of Megiddo were, very clearly, a likely spot for a battle.

Those slopes themselves were a part of its long legacy. Megiddo did not lie on a mountain, or even a natural hill. But the city was already ancient in ancient times. The effect of building a settlement on top of a previous settlement, built on top of a previous settlement – twenty layers in all – had created a pronounced incline up to it. And at some point, someone decided to call that rise Mount Megiddo – or in Hebrew, Har Megiddo.

And it was this term that John of Patmos transliterated to the Greek in which he composed the Book of Revelation, and so bequeathed us the word we still use today. The word that means the climactic, all-consuming battle that will be joined at the end of days:

Armageddon.

Of all the crises that can befall a society, and of all the means of destruction that threaten us, war has a special place in our apocalyptic imagination.

The other terrors of existence are mostly optional in the pantheon of doomsday stories. Not everyone lives near an earthquake zone, after all; people in the desert are rarely concerned about a *fimbulwinter.* Floods remain a popular choice, but even they aren't present in every apocalyptic narrative. But pretty much everybody telling tales of the end times, and deciding what tribulations will mark their final days, will eventually choose violence.

As we've already noted, Jewish apocalypticism both began and became entrenched during periods of conflict. In

Christianity, two of the Four Horsemen of the Apocalypse were (probably) symbolic of one form of war or another. In Chinese eschatology, there's very little talk of pestilence, but a huge focus on the fear of invasion or civil war. Hinduism foresees a great battle at the end of the *kalpa*. Secular predictions of doom may see many causes of our downfall – but almost all of them envision combat as either a result of, or a catalyst for, whatever catastrophe will consume us.

This apocalyptic certainty has been reflected in wars down the ages. 'Mine eyes have seen the glory of the coming of the Lord,' goes 'The Battle Hymn of the Republic', Julia Ward Howe's stirring song from the American Civil War. It's a familiar refrain, and much loved ('Play it again!' was reportedly Lincoln's delighted reaction when he first heard it). It's also a deeply apocalyptic one: the song's lyrics are unambiguous in seeing the Civil War as the final battle prophesied in Revelation. The Day of Judgement isn't just imminent; it's *here*. (In case the message wasn't clear, the lyrics go on: 'He has sounded forth the trumpet that shall never call retreat / He is sifting out the hearts of men before His judgment-seat'.) This wasn't a weird outlier: one historian has written of 'the sheer intensity and virtual unanimity of Northern conviction . . . that the war was not merely one sacred battle among many but was the climactic test of the redeemer nation and its millennial role'.

Why, exactly, does war play such a central role in apocalyptic tales? And – to flip the question – why do apocalyptic tales play such a central role in war?

Partly, it's simply because war is very close to being a human universal. Almost every society in history has experienced war as a fairly regular occurrence – 95 per cent of all cultures across time, according to some estimates. Those societies who've managed to largely avoid it tend to do so by being either very small or extremely isolated or both, and basically hoping that nobody notices them or cares enough to bother having a war at them. The Battle of Megiddo may have provided history with its first written body count, but the butcher's bill extends much further back in time. The earliest archaeological evidence for something that looks a lot like a war is fourteen thousand years old. War was already a grizzled veteran of human destruction when the apocalypse was just a twinkle in Zoroaster's eye.

War, bluntly, is just a thing that humans do. A catastrophic, all-destroying war is not just a constant anxiety for human culture, it's also something that's easy for people to picture. In pre-mass-media eras, you might not have a good sense of what, say, a volcano looked like, unless you were unfortunate enough to live next to one. But bad men with weapons, slashing and burning their way through your world? Yeah, you could imagine that. It turns the planetary into the personal.

But there's another reason why apocalypse and Armageddon are so entwined, and that's because there's a cause-and-effect loop that other catastrophes simply don't have. What I mean is: if you think that your world is soon to be wiped out by a flood, that belief doesn't actually *cause more floods*. (Assuming you don't get really into diverting rivers in order to fulfil the prophecy, that is.)

But war? That's different.

After all, one of the major causes of war is the belief that someone else is about to start a war. It's the inescapable logic of the arms race: you see someone else marshalling their forces down the road, so you begin to think that, uh, maybe you should marshal your forces too. And the apocalyptic belief in a great climactic battle is not just a prediction: it's a call to arms. When James VI demanded his people be 'armed spiritually and bodily', it wasn't a metaphor.

If you start summoning your followers to prepare for the final conflict, other people are going to notice. They're going to respond in kind. Even if they don't think this is in fact the ultimate battle for the soul of the world, they're still going to do the things people do if they're worried about a regular battle. And those things will only heighten your certainty that the great war is, in fact, extremely nigh.

So apocalyptic expectation and a thirst for battle can reinforce each other in a particularly vicious cycle: the rising threat of war fuels apocalyptic belief, and apocalyptic belief lights a fire under the threat of war.

On a small scale, the way this plays out is very familiar to us.

Vicki Weaver began having visions of the end of the world in the late seventies. She and her husband Randy already believed the apocalypse was imminent: they'd been heavily influenced by the economic and political turmoil of the decade, the televangelists of America's rising religious radical right, and Hal Lindsey's 1970 doomsday book *The Late Great Planet Earth*. When Vicki began to have her own prophetic experiences, usually while having a bath, it only solidified their certainty that a great and terminal conflict was looming. In the bad days of the Cold War, they were hardly alone in that feeling.

And so they did what many others were doing at the same time: they sold their possessions and left behind their life in Cedar Falls, Iowa, and headed west, to the remote mountains of northern Idaho, up near the Canadian border. Here, they thought, far from population centres and the federal government and the corrupting influence of the sick modern world, they could ride out the terrible conflagration, dedicate themselves to God, and be among the saved when the final day arrived. The area attracted plenty of like-minded people: a toxic mishmash of outsiders, religious zealots, survivalists and neo-Nazis, united by their distrust of the government and the sense that they needed to prepare for violent times ahead.

The Weaver family set about building their mountain cabin, in a spot named Ruby Ridge.

Randy Weaver was not trying to start a war, and what happened at Ruby Ridge in 1992 was a small, grubby burst of killing that fell a long way short of one. But it illustrates the dynamic that plays out time and again, on scales small and large: once you introduce the idea that conflict is looming, it can become self-fulfilling. Every action that one side takes confirms the most paranoid fears of the other. Their reaction to those fears then confirms the fears of the first side. Escalation, escalation, escalation.

In this case, a family who saw the federal government as a malign force and had been taught to interpret events through a lens of apocalyptic expectation ran up against federal agencies scrambling to get a grip on a rising tide of far-right anti-government domestic terrorism that they didn't fully understand. The Weavers' beliefs were perhaps too personal and specific to fit neatly into any box, but Randy Weaver sure as hell hung out a lot with Aryan Nation members, so you get where they were coming from. An attempt by US marshals to enforce a firearms warrant against Randy spiralled into a shootout in which everybody's worst fears about the other side were confirmed again and again. The family dog ran at the marshals, they shot the dog, the family shot back. The first shootout claimed the lives of Randy's son Samuel, US Marshal Bill Degan, and Striker the dog. In the following stand-off, Vicki Weaver was fatally shot by a sniper.

Not a war. On the basic death toll, not even that notable for the US: deadlier firearm incidents happen in malls and schools and the former workplaces of disgruntled ex-employees all the time. But the dynamics of the escalating conflict are familiar – and those dynamics would echo forward from Ruby Ridge.

Six months later: another apocalyptic group, another ham-fisted government response that acted simply as confirmation. This time it was a niche splinter sect of a niche splinter sect, who'd been expecting the apocalypse to arrive any day now since the mid-fifties. Their original prophet, a chap named Victor Houteff, had died, after which his widow took over, moving the group to a hilltop compound and starting to groom a successor prophet. With an eye to the Bible, they named their compound Mount Carmel: just up the road from Armageddon.

This sect had all the usual personal dramas you associate with such groups: accusations of corpse desecration, one non-fatal shootout between factions, and an axe murder. It was in the aftermath of the latter that the successor prophet, a troubled young man named Vernon Howell, seized control of the group, and turned it into an abusive sex cult while assembling what he termed an 'Army for God' in preparation for the final conflict. He also changed his name, rechristening himself after the Hebrew name for Cyrus the Great, the Achaemenid emperor who freed the Jews from their Babylonian exile. His new name was David Koresh.

The eventual conflagration at the Mount Carmel compound near Waco, Texas – a shootout between law enforcement and Koresh's Branch Davidian followers that left ten dead, followed by a fifty-one-day siege, and a final raid in which the Davidians torched their own compound, killing seventy-six – would only fuel apocalyptic expectation in the wider culture. Coming so soon after Ruby Ridge, it seemed to be confirmation that a violent end was nigh. It entrenched the view of the government as an evil force in the paranoid mixture of end-times religion, conspiracy theories and far-right politics that had been brewing in American culture. Neither of these events was a war, unless you really wanted to see them as a war. Two years later, Waco and Ruby Ridge would inspire the bomber Timothy McVeigh to kill 168 people at a federal building in Oklahoma.

Violence is inherently escalatory; we've got the term 'cycle of violence' for a reason. When you add in a belief system that says conflict is inevitable, necessary and morally righteous, then escalation is even more likely.

In the same way, Hong Xiuquan's Taiping Rebellion didn't start with a plan to provoke one of history's deadliest wars – the bloodiest of the whole nineteenth century, one that may have killed up to 10 per cent of China's population. It started small. Then it escalated.

To recap: Hong Xiuquan had a breakdown after he repeatedly failed China's civil service exam. The imperial exam was a big deal: it was the path to government employment. This made it the major driver of social mobility under the Qing Dynasty – it allowed those from humbler backgrounds to rise to positions of power and wealth, forming a class of their own. (The Chinese civil service, with its novel idea of hiring candidates on merit rather than cronyism or nepotism, would be an inspiration for the modernisation of both the UK and US civil services later in the century.) For Hong, the son of an ethnic minority farmer from a provincial village in Guangdong province – not poor, exactly, but definitely from the margins – this was what he'd pinned his hopes for the future and his sense of self-worth on.

In his feverish mental turmoil after his third exam failure, Hong experienced puzzling dreams of a heavenly figure. The meaning of this vision only became apparent to him after he recovered somewhat – and promptly failed the exam for a fourth time. In his despair, he started reading literature he'd picked up from Christian missionaries when he was in the city of Guangzhou for the exams. The heavenly figure, he realised, was his father, who was the God of the Bible; Jesus was his brother. He saw himself in the story of the great flood that wiped the earth clean: literally saw himself, because *hong* means 'flood'.

How things turned out may have had something to do with the flavour of Christianity Hong picked up. Many of the missionaries were American; this was the early 1840s, near the peak of the Second Great Awakening, a revivalist movement that had swept the USA. New microchurches and sects-within-sects were springing up everywhere, combining a socially reforming zeal with – usually – apocalyptic expectations of the imminent Second Coming.

Hong took these fundamentals, and reshaped them to his context. He blended the piecemeal Christianity he'd picked up from sermons, pamphlets and unevenly translated Bible verses with aspects of Taoist eschatology and traditional Chinese folk religion. Like the American revivalists, he diagnosed a great sickness in his society, but where they imagined America as the location of the new Kingdom of Heaven, he saw it as a place he would build; and where they expected the return of Christ, he inserted himself, the divine sibling come to usher in a new world.

He started small: preaching his new combination religion with a friend to tiny groups of interested parties in rural villages around Guangdong. His faith promised a world reborn: simultaneously new and ancient, tearing down the rotten present and restoring an imagined past. He found some sympathetic ears in an area riven by crises – the Qing Dynasty was flailing, famine was common, and many were forced to turn to piracy and banditry, which only accentuated the sense of a society fracturing apart. The foreigners who had brought Hong the news of his Heavenly Father had also brought other, brutal disruptions: Hong began his preaching in the aftermath of the First Opium War, the Chinese Empire routed by the British in a dispute over whether the Brits were allowed to sell drugs.

Violence was present from the start. In his crusade against the Confucian order that had snubbed him and the worship of gods he wasn't related to, Hong began with small acts of symbolic destruction. He carried a huge sword inscribed with the words: 'Sword for exterminating demons'. He didn't use it to do much actual demon-slaying, instead focusing on vandalising religious statues – provocative shock tactics of which the Ranters might have approved. Naturally, this led to an angry reaction from local authorities, which only reinforced Hong's sense that he was in conflict with them.

Bit by bit, things escalated. As he gained followers, they

started to form into impromptu militias to take on the gangs of bandits that plagued the countryside – something that only won them more fans. (Hong himself had been a victim of one such gang, who robbed him of all his money and, most painfully, stole his prized anti-demon sword.)

Hong's sect also expanded as it absorbed members of another eschatologically minded group – the Tiandihui, or the Heaven and Earth Society. From a similar lineage to the White Lotus sect that had fought a long war against the Qing Dynasty at the turn of the century, the Tiandihui was a loose mixture of a Freemason-like secret society, a criminal protection racket, a revolutionary movement devoted to overthrowing the Qing, and a millenarian cult. For many people, they offered their members a way to avoid getting robbed by bandits and pirates – because lots of the bandits and pirates were members too. But for Hong, they would also provide him with a growing body of allies comfortable with violence and primed for conflict with the ruling dynasty.

(The Tiandihui also had another name, one that's become synonymous with violence in our time: the Triads. It's used today as a catch-all term for Chinese organised crime, because British imperial authorities in Hong Kong heard the name and blithely assumed that all criminal gangs were the same thing. Classic British imperial authorities.)

The escalation continued. Hong and his followers marched from their mountaintop base to destroy a statue of a much-worshipped local spirit called King Gan. This outraged local dignitaries, naturally, who whipped up a militia against them and attempted to put several members on trial. In the following years, the cycle of outrage, reprisal and revenge spiralled upwards: Taiping members would be jailed, tortured and killed, and Hong's followers would respond with further raids, all the time growing their forces as the crackdowns against them fuelled their certainty that they were on the righteous path.

The dam broke in early 1851. The Qing authorities, still bruised from the opium conflicts and remembering the unthinkable scale of the White Lotus war, realised that Hong no longer had followers – he had an army, one that numbered in the tens of thousands. They sent a military expedition of the imperial army to crush the rebels. The Taiping forces, now in open revolt, obliterated them. The Qing sent more forces, which had the effect of squeezing the Taiping out of their mountain stronghold – something that turned out to be bad news for the Qing, because it forced them to go and conquer new territory instead. By 1853, they had taken Wuchang – part of modern-day Wuhan – and from there controlled much of the Yangtze River. Their army exploded in size: from 70,000 when they besieged Wuchang to 750,000 by the time they marched on Nanjing, which fell after a two-week siege.

Hong made Nanjing his capital, where he lived in luxury while ruling by divine decree. For the rest of the decade, the Taiping war raged across much of the country: the Qing besieged Nanjing, the Taiping mounted strikes to capture new territory. Millions upon millions of people died, either directly from the fighting or from famine and disease.

In the end, the Taiping did not usher in a new world. Things played out in . . . well, fairly familiar ways. The Taiping were riven by internal struggles, pervasive paranoia and occasional bouts of political murder – which is the sort of thing that tends to happen when you have one person who claims to be God's son, and several others who also say they talk to God regularly. The Qing, meanwhile, were belatedly doing sensible government things: diplomacy got them European help in the war, while they put talented military leaders in charge of their efforts.

By 1864, the besieged Nanjing was on the brink of starvation. Not to worry, said Hong: the Bible said in Exodus that God would send manna for the people to eat. When people weren't entirely sure what he meant by that, he demonstrated: he went around the palace grounds collecting weeds, and ate them. He died (probably from eating weeds) shortly after.

Nanjing fell a few months later.

In a final irony, one of the Qing military leaders who ultimately defeated the Taiping was a chap named Zuo Zongtang – who'd also repeatedly failed his imperial exams before simply giving up. Maybe Hong Xiuquan shouldn't have let it get to him so much.

War may long have been linked to the apocalypse, but the nature of that connection changed forever on 6 August 1945.

For most people at most times throughout history, war must have seemed a pretty plausible way the world could end. After all, the world was what you knew around you. *Your* world could absolutely be ended by war, if it decided to pay your neighbourhood a visit. The early apocalypses were local affairs.

But could a war actually destroy the *whole* world? Once your perspective shifts to the understanding that there's an entire planet out there, even the most devastating regional conflict might seem a bit . . . sub-apocalyptic? Even in the age of empire, when wars stretched way beyond national boundaries to the far side of the world, they still weren't all-encompassing.

That's why the apocalyptic wars from the Middle Ages onwards were seen as moral crusades of good vs evil, or as taking place on lands that held a divinely appointed role in the cosmic plan. The war would be pivotal in deciding the fate of the world, but it would not on its own be the sole agent of destruction.

Then, at 8.15am on a sunny August day, the United States dropped the atomic bomb on Hiroshima.

The age of nuclear weapons brought back with a sudden shock the full apocalyptic potential of war. Now not only was the war a fight for the soul of the world, but it also had a plausible mechanism by which it could genuinely be the end of the world. Even before the great powers of the twentieth century had fully begun their nuclear arms race, both religious and secular prophets of doom were racing to incorporate its possibilities into their tales.

'Peter says, "That it melts with fervent heat, that all these things are dissolved." Dissolved! How scientific is the New Testament after all!' wrote one pastor, Sam Swain, in his 1946 *The Atomic Bomb and the World's End.* For many religious people – especially those in America's dispensationalist tradition – the coming of the bomb was proof that the end was near, and that the prophecies of the Bible were accurate.

For those of a more scientific mind, meanwhile, the nuclear age provided a mechanism by which they could tie their concerns about the world to a familiar narrative structure. Secular apocalypticism had been rising in the culture since the nineteenth century – scientists, of course, are just as prone as anybody to look at the world and think it's going to shit – but the actual mechanics of it remained speculative. Disease, perhaps, some speculated. Astronomical catastrophe, claimed others. Demographers warned of overpopulation and starvation; eugenicists warned of inferior humans outbreeding the superior humans, leading to the degradation of the species.

The bomb rapidly became the runaway favourite in the non-religious doomsday stakes. In a large part, this was driven by nuclear scientists themselves – both those who had helped build the bomb in the first place and were having second thoughts, and also those not involved and horrified by the whole thing. In 1947, the *Bulletin of the Atomic Scientists* introduced the 'Doomsday Clock' – the symbolic representation of how close humanity was (in their opinion) to destroying itself. The clock started at seven minutes to midnight; it's since fluctuated between seventeen minutes and ninety seconds to midnight in a somewhat idiosyncratic fashion. But even when it hasn't been an especially accurate guide to the real threat of catastrophe (it somehow missed the Cuban Missile Crisis entirely), it's remained a stubbornly potent symbol of secular apocalyptic anxiety.

But while the methods of war have changed, some things remain the same. Megiddo itself may be long gone – an archaeological site of great significance, but little else – but the fight to control the lands around it continued down the ages. Apocalyptic prophecies around Jerusalem helped motivate the Crusaders; to this day, large numbers of Christians, especially in America, support Israel not from a love of the Jewish people, but because of a belief that their presence in the Holy Land is essential for the apocalypse to come about. And apocalyptic prophecy doesn't just fuel war in that small patch of land alone.

In the 2000s, the rise of the Islamic State was driven by a powerfully eschatological goal: bringing about the final conflict between the Muslim world and the West that they believed must be imminent. Theirs was a very different style of war to those in previous ages: one of atrocity videos and online propaganda. As part of this, ISIS produced what can best be described as a jihadi lifestyle magazine: titled *Dabiq*, it was published on the dark web and featured exhortations to join their fight, along with articles about how great life was under ISIS rule.

Why was it called *Dabiq*? Because in the hadiths of the Islamic tradition, the final battle at the end of days will not happen in Megiddo. Instead, the site will be a small Syrian town: Dabiq. Every issue of the magazine included a quote from an ISIS leader promising that their battle will be a conflagration that 'burns the Crusader armies in Dabiq'.

Dabiq ceased publication in 2016, after ISIS lost control of the actual town of Dabiq. It was replaced with a new magazine called *Rome* – so named because of a prophecy that says that city too will fall.

Humanity may not have managed to wipe itself out in the fires of war just yet, even if it's not for lack of trying. But the thing about apocalyptic belief is that it never runs out. There's always another battle just over the horizon.

9.

Prophecy and Portents

It's always a special day in Kyoto when the cherry blossom reaches full bloom.

The flowering of the cherry tree occupies a special place in Japanese culture, and people flock from across the world to take part in the tradition of *hanami* – the simple pleasure of looking at flowers. Unlike quite a lot of 'traditions' (you know, the kind that turn out to have been invented for a department store marketing campaign in 1936) this is a truly old custom; for more than a thousand years, the people of Japan have made a point of lounging and eating beneath the freshly opened petals, giving over their busy lives to calm moments of contemplation and beauty.

It's transcendent, but also transient. A brief week or two is all you've got before gravity and decay win the battle, the tree gives up its petals, and your streets are suddenly full of cherry blossom mulch. For anybody who wants to arrange a *hanami* trip – or, somewhat more importantly for the local economy, organise the spring festival – this short window demands foresight: when, exactly, will the blossoms bloom? It's usually some time in April, ish, but it's a movable feast. Which means that getting an accurate blossom forecast has become kind of a big deal.

Forecasting is the business of moving from observation to prediction. And so, for as long as the people of Japan have longed to sit blissfully beneath a burgeoning cherry tree, they've also paid close attention to exactly *when* the flowers appear. The result is a record stretching back more than a millennium, dutifully noting the day of the year that the cherry trees burst into bloom. In the ancient capital of Kyoto, the earliest records – sourced from court histories, diary entries about blossom parties, or even the titles of poems – date as far back as 812 CE. Together, they provide perhaps the most complete chronicle we have of what plants, historically speaking, have been up to.

Now, if you're the kind of person who gazes upon the beauty of the natural world and thinks, 'Oooh, I could make a graph out of this,' this is terrific news. It makes a cracking scatterplot: year along the bottom, full flowering date up the side. The result is a big, bushy mess of dots – the date of the blossoming zigzags around year by year, seemingly at random. And (as many data visualisers have realised) if you replace the dots with cherry blossom emojis, then the chart looks . . . well, it looks pleasingly like a cherry tree.

But here's the thing: the tree is starting to lean over at one side.

For a thousand years, the full flowering date doesn't seem to follow any discernible pattern. Some years it's early, some years it's late, most years it's kind of middling. But then on the right-hand side of our tree chart – the last few decades, in other words – our little cherry blossom data points suddenly plunge lower in unison. The tree droops, like its branches are weakened by some sickness. Like it's being buffeted by an unseen wind.

The blossoms, you see, are appearing sooner. Because the spring is arriving earlier. Because, inexorably, our world is getting warmer. On average, the flowers now emerge eleven days earlier than they used to; in 2021, the blossom came sooner than it has at any time in the previous 1,200 years.

The cherry trees of Kyoto offer us a window into the past – and in doing so, they also offer us a glimpse of our future. They help us move from observation to prediction. With them, we can do something that humans have done for thousands of years – look at the world around us, searching for signs that might answer the question which has obsessed us down the ages: *What happens next?*

Unfortunately, quite a lot of the time the answer to that question has been 'nothing good'.

* * *

Knowing what's going to happen next has very obvious advantages in life. Will a light jacket do, or do you need the Big Coat? Would it be wiser for your company to invest in Betamax or VHS as the default format for home video? If we have a war, are we divinely assured of a glorious victory over the forces of darkness, ushering in the final age of mankind and establishing paradise on earth? That sort of thing.

In our age, we understand this well, and a huge amount of time, effort and resources are poured into trying to work out what lies just out of sight over the time horizon.

My phone will try to tell me, to the minute, when it's going to start raining (and sometimes it's right). The political fortunes of governments rise and fall on forecasts of growth, spending and debt. Covid-19 saw angry debates about obscure aspects of epidemic modelling, as vital decisions about health and liberty hinged on the error bars around a predictive curve. The bestseller lists regularly feature books that confidently assert their authors can foretell the path of society in the coming decades. Billionaires are made and unmade based on whether investors buy in to their corporate vision for the next five years. The internet is awash with desperate people betting their life savings on the hope that some anonymous dude with a statue avatar is right when he prophesies what's going to happen to the price of a stock, or a cryptocurrency, or an ugly jpeg of a cartoon ape.

In short, we expend a lot on attempts to see the future, and the rewards for getting it right – or, at least, for convincing enough people that you've got it right – are huge.

But while the forecasting techniques we use may have changed, as have the types of future we obsess over, this basic dynamic has held true across history. The gift of foresight has long been one that promised to unlock the doors of power and wealth.

For example: the polymathic mathematician and occultist John Dee was for some time one of the most influential people in Elizabethan England, based on his esoteric claims to be able to divine the future. He would cast horoscopes, and possessed a mysterious glass which – it was rumoured – gave him insight into what was to come. (This object is usually interpreted as something like a crystal ball or a scrying glass. Some historians have suggested that it may have simply been an early funhouse mirror, and the excitement it generated was purely because it made you look weird.)

Dee was one of Elizabeth's most trusted advisers – albeit one who operated in secrecy, on the fringes of acceptability. His influence was significant. He advised on preparations for the defence against the Spanish Armada, and advocated for the colonisation of the Americas and the creation of an empire. (Indeed, he may have been the first person to ever use the term 'British Empire'.) Whether John Dee could actually see the future is almost immaterial; in convincing others that he could, he helped create it.

But if claims to see the future could be a route to great power, it was also a dangerous one, so potent was the belief in the power of prophecy. Elites craved the knowledge it offered, but also feared it being used against them. Dee's vast personal library would be ransacked and pillaged, and he himself had been charged with treason before Elizabeth came to the throne, accused of 'calculating' horoscopes for the royal family – something that the sitting Queen, Mary I, was not best pleased about.

Particularly dangerous was foretelling the death of a

monarch – it could encourage talk of succession, and prompt aspiring claimants to plot and scheme. Under Henry VIII, at least two such prognosticators – the monk Nicholas Hopkins and the visionary nun Elizabeth Barton – had been executed for predicting the King's demise. Even listening to prophecy could be deadly: that the Duke of Buckingham had sought and heeded Hopkins's prophecies was what sent him to the axeman's block as well, convicted of 'imagining' the death of the king.

Prophecy, in other words, was serious business. And intimately wound up with the business of prophecy is that of the apocalypse.

Apocalypse and prophecy go together like a pale horse and rider. On the one hand, to talk of the last day is inherently to indulge in prediction of the future: there is no apocalypse without prognostication, even if you're being careful to not put a firm date on it. And on the other hand, those who try to see the future can be irresistibly drawn to the apocalyptic. Think of Dorothy Martin in 1950s Chicago, whose UFO predictions started with talk of cosmic harmony and enlightenment, and over the course of just a few months evolved into an all-consuming flood and an immediate need to evacuate the planet. Once you start foretelling stuff, it seems, there's a pretty good chance that you'll end up foretelling some sort of doomsday.

Of course, this could simply be the marketplace at work. People will pay more attention to prophecies that are more dramatic. An ancient shaman casting the bones might draw more followers if he saw a coming Great Storm than if he saw, say, a light drizzle clearing up around lunchtime. 'Soon the King will die childless' will result in many more ambitious nobles paying you a visit – and get you recorded in a lot more history books – than 'on 7 October, the King will stub his toe', even if the latter turns out to be more accurate. And there is no prediction more attention-grabbing than that of the world's end.

As a result, for many centuries, an awful lot of people have very confidently predicted the end of the world. Spoiler alert: they haven't got it right. Yet.

Admittedly, some of the time it's not clear that these prophecies were even *trying* to get it right. The fact that prophecy was politically useful – or potentially lucrative – was motivation enough. You didn't need to be right. You just needed people to think you might be.

Take, as one example, the Prophecy of the Popes – a document attributed to Malachy, the twelfth-century Irish saint, which claims to be a predictive list of the 112 future popes who would reign until the end times arrived. This list was supposedly lost for centuries, only to be rediscovered – how fortuitous! – and subsequently published by a Benedictine monk called Arnold in 1595.

The nature of this particular prophecy becomes apparent when you note that it's remarkably accurate about all the popes between the 1140s (when Malachy supposedly wrote the prophecy) and the text's 'rediscovery' in the 1590s . . . and then goes wildly off the rails immediately after that point.

At first, you see, the popes are identified both by name and by abstract phrases that play on things like the popes' heraldic symbols, birthplaces or previous jobs. So, for example, the fifty-fifth entry – 'pasturing ox' – matches up with the actual pope in the sequence, Pope Callixtus III from the 1450s, whose coat of arms was indeed an ox standing in a field. What an excellent prophecy. Top marks.

But the thing is, after pope number seventy-seven in the sequence – Clement VIII, who *just so happened* to be pope at the time of the prophecy's publication – the predictions suddenly get incredibly vague. It stops giving us names for the popes, and we're left only with the increasingly abstruse mottos such as 'wavy man' (who, per the sequence, should be Leo XI, who became pope in 1605), 'swift bear' (Clement XIV, 1769–74), or 'glory of the olive' (Benedict XVI, 2005–13). By the time the list has got to pope ninety-nine – described merely as 'religious man' – you really begin to sense the author is losing steam. They may have decided to end the world at pope 112 simply because they'd run out of ideas.

Naturally, there have been many tortuous attempts by prophecy fans down the years to fit these riddles to the details of actual popes. But despite these efforts, there remains no plausible sense in which Leo XI – one of the powerful Medici family, who died a scant twenty-seven days into his papacy from a cold he caught at one of his inaugural ceremonies – can be described as an especially wavy individual. Clement XIV was neither especially speedy nor notably ursine. Nor, for that matter, did the Palpatine-faced German traditionalist Benedict even remotely embody olives, to say nothing of their glories.

It has been suggested that the 'prophecy' may have been created at some point in the 1580s or 1590s as a simple piece of propaganda – an attempt to boost the fortunes of one particular candidate for the papacy, who would conveniently fit the description given. Whatever the motivations of the author, it doesn't seem to have worked terribly well.

Given all this, the prophecy would be of only passing interest, were it not for one point that makes it especially salient right now. The thing is, we're currently on Future

Pope 112 – that is, the one whose papacy is supposed to coincide with Judgement Day. If the list is correct (and despite everything, you'll find no shortage of websites and YouTube videos insisting that it is), then we're due an apocalypse any day now.

Now, granted, it's a bit hard to see how Pope 112's motto ('Peter the Roman') applies to a guy originally called Jorge from Buenos Aires, and prophecy believers have struggled mightily to find any way to make the clue fit. Nonetheless, if the world *does* end while Francis sits in the Vatican, the previous paragraphs about how the Prophecy of Pseudo-Malachy is a transparent forgery are all going to look a bit silly. For that reason – among others – let's hope that doesn't happen.

This is far from the only mercenary use of spurious apocalyptic prophecies in history. For an even more transparently avaricious example, let us now turn our attention to the Prophet Hen of Leeds.

This was . . . well, a hen. Which was from Leeds. In 1806, the hen laid an egg that had the words 'Christ is coming' clearly visible on its shell. This was, not unreasonably, interpreted as a sign of the imminent end of days – a feeling that was only accentuated when the hen subsequently laid several more eggs bearing the same message. The hen, as you might expect, became the talk of the town.

The owner of the hen, one Mary Bateman, wished to share the important news of the imminent Second Coming with the world. She did this by putting the eggs on display, and charging people a penny a time to look at them. In addition to the egg-viewing fee, she also sold small tokens that, she said, would ensure the holder entry into heaven when the Day of Judgement arrived.

At this point, an attentive reader such as yourself *might* be starting to discern the truth of what was going on here.

Indications soon emerged that the apocalyptic eggs of the Prophet Hen of Leeds were not all they were cracked up to be. A doctor, upon examining one of the eggs, noted that the inscription appeared to be inked upon the shell, rather than being an integral part of it. Also 'Christ' was spelled wrong, which you probably wouldn't expect from a divine intervention. Furthermore, when the hen was taken from Mary's possession, it mysteriously stopped laying the miraculous eggs.

It turned out that, yes, Mary Bateman had simply been taking eggs from the hen, writing 'Crist is coming' on them, and then . . . forcing them back inside the unfortunate hen, whereupon she would simply wait for them to be 'laid' all over again. A second coming of sorts, sure, but not quite the one claimed. Needless to say, the world did not end in 1806, although the poor hen may well have felt like it was ending.

Mary Bateman turned out to be a career criminal and a habitual grifter, who had already been linked to a large number of robberies, and at one point defrauded people of charitable donations intended for the victims of a fire. A few years after the hen debacle, her world did indeed end – she was convicted and executed for fatally poisoning a sickly woman to whom she had been selling fake magical cures. In a nasty bit of irony, after she was hanged for her crimes, Mary's body was put on display – and people were charged three pennies to view it, while strips of her skin were sold as good luck tokens.

The world is impermanent, but the grift is eternal.

But the thing is, while Mary was simply a habitual scammer with a severe conscience deficit and a low regard for the feelings of poultry, she had been inspired to stick doomsday eggs up a hen's arse by another apocalyptic prophet – one who very sincerely believed in the truth of her visions.

This was the remarkable Joanna Southcott, a domestic servant from Devon who had lived a fairly mundane life until 1792, when, at the age of forty-two, she began to experience dreams and visions that told her the end of time was imminent, and that she had a starring role to play in the drama that was to come. She herself was the Woman of the Apocalypse that Revelation had predicted; her visions would help to guide the world through the dark days before the Second Coming.

Southcott became an incredibly prolific author, detailing her visions in around sixty works over the next two decades. Known as the Prophetess of Exeter, she began to attract a large and enthusiastic following. Her fame grew and grew – she's namechecked in the opening of Dickens's *A Tale of Two Cities*, and her notoriety was such that he felt no need to explain to his readers who she was.

Among Joanna's followers was the noted engraver William Sharp – a man who desperately wanted an apocalyptic prophet to believe in. He'd been through two already; the latest had been a chap named Richard Brothers, who preached that a New Jerusalem would be founded with himself as the prince of the Hebrews, but who was currently in an asylum for the criminally insane after being charged with treason for – that's right – prophesying the death of the King. Sharp had grown disaffected with Brothers in late 1795, after his prophecy that he would be revealed as the ruler of the world on 19 November had failed to come to pass. Instead, he found a fresh harbour for his belief in Joanna Southcott.

Sharp persuaded Southcott to come to London, and it was here that her fame really exploded. Not only that, but she also found a lucrative business in selling small paper seals that, you guessed it, would grant her followers admission to heaven come the day of the Lord.

But while this was what inspired Mary Bateman into her egg-based scam, Joanna herself seems to have viewed the endeavour entirely in good faith. Her apparent sincerity and kindly demeanour were a large part of what drew followers to Southcott – a number that probably peaked at around 100,000, and included some notable names. ('I should like to buy one of her seals,' wrote Lord Byron, who was fascinated by her, '[for] if salvation can be had at half-a-guinea a head, the landlord of the Crown and Anchor should be ashamed of himself for charging double for tickets to a mere terrestrial banquet.')

Southcott's tale has a tragically ironic ending. In 1814, she proclaimed that – although she was sixty-four years old, and a virgin – she was pregnant with the new messiah, who would usher in the next world. And indeed, she seemed to be speaking truth. Over the following months, her belly swelled and her followers eagerly anticipated the birth of the holy child, while the media had a field day. And then . . . nothing. The pregnancy had been a phantom. Joanna's distended belly was not the herald of the heavenly age, but the symptom of a sickness that would kill her just two months later.

Some movements die out after a failed prophecy or the death of their prophet, but not Joanna Southcott's. While some followers drifted away or moved on to the next prophet, a core of devotees stayed true to her visions; indeed, she still has followers today, although they're now relatively few in number. And a big reason for this is that while Southcott may have died, the alluring potential of prophecy was able to outlast her. Joanna Southcott, you see, left a box behind.

This box, she said, contained her prophecies for the future. It was not to be opened until a time of great national crisis, and only then in the presence of all the bishops of the Church of England, who would be required to spend several days in prayer and contemplation before the opening.

Naturally, this box served to sustain interest in Southcott's teachings down the centuries; the possibility of hidden knowledge locked away, of wisdom revealed at the time of greatest need, has been too compelling to ignore. There is, let's be honest, very little more fascinating than a box you're not allowed to open. Equally predictably, it's led to decades and decades of arguments over when and how the box should be opened – along with long-running disputes about who actually has the box in the first place.

In 1927, a psychic investigator claimed to have possession of the box, and found a bishop willing to stand next to him while he opened it: it turned out to only contain a lottery ticket and a gun, which aren't especially useful as prophecies (even if they're exactly what you'd expect to find in a time traveller's luggage). But it's doubtful this was actually the true box, if a true box even still exists; certainly the contemporary followers of Southcott insisted that the box was fake, and they had the real one.

A group of Southcott devotees named the Panacea Society insists to this day that they still hold the true box at their headquarters in Bedford (they believe that Bedford was the original site of the Garden of Eden, which will be a surprise to many people). Throughout the 1960s and 1970s, they regularly placed adverts in the national press imploring the Church of England to assemble its bishops so that the box might be opened, our great national decline halted, and the world better prepared for the tribulations to come. The Church of England, not unreasonably, has long taken the view that they want absolutely nothing to do with any of this nonsense.

At the time of writing, the box remains unopened. It may never be opened. It may be opened and found to contain nothing. There may not even be a real box at all; and if one box is opened and disappoints, you can bet somebody will quickly claim that this box was false, and another box is the true box. Whatever happens, the tantalising possibility will always remain: that somewhere, there's an answer to the question of 'What happens next?' – an answer that's just the turn of a key away.

Unfortunately for us, the actual answers to that question are rarely so easy to uncover. The business of moving from observation to prediction can be a painful one.

Okay, granted: it's actually relatively easy when what you're observing is 'this really weird dream you had', which is why that's always been a very popular source of prophecy. At that point, how much attention people will pay to you rests almost entirely on your personal charisma and how well your story resonates with the narrative needs of the day. Tell a good story, and people will always listen. But if you're actually trying to look at the real world around you, and work out what it truly tells you about the future, you've got a much harder job – not least because it often requires an awful lot of observation before you can even begin to make a stab at it.

Take something extremely simple: the fact that lunar

eclipses happen on a roughly eighteen-year cycle in any particular part of the world. That's a fact that was discovered independently by numerous ancient civilisations thousands of years ago. You can see how it might be a socially useful thing to predict – you can either reassure people they don't need to freak out, or you can convince them you're a wizard, depending on your vibe.

But now think about the process of actually spotting that afresh for yourself: it would be thirty-six years before you could even begin to speculate that there was a pattern here, and fifty-four before you might feel confident enough to make a prediction for next time. Seventy-two years to see if your prediction holds up. A whole lifetime just to spot one simple repeating pattern, and a high risk of simply carking it before you even get to find out if you were right (never mind using it to convince people you're a wizard).

Given these difficulties, it's not surprising that a lot of apocalyptic prediction has focused not on the regular, but the irregular. For all that humanity has spent large parts of its history searching for meaning in patterns, we're also drawn to look for deeper meaning in the things that *break* patterns – the unexpected, the inexplicable, the weird and the terrifying. The search for signs of the end, in other words, often focuses on the interpretation of omens and portents.

The Augsburg *Book of Miracles*, a wonder of sixteenth-century art, is a mammoth collection of lavishly illustrated scenes depicting a dazzling array of strange occurrences. There are eclipses and volcanoes and rains of blood, alongside sea monsters, strange beasts, two-headed calves and – in one slightly underwhelming case – an 'extremely small horse'. There are an awful lot of comets, and enough strange optical effects in the sky (sun dogs, halos and that sort of thing) that you begin to feel people should have realised that they're not actually *that* unusual.

While the pictures are both beautiful and fearsome, what's also interesting for our purposes is the short text accompanying each of them. It insists, over and over again, on the predictive power of these events. The sun is seen sweating blood, and afterwards many people die in Venice. The sun goes dark, and many great wars follow across Europe. The coming of comets presage plagues, and famines, and political disagreements between the pope and the emperor. Tiny crosses apparently fall from the sky in 1503, and later that year there are three popes in the space of a few weeks. Rainbow rings appear around the sun in 1519, and the next day the Emperor Maximilian dies.

And having established that these events are meaningful, the *Book of Miracles* leads its reader to its conclusion – because the final images in the book don't depict contemporary happenings, but the series of events that will lead up to the apocalypse. It goes straight from a depiction of a particularly smelly hailstorm that hit Dordrecht in 1552 to depicting passages from Revelation – visions of Christ, the four horsemen riding across the world, and stars falling from the heavens. Having convinced the reader of the predictive power of portents, it asserts that this predictive power will follow through to the imminent portents to come.

It has the structure of a logical argument – even if it's mostly just drawing scary pictures, pointing at them and going, 'Weird, huh?'

Of course, one problem with omens as a predictive tool is that . . . well, they usually aren't predictive. That's most obviously true in the very literal sense that they have nothing to do with the thing you're foretelling – comets do not cause plagues, guys. They're just an attention-grabbing dramatic peg on which to hang your preferred story. But it's also the case that rare events simply aren't especially useful for prediction, full stop. Even ones with obvious causal links – 'Uh, the dormant volcano seems to be producing a lot of smoke; it's never done that before, do we think that's bad?' – won't necessarily tell you what you want to know with any certainty. (It might be a good idea to move away from the volcano, though.)

The other problem with omens is that once you start looking for them, you begin to see the bloody things everywhere.

In truth, there's almost nothing that can't be an omen if you want to find omens badly enough. Every weather change, every astronomical event, every quirk of nature and every societal shift: all omen-fodder. Just look at how we do it in our own lives. Find ten pence in the street? Your annual performance review today will go well! Spill coffee down your shirt? That stock you bought on the advice of a guy from Reddit will fall 37 per cent. 'Is the universe is trying to send a message?' we ponder to ourselves, as we're narrowly missed by a falling piano for the fifth time today.

Go on social media, and you'll see an awful lot of people pegging an awful lot of events as signs of the apocalypse (usually in that mostly-joking-but-also-not tone that's the default for online discourse). As I write this section, the news tells me that – in the words of the *Times* – 'Riderless blood-soaked horses race through central London', and people are having a field day. And who can blame them? It certainly *feels* like the sort of thing that happens when mere anarchy is loosed upon the world. It has distinct omen-like qualities. The possibility that, well, some horses just got spooked seems insufficient to bear its symbolic weight.

So the question is: what omens should you pay attention to?

For the religious, of course, holy texts can offer a steer on the particular types of omen to be on the lookout for. That's the argument that the *Book of Miracles* is making: that portent is predictive, and we have an established list of particular portents that will predict particular things. The difficulty is that the texts themselves are rarely that specific. Christianity's Revelation is a psychedelic fever dream of images that are too weird to be useful if taken literally, and are open to virtually any interpretation if taken metaphorically. In Islam, depending on exactly how and what you count, there are somewhere in the region of fifty signs that the Hour is imminent – but they range from the very helpfully precise (the Euphrates runs dry, three landslides occur in particular parts of the world) to the rather less helpfully vague (an increase in commerce, a loss of trust).

Attempting to work through this problem leads to one of the more surprising things about the history of apocalypse and the predictive arts.

We tend to think of doomsday predictions as being, well, the opposite of rational inquiry. Someone standing in the town square with a 'The end of the world is nigh' placard is a universal shorthand for 'you should slowly back away from this person'. And yet, at the beginning of the scientific revolution, this distinction simply didn't exist. In fact, the opposite was often true.

The apocalypse inherently implies a structure to history and a plan for the world. And if that structure exists, then the clues to its nature can be discovered – not through the free-form interpretation of emotionally heated events, but through dispassionate and systematic study. The possibility of predicting the world's end offers hope that the world is, at least, in some sense predictable.

And so for many centuries, the search for a better understanding of the world went hand in hand with the attempt to discern its end. Pioneering thinkers at the birth of the age of science, such as Francis Bacon and Tommaso Campanella, straddled the theological and the empirical – with the logic of an historical progression towards the apocalypse providing a unifying framework, one that meant the divine mysteries of the world could be understood through rational processes. Isaac Newton deeply pondered the final moments, and saw the laws of nature he was uncovering as evidence that those same laws could be rewritten upon the final day. For many thinkers, this very process of discovery, of better understanding God's plan, was a central part of the enlightenment of humanity that would lead it towards its final paradise.

Attempts to understand the world and predict the future that today we might find laughably untethered from reality were, in their time, attempts to be *more* systematic and accurate than the alternative. Astrology and astronomy are very different things today (and astronomers get very annoyed when you say the wrong one) but the distinction is a relatively recent one. Many of the pioneers of modern astronomy were professional astrologers: Galileo funded his work by compiling horoscopes for rich patrons; Tycho Brahe's job in the Danish court was giving the nobles a heads-up on what political upheavals the planets predicted for the coming year.

Attempts were also made to determine the precise age of

the world – a vital tool of apocalyptic prediction, given the widespread assumption that the world would last for seven millennia (mirroring the seven days of the creation). The Irish archbishop James Ussher – who famously pegged the date of Creation to 22 October 4004 BC – may have been off by a few billion years, but his knowledgeable and scholarly approach to the cataloguing of history was a genuinely impressive feat, a far more disciplined approach to the discipline of history than many of his contemporaries. It's perhaps no surprise that Pierre d'Ailly – the theologian whose work may have influenced Columbus, as we saw in Chapter 5 – was interested in the precise mapping of both the physical world and its history. Even if he wasn't that great at either.

Perhaps nobody embodies this better than John Napier – an eccentric Scottish aristocrat whose enthusiastic dabbling in mathematics would revolutionise the field. Napier did plenty of impressive things – invented one of the first mechanical calculating devices, popularised the use of decimal places, convinced a lot of people that he was a wizard – but he's best remembered today as the main discoverer of logarithms: one of the most influential and useful breakthroughs in the history of mathematics. By simplifying complex calculations, it enabled a slew of advances in physics, engineering, navigation, economics and many other disciplines. One biographer described it as 'one of the very greatest scientific discoveries that the world has seen'; a huge amount of the modern world around us is underpinned by the work logarithms enabled.

But Napier would have been surprised to discover that his life's work was still being used in fields from statistics to acoustics all these centuries later. Not because he didn't think it was an important discovery – he had a healthy enough ego about his accomplishments – but because of his *other* life's work.

John Napier, you see, used his mathematical genius to try and calculate the date of the apocalypse. He would have been surprised to find us using logarithms in the twenty-first century for the simple reason that he didn't think there was going to *be* a twenty-first century. He wasn't even sure there was going to be an *eighteenth* century.

Napier's work was very much of its time and place. His 1593 book of apocalyptic predictions, *A Plaine Discovery of the Whole Revelation of Saint John*, was published just five years after King James VI's own doomsday tract – and, in a savvy political move, was dedicated to the Scottish monarch. Like that work, it made no bones about identifying the Catholic Church as the seed of apocalypse: 'The pope is that only antichrist prophesied of,' Napier wrote, as we saw in Chapter 5.

But his book was also, in its own way, a radical break from the norms of the age. It was systematic and methodical in a way that few previous books had been. It had charts showing the logic of his argument; tables cross-referenced the verses of Revelation with historical events to establish a chronology. The final trumpet of the apocalyptic drama had begun to sound in around 1541 with the consolidation of Protestantism in Britain, he argued; the final crisis would begin in around 1639, ushering in decades of dire conflict before the ultimate triumph of righteousness.

In unleashing his mathematical talents on predicting the end date, Napier offered his many readers a persuasive sheen of certainty. But he also brought something familiar from our modern understanding of systematic prediction: a carefully calibrated window of *uncertainty*. Just as your weather app will tell you there's a 90 per cent chance of rain, or a polling aggregator will inform you Hillary Clinton has a 71 per cent chance of winning the election, the sensible forecaster doesn't trade in false certitude. Rather than pick one single outcome and hang their hat on it, they'll offer a range of outcomes, weighted by likelihood.

So it was with Napier's calculations. He gave his readers an upper bound for the end of the world: 1786, he determined, was the last possible year for the Big Day to arrive. But it would probably be much sooner than that (mostly because God wouldn't be mean enough to put his elect through a century and a half of tribulation). The range he identified was between 1688 and 1700. Somewhere within that window was when the final day would dawn: 90 per cent chance of apocalypse, becoming earthly paradise later.

Now, you'll have noticed that this didn't happen. For all his charts and tables and mathematical wizardry, Napier was still trying to retrofit historical observations to ancient prophecy, all filtered through the distorting theological and political assumptions of his time. His approach may have been methodical; the method itself left something to be desired.

But the burgeoning intellectual movements that Napier was part of – towards the systematic observation and collection of facts, towards an attempt to uncover the underlying structures of the world, and towards more honestly delineating the boundaries between certainty and uncertainty – would lay the foundation for something very different. What began as a search for God's plans would end up removing the need for God entirely. The business of prediction offered the possibility that we could discover whole new catastrophes awaiting us, not buried in the metaphors of an ancient text, but lying ready to be harvested from fields of data. The idea of a secular apocalypse was being born.

One result of this is that, several centuries later, when an argument between two Catholics about the imminent end of the world became a months-long media sensation, the root of their dispute wasn't a matter of doctrine or exegesis. It was one of science.

Father Jerome Sixtus Ricard was both a man of faith and a man of reason. A Jesuit by training, he was ordained in 1886, but in 1900 he took a course in astronomy and realised that this was his passion; by 1907, he had become the director of the University of Santa Clara's observatory. More to the point, he was a massive sunspot enthusiast and a pioneer of weather forecasting. His core theory was that a close monitoring of sunspot activity – an only recently discovered phenomenon at the time – could be the key to unlocking the accurate prediction of weather. And for several decades, Father Ricard managed to provide the farmers of the Pacific coast with remarkably accurate forecasts. (At least, they were perceived as accurate, given the state of forecasting at the time.) So valuable did the people who relied on his forecasts find them, they came to call him the 'Padre of the Rains'.

If Father Ricard had a flaw, it was that he was rubbish at hiring people. Later in life, this would manifest in him completely failing to build his university a massive telescope – an extremely expensive pet project of his – due to his hiring people who didn't know how to build telescopes. But in 1913, this flaw manifested in his hiring Albert Porta to do some sums.

Porta was a fellow Jesuit who had taught for a time at Santa

Clara College. He wasn't trained in astronomy – his academic background was in civil engineering and architecture – but like Ricard, he had recently discovered a passion for it. So it seemed a great fit when Ricard was looking for someone to do some temp work on the complex calculations required to turn observations of sunspot activity into weather forecasts; Porta was a mathematical whizz, and could – Ricard felt – be trusted to keep his head down and bury himself in the numbers.

Albert Porta . . . did not do that. Instead, he took the scraps of knowledge he'd gained from a few months' work under Ricard, plus the reputational boost of having worked with the famed Padre of the Rains, and promptly founded his own rival forecasting business.

Porta had zero expertise in the field; the man didn't even own a telescope, Ricard would bitterly complain, and he simply based his predictions off someone else's astronomical tables. It was as much astrology as astronomy. But Porta did have a knack for publicity, one that managed to encompass both coasting on the reputation of the Santa Clara Observatory while also slagging it off as an inferior competitor to his grandly titled Institute of Planetary Sciences. Living just a few years after the devastating 1906 earthquake in San Francisco, he realised that weather forecasting wasn't the only market he could serve, and claimed he could predict earthquakes as well. In the space of a decade, Porta had developed a reputation as one of the foremost – certainly one of the best-known – forecasters in the country, and his monthly predictions were syndicated to newspapers across America.

And then, in the summer of 1919, he calculated that a terrible cataclysm was just months away.

Porta's theory, such as it was, held that sunspot activity was caused by planetary alignments. (It isn't.) Starting on 16 July newspapers began to print his warning. 'PLANETS MOVING INTO HUGE DANGER-ZONE' ran headlines in the *Sheboygan Press*, the *Arizona Republican*, the *Washington Herald*, the *Buffalo Times* and many more, accompanied by a lurid 'scientific drawing' of Porta's 'Terrifying Prophecy'.

In the article – grandly by-lined 'by Prof. Albert F. Porta, Noted Sunspot Forecaster and Discoverer of "Porta's Weather Laws"' – Porta informed his readers that 'on December 17, 1919, no less than seven planets will pull jointly on the sun . . . Six of them – Mercury, Venus, Mars, Jupiter, Saturn and Neptune – will be in conjunction,' while 'directly opposite . . . will be the huge planet Uranus'.

The effect of this would be catastrophic. 'The magnetic currents between Uranus and the Six planets will pierce the Sun like a mighty spear,' Porta wrote, producing a 'gigantic explosion of flaming gases . . . rich enough in electro-magnetic energy to fling the atmosphere of our planet into a disturbance without precedent'.

The resulting calamities would include 'hurricane, lightning, colossal rains . . . gigantic lava eruptions, great earthquakes, to say nothing of floods and fearful cold'. Of course, while insisting that his findings were a 'mathematical certainty', Porta also hedged just a little on precisely *how* apocalyptic the great sunspot catastrophe would be: 'What will be the outcome? My knowledge does not permit me to state beyond the fact that the storms, eruptions and earthquakes will be tremendous in their strength and scope.'

Oh, and he was at pains to point out that he was informing his readers of his 'startling prophecy' with, he insisted, 'no desire to be merely sensational or alarming'. Hmmmm.

Predictably, Porta's prophecy did indeed become an alarming sensation. His warnings were reprinted over and over in newspaper after newspaper across America in the following months, up until just days before the supposed doomsdate. The prophecy became gleefully embraced fodder for the media churn, deployed for the purposes of either panic or merriment, depending on how the mood took each particular newspaper. (Also depending, you suspect, on whether the newspapers had previously carried Porta's less apocalyptic forecasts.)

Of course, his claims didn't go without pushback. Observatories and astronomy departments across the nation found themselves flooded with worried letters from concerned citizens. Once it became apparent that this was very much A Thing People Would Not Stop Asking Them About, astronomers rallied to pooh-pooh the predictions. In Britain, the Astronomer Royal derided it as 'just American sensationalism'. Professor William Hussey of the University of Michigan gave it short shrift in comments to the *Detroit Free Press*: 'all bosh, nothing to it'. One amateur astronomer in Montana pointed out that a similar alignment had occurred just this past May, 'and the worst that happened was a shortage of sugar'. There was no reason to believe that – as the *Shelby Promoter* delightfully phrased it – 'the planets would be in such a hopeless jumble that that earth would go flooey'.

In November a lengthy syndicated article by Isabel M. Lewis of the United States Naval Observatory (a pioneering woman astronomer, who would go on to a decades-long career as a science populariser) explained, in a tone of infinite weariness, that no, that's not how sunspots work, and furthermore, 'such groupings of the planets have already taken place several times during the present year, with no abnormal results'.

Unfortunately, the effect of Lewis's debunking may have been slightly reduced by the fact that it ran below a reprint of Porta's original warning, underneath a massive headline reading 'Tremendous World Catastrophe to Happen on Dec. 17?', and illustrated with a nightmarish depiction of a scene from Revelation by the nineteenth-century Irish painter Francis Danby. The casual reader, perhaps, may not have been left with the impression that the answer to the headline's question was 'no'.

Even this pushback could backfire on those who attempted it. After the University of Michigan's Professor Hussey gave his verdict, wires got crossed somewhere, and by early December newspapers across America were describing Porta himself as being a professor at Michigan – 'the distinguished Ann Arbor savant', as the *Salt Lake Tribune* described him – despite him actually holding no university affiliation. The unfortunate university had to scramble to tell anybody who would listen that he was nothing to do with them. ('President Hutchins of the university informs the *Times* that Professor Porta has never been connected with that institution,' the *New York Times* corrected itself in a small note on page seven two days later.)

Father Ricard himself, still stung by Porta's abuse of his reputation, fulminated against the prophecy, echoing Lewis in saying that 'there is nothing strange or new in planets getting together sometimes'. On the eve of the supposed apocalypse, he said that 'fear that the world will end tomorrow is absolute folly', labelling the prediction 'a flight on the wing of an extremely bad imagination'. He suggested that rather than an apocalypse, 17 December would see good weather across the West Coast, perhaps with some light cirrus clouds.

For all the media circus that it stirred up, how many people really believed Porta's claims? It's unclear. Certainly, neither the US nor the world ground to a halt as people locked themselves away in terror. Church attendances were generally said to be up, and there were reports from Oklahoma of miners refusing to work because they feared being trapped underground by the upheaval. In Paris, a butcher was said to have hanged himself, while in London it was reported that a large part of the population 'stayed awake all night and midnight prayers were said in thousands of homes'. In Cleveland, a sixty-five-year-old farmer related that he had been scammed out of $15 by two men who told him he could reserve a seat to watch the end of the world occur; in New York, a restaurateur was convicted of disorderly conduct after locking up his business, emptying the cash register and going on one final bender. (All these reports may require a pinch of salt.)

When 17 December dawned, it was – you'll be astonished to learn – a perfectly normal day. Along most of the West Coast, it was bright and clear, if cold. Thick fog shrouded Vancouver, and there was a heavy storm off Ketchikan in Alaska. It rained across much of the UK, and flooding in Stalybridge was reported to have claimed the lives of a number of chickens. Once again, poultry appear to have borne the brunt of apocalyptic expectations.

Chickens aside, you'll note that none of the above is, well, particularly unusual for December. But Porta, whose public statements in the run-up to the fateful day had been a curious mixture of backpedalling and doubling-down, seized on the not-at-all-weird storm in Alaska to hit back at his critics, grandiosely declaring to the United Press that this was the first harbinger of the tumult to come, and that: '[W]hen events themselves have proved I was correct I will rise like a lion and show them I know whereof I speak.'

If the cataclysm he predicted turned out to be, perhaps, a little underwhelming, he insisted that this was simply because the worst effects had been 'prevented by the sun's rotation' – the great solar eruptions were real, but were conveniently pointed in the wrong direction. (You wonder why this possibility hadn't occurred to him before.)

On the contrary, one professor of astronomy in Pittsburgh said his team had taken observations that day and found only minimal sunspot activity. These observations, he noted dryly, were only made possible by the clement weather and clear skies.

The press, of course, greeted the continuation of the world in the same gleeful manner with which they'd printed the news of its demise. 'Fake! Bum Show! World Is Intact!' hooted the *San Francisco Chronicle* the following day. 'To our relief, we found that not even a milk churn had been upset by the Planetary conflagration' recalled the *Welshman* on 26 December.

From his previous position as a respected seer, in the space of a few days Porta fell to being used as an all-purpose punchline. 'In order to retrieve his reputation,' japed the *Liverpool Evening Express* on 31 December, 'Professor Porta has now predicted that the year will come to an end about the last day of this month.' Over the next few years, all but one newspaper dropped Porta's regular forecasts from their pages. He would die four years later, the world still very much unended.

The thing about Porta's predictions, and his decade-long feud with Father Ricard, is that while Porta was demonstrably wrong . . . so was Ricard. His belief that sunspots were the key to unlocking the mysteries of the weather has proven to be, at best, wildly optimistic. Not entirely groundless: solar activity probably does have some edge effect on Earth's climate, but the impact is minimal: one signal among many, hard to discern, and overwhelmed by the far larger fundamentals that shape the complexities of our weather systems. Ricard's theory – to quote his *New York Times* obituary – 'that sun spots were responsible for all weather disturbances, and also induced earthquakes' is, quite simply, not true.

But if there was a key difference between these two religious men who embraced the possibilities of scientific prediction, it was that while both were wrong, Ricard was at least wrong in the right way. Where Porta ploughed ahead in proclaiming the 'mathematical certainty' of a hypothesis that was entirely untested against reality, proceeding from the assumption that his beliefs were correct and that all else flowed logically from that, Ricard stressed the need to actually observe the world and see if it matched up with your beliefs. In one of his critiques of Porta – written four years before his wayward protégé had even predicted the end of the world – Ricard was scathing about Porta's failure to even examine the phenomena he was claiming to derive knowledge from. 'Without instruments of observation,' he wrote, 'one is no more able to launch, intelligently and trustworthily, even a mere general weather forecast . . . than a log can fly.'

Forecasting: the business of moving from observation to prediction.

Let's return to where we came in, because it might be worth clarifying something:

Our understanding of the future path of the world does not hinge on looking at some cherry trees in Kyoto.

That would, let's face it, be pretty silly. There could be a hundred explanations for any year's flowering date, and for the trends over time. On their own, they tell us very little; they don't even tell us enough to predict next year's cherry blossom day, outside of a vague, 'Eh, might be earlier than normal.' Asking them to predict much else is more weight than their little petals can bear.

They are an observation, and a series of observations; they are not themselves a prediction. To treat them as such would be to make the same mistakes as those in history who fumbled their way towards seeing the true future – relying on a single sign for insight, placing all your faith in one interpretation of that sign. It would be treating them like an omen, rather than a data point.

But they are, of course, far from the only data point.

Even if all you want is evidence that spring has Gone Weird, there's plenty available. You can look to another large temperate island with a long history of botany nerds obsessively recording what flowers were up to: plants in Britain are now blooming around a month earlier than the historic average. You can look to Vermont, where the sap which produces the state's famous maple syrup needs to be tapped at a precise point in winter's thaw; an event that used to happen in March must now happen in January or even December, shortening the season. You can look to Greenland, where the warmer spring has rendered the emergence of different plant species chaotic and unpredictable, throwing ecosystems out of sync. Like many creatures, caribou time their migration to verdant breeding grounds by the length of the day, not the temperature. When those two signals diverge from their usual relationship, things fall apart: when the caribou arrive to bear their calves, they can find the food they expected to be flourishing has already been and gone.

Or if you'd like to respect prophetic tradition and focus on chickens, well, they lay fewer eggs when it's hotter. Bengal's seen a 25 per cent drop in egg production as heatwaves sweep India. You don't need a scammer to write messages on the eggs to get a sense of what they might be telling us.

All these small observations, and tens of thousands of others like them, add up to something far more powerful than any omen or portent ever could. The solution to the problem of observation – that the observations required to discern the true patterns of the world are usually beyond any single person's capacity – is collaboration. The steady accumulation and sharing of observations from many sources; the communal testing of predictions against reality.

This collaboration can happen across space – to pick an obvious example, the reports of the Intergovernmental Panel on Climate Change involve hundreds upon hundreds of scientists from all around the world – but also across time, as observations in our time form a dialogue with those made by the long dead. Just as our cherry blossom data is a collaboration between modern scientists and courtiers and poets from centuries ago; just as our approach to prediction is a collaboration with theologians looking to better understand God's plans.

And with this comes something that John Napier may have recognised: understanding the limits of prediction. Truth lies in the error bar and the confidence interval, not in the false certainty of an absolute proclamation. We are more accurate when we have rigidly defined areas of doubt, not less. It is, in fact, useful to know that there's a 50 per cent chance of rain, even if it is also kind of annoying. You should probably wear the Big Coat just in case.

We can seem irresistibly drawn to the singular: the One True Omen that shows us what is to come, the Lone Visionary with unique insight into the path that lies ahead. But the same principles apply equally to omens and data points, prophets and forecasters: truth comes not from one, but from many.

10.

'I Waited All Tuesday and Dear Jesus Did Not Come'

Erin Prophet was deep underground when the bombs didn't fall.

Along with hundreds of other members of the Church Universal and Triumphant, she had spent the previous hours pushing carts filled with supplies along train tracks through the tunnels they'd built. They had, they hoped, thought of everything. They'd ploughed $12 million into the vast bunker complex; it was the largest nuclear shelter in the USA not owned by the government. They had enough non-perishable food to last them for seven years. They had pick-up trucks, hazard suits, radiation monitors and body bags, plus a large cache of guns and millions of dollars in gold and silver coins. The narrow bunkbeds had seatbelts, so that the tremors from distant nuclear blasts wouldn't cause injuries.

The one thing they hadn't thought about – not *really*, not outside of brief snatched moments of doubt, not in the frenzied rush of events and the sense of community and the hope of the golden age that would follow the nuclear horrors – was what would happen if the world didn't end.

It's worth pointing out here that Erin Prophet, despite her name, wasn't really a prophet. That would be silly. No, the prophet was her mother, Elizabeth Clare Prophet, and before that her late father, Mark Prophet. The Prophets were both prophets. (No deed polls were involved – Prophet really was the family name, although as far as we know, none of Mark Prophet's other relatives took this as a cue to become prophets.)

Erin was, however, in the process of being trained up as a prophet. Privately, she had been having doubts about whether she was cut out for the family business. She believed in her mother; she wasn't as sure she believed in herself.

The thing she hadn't admitted to anybody was that *she* was the one who'd come up with the date for the end of the world. Her mother had been ill, and needed assistance in firming up the details of the apocalypse she'd already announced. She'd asked her protégé Erin to visualise the date for the upcoming cataclysm. Erin hadn't wanted to let her mother down. She had tried her best. She'd picked 15 March 1990 – the Ides of March, because she remembered the quote about it being something to beware of.

'I began to feel the prophet's trap tightening around me,' she would later write in *Prophet's Daughter*, her memoir about her life in her mother's church. The trap: making a prophecy so specific that it can be proven wrong, but which also locks you into a course of action. Power as a prophet relies both on people accepting the truth of your prophecies, and on them being motivated to act as a result. This means you need to walk a fine line between specificity and vagueness. Get too woolly, and your prognostication loses force. But trip over the line and give too many details . . . well, now you're committed. How can you ever go back?

Which is why hundreds of people were now waiting, nervous and giddy and hopeful, beneath the mountains of Montana. Prophet would later write that a 'fey sense of purpose and imminent completion replaced whatever healthy skepticism might have kept us from putting ourselves and our children through this ordeal'.

That ordeal would last, in total, for just under two stop-start weeks. They knew the bombs had not come on the first night; this was passed off as a 'drill'. The date was reset; nothing happened again. Another drill. Some members left after that first failed prophecy. But most, having put so much work and belief into the project, stayed, even as doubt began to creep in. They took a 'wait-and-see' approach, Prophet writes; experiencing 'disappointment and relief, but not yet disillusionment'.

But the end could not be put off forever; belief could not be sustained indefinitely. For those who still kept the faith, there was the horrible fear that members would give up, depart and return to their former lives, and then be caught in the cataclysm. Their group, their community, *needed* it to happen. A quiet desperation began to creep in. A new date was named.

The Church Universal and Triumphant had always stated publicly that they didn't *want* the nuclear war and the years of societal collapse that would follow. There was no glee about the imminent death of almost everybody on Earth. But on the last night, the night when it was definitely going to happen this time, as they gathered together in the bunkers once more,

Elizabeth Clare Prophet led them in prayer to summon the bombs and unleash destruction on their fellow humans.

The next day, the world was still there. Emerging into the morning light, dazed and uncertain, the members of the church began a slow, unsteady journey that so many others had been on before them – the journey of trying to make sense of two competing certainties that couldn't both be true.

In other words, they were confronted with the question: what happens when the world doesn't end?

That dizzy, sickly feeling you get when your brain tries to hold on to two contradictory things at the same time has a name. You're possibly familiar with it: cognitive dissonance. Our brains really, really don't like this feeling. We experience it as stressful, uncomfortable, a persistent itchy wrongness that we're desperate to shake. When our own actions fail to live up to our self-image, say, or when events don't fit with our preconceived beliefs, our minds will desperately scramble to find some way to reconcile the irreconcilable.

Sometimes this can be a good thing – indeed, it's an essential part of growth. We can adjust our beliefs to take account of new evidence, or moderate our behaviour to better fit our values. Well done us: we're listening and learning and doing the work.

But at other times, things go . . . less well. Especially when the conflict touches something core to our identity – our most deeply held beliefs, our sense of community, the goals we've worked hard to achieve, our fiercest desires – then something else will often give. We may end up bluntly denying reality, or constructing massive, baroque structures of justification for the unjustifiable. Our minds will go to great lengths to fool us into rejecting the obvious, or to distract us from a contradiction that would otherwise be unbearable.

An example of this is what happens when you firmly believed the world was about to end, and then it didn't.

In fact, that's not just *an* example of cognitive dissonance. It's *the* example. The theory of cognitive dissonance was first proposed by the social psychologist Leon Festinger in the 1950s – and it developed out of his study of a small group in Chicago who believed that the world was about to be consumed in floods, but that they would be rescued before the calamity by aliens from the planet Clarion.

This group was, of course, the Seekers: the followers of Dorothy Martin. We met them at the beginning of this book, when they were standing in a suburban backyard waiting for flying saucers that never showed up. Their identities are disguised in *When Prophecy Fails*, the classic book about the group's travails that Festinger wrote with his colleagues Henry Riecken and Stanley Schachter – Dorothy Martin becomes 'Marian Keech', Chicago is renamed 'Lake City', and so on. But it's them.

Festinger's theory of cognitive dissonance predicted that, when their belief in Martin's prophecies was proven wrong, the group wouldn't collapse in disillusionment as you might expect. Instead, they would double down on their belief, and specifically they would focus harder on trying to convert new members. This proselytising would be their way of reconciling the dissonance – building up the force of their own belief until it drowned out the contradictions. After all, if new members join, then that's a sign that the beliefs must be correct, right?

This was exactly what they found . . . or, at least, it's what they *thought* they'd found. Festinger's study of the Seekers has come in for more than a little methodological criticism down the years – not least for the fact that at some points, almost a third of the 'members' of Martin's group were actually undercover psychologists. Even with good intentions, their presence simply couldn't avoid influencing the events in question.

More to the point, as one critic notes, *When Prophecy Fails* 'does not offer unambiguous evidence that Mrs Martin's followers went on a preaching rampage after the world failed to end'. The Seekers had drawn a huge amount of gleeful attention from the media – that's how Festinger and his colleagues heard about them in the first place – and much of the extra 'proselytising' was just them giving face-saving statements to the press. They didn't initiate it; they were largely responding to outside prompts.

When Prophecy Fails is most commonly remembered as a short factoid summary of its delightfully counterintuitive conclusion: that apocalyptic movements aren't doomed by failed prophecy. They can survive, because when presented with evidence that their beliefs are wrong, human beings will double down on that belief instead of changing their minds.

And the thing is, although some of this is basically true, the study of the Seekers *didn't actually show this at all.* Numerous studies of other doomsday groups in the decades since have backed up the main aspects of this core claim, although they've added a bunch of caveats and changed our understanding of how it all works. But in the case of the Seekers, the group did not survive. It didn't last for more than a few weeks after their appointment with the inhabitants of Clarion fell through. The book is clear about this: 'By January 9, there was no group in Lake City.' Many members had already grown sceptical of

Martin's claims in the run-up to the date of the prophecy, and several of them quit the group in the immediate aftermath. Even fervent true believers became rapidly disillusioned.

There was a core group whose belief persisted, but it all fell apart anyway. Fearing legal consequences, Dorothy Martin fled the area, as did Charles Laughead, another leader of the movement. A small collective held out for a few extra days, gathering in an ad hoc support group, but they quickly dispersed too. Some members tried to strike out on their own, attempting to spread the word of their beliefs as solo preachers, largely unsuccessfully. Dorothy Martin ended up moving to Arizona, where she joined a Dianetics centre and later acted as a medium under the name of Sister Thedra.

In this, the Seekers were actually a bit unusual. Of the apocalyptic groups in the twentieth century whose failed predictions have been studied in detail, most persisted in some form after their expectations were dashed. Around half continued at full strength, the disconfirmation of their beliefs not ultimately doing them much damage at all. And around half endured, but in a weakened form, losing a significant number of members and struggling to attract replacements. Only one (aside from the Seekers) fell apart entirely.

But all of them had to deal with that same dizzy, sickly feeling of encountering a reality that contradicts something your brain had been utterly convinced was true.

'I waited all Tuesday and dear Jesus did not come,' Henry Emmons wrote in 1845, recalling the events of the previous year.

It may sound like someone wondering why their Amazon package never turned up, but Emmons had been through a far more distressing experience. 'I waited all the forenoon of Wednesday, and was well in body as I ever was,' he continued, 'but after 12 o'clock I began to feel faint, and before dark I needed some one to help me up to my chamber, as my natural strength was leaving me very fast, and I lay prostrate for 2 days without any pain – sick with disappointment.'

This profound soul-sickness was understandable – and Henry Emmons had been far from alone in feeling it. He had just, much to his surprise, lived through one of the largest and most famous failures of prophecy in history. On 22 October 1844, across a swathe of the USA centred on Massachusetts and New York, as many as a hundred thousand followers of the preacher William Miller had prepared to be lifted up to heaven shortly before the Earth was scoured with fire.

Their hopes were dashed, and they remained firmly earthbound. This was the event that became known – often mockingly – as the Great Disappointment.

Emmons may have despaired and stayed in bed for two days, but if anything he was coping a bit better than some of his fellow believers. 'Our fondest hopes and expectations were blasted, and such a spirit of weeping came over us as I never experienced before,' wrote Hiram Edson, a leading disciple of Miller's. 'It seemed that the loss of all earthly friends could have been no comparison. We wept, and wept, till the day dawn.'

The trauma Edson was experiencing was exactly that dissonance between the evidence of his eyes and a foundational aspect of his identity. 'My advent experience has been the richest and brightest of all my christian [sic] experience,' he would write later. 'If this had proved a failure, what was the rest of my christian experience worth? . . . Is there no

God – no heaven – no golden home city – no paradise? Is all this but a cunningly devised fable? Is there no reality to our fondest hopes and expectation of these things?'

For the Millerites, it was not only their inner turmoil they had to wrestle with – it was also becoming the butt of a national joke. The movement was mercilessly jeered in the press; its members were sneered at by their neighbours behind their backs, and small children would openly take the piss out of them in the streets. William Miller himself, in a letter written that December, described the experience of very suddenly becoming the Main Character of society: '[T]he next day it seemed as though all the demons from the bottomless pit were let loose upon us. The same ones and many more who were crying for mercy two days before, were now mixed with the rabble and mocking, scoffing, and threatening in a most blasphemous manner.'

Amidst all this, the Millerites were faced with a question that was as obvious as it was hard to answer: what now?

The thing is, it wasn't the first time they'd had to answer that question – because 22 October 1844 was not the first date given by Miller's predictions. In fact, that date didn't even come from Miller himself.

There had been no great crisis that precipitated the Millerite fervour – other than, perhaps, the disorientating ongoing crisis of being a person who is alive during history. For William Miller himself, this must have felt particularly acute. He'd been born in 1782 in a country that wasn't quite a country yet; one year after the British surrendered at Yorktown, years still before the USA would have a constitution or elect a president.

In between that date and his predicted end of the world

was a period of dizzying change, as the agrarian world of his rural New York childhood transformed into landscapes of steel and smoke. Cities bloomed, railroads sprouted, printing presses scattered the seeds of radical ideas far and wide; a few months before the world was due to end, Samuel Morse sent the first telegraph message ('What hath God wrought?'). Not even the map of his nation would stand still, as new territories were purchased, ceded or seized. A rapidly growing country – but also one that was increasingly divided by the great moral and economic schism between the industrial north and the slave-holding south.

This was the backdrop for the USA's Second Great Awakening – the wild upsurge in religious fervour that swept the new nation in the decades after its founding. New movements, sects, churches and revelations sprang up at a frantic pace. So bright did the spiritual flame blaze that one region of New York would later be named 'the burned-over district' (it was here that an impoverished young farmer and supernatural treasure hunter named Joseph Smith would have the visions that revealed the Book of Mormon to him).

It was both an emotional reaction against the rationalist currents that had influenced many of the Founders, and an extension of that same desire to build a new nation. Many of the Awakening's movements did not expect the return of Christ to solve their problems; instead, they would need to create the perfected world before the Second Coming could even occur. In a potent blend of the ecstatic and the pragmatic, they believed that spiritual salvation would follow worldly progress.

Miller's prophecies hit near the end of this period – the Awakening experiencing a final surge of energy before bedtime. They were far from an overnight success, however.

Miller's predictions were not based on visions or divine revelation, but on his own research. Like so many prognosticators before him, he went deep into textual and numerological analysis of the Bible, cross-referencing it with historical events. The Book of Daniel says that the sanctuary will be cleansed after 2,300 days; 'days' in this context should be read to mean 'years'; and the countdown started, for reasons that were apparent to Miller, in 457 BCE, when King Artaxerxes I of the Achaemenid Empire issued a decree regarding the governance and restoration of Jerusalem. Add 2,300 to –457, and you get the year of the cleansing: 1843.

Miller reached this conclusion in the early 1820s . . . and then decided not to tell anybody about the end of the world for the best part of a decade. (He did write down his prediction, but didn't show it to anyone.) Perhaps unusually for an end-times preacher, Miller was not a natural attention-seeker; he hated being called a prophet. He only began preaching and writing publicly about his theories in the early 1830s, and his local following grew steadily, but slowly.

What put a rocket under Millerism was not really Miller himself: it was the enthusiasm and energy of his new followers as the great date loomed into view. In particular, it was their fondness for the printing press. A Boston preacher named Joshua Himes launched a periodical called *Signs of the Times* in 1840, which acted as a vehicle for Millerite prophecy. This was quickly joined over the following years by a host of others: the *Day-Star*, the *Jubilee Trumpet*, the *Advent Harbinger and Midnight Alarm*, the *Midnight Cry*, the *True Midnight Cry*, the *Southern Midnight Cry!!*, and the *Western Midnight Cry!!!* (They liked their exclamation marks.) In all, nearly fifty Millerite publications were printed across the US – some of them regular papers with sizeable subscription bases, others little more than one-off pop-ups that appeared whenever Miller's fans passed through an area, or had something they wanted to get off their chests.

This all started to peak in 1843, which you might remember was the year in which Miller had predicted the world would end. There was little more specific to go on, because William Miller was (by the standards of doomsday prophets) cautious. He would not give a fixed date. All he could know was that his calculations showed the end would likely come at some point in 1843. Also, for various complex reasons involving religious calendars, the year 1843 wouldn't start until 21 March, and would run until the same day in 1844.

All through this year, tens of thousands of Millerites thrummed with expectancy, but without the focal point of a specific date to channel their fervour towards. This meant that the disappointments, when they hit, were not catastrophic to the movement: some had expected it on the first possible day in 1843, others on New Year's Eve that year. Even when 21 March 1844 passed without anything noteworthy happening, there was little sense of despair.

Some followers suggested April was a more suitable date, based on lengthy discussions of different Jewish calendar systems in *Signs of the Times*. Others pointed to biblical passages that suggested an unspecified 'tarrying time' after the appointed day before things really kicked off. Like many other puzzled doomsday enthusiasts, the Millerites adopted a wait-and-see approach.

But wait-and-see can't sustain a movement built on urgency and expectation for very long. That Millerism ended up focusing all its expectations on 22 October was due to, effectively, apocalyptic fanfic. Miller didn't come up with the date, as I've said – instead, it was a recent convert named Samuel Snow, who had become obsessed with Miller's work and decided to expand on it. He'd originally proposed his alternative date that February, before Miller's doom window had even closed, but it exploded in popularity over the summer as Millerites looked for answers.

Many of the movement's leaders were initially hesitant about endorsing it (and Miller himself remained silent), but they swung into line when they saw how giving a clear, single date was motivating believers and holding the movement together. The battle between vagueness and specificity was over. From that point, the Great Disappointment was locked in.

In the annals of failed doomsday predictions, the name of Harold Camping stands out as one of the more determined prophets.

An American radio preacher with a significant reach, Camping had an apocalyptic career that spanned decades, and included as many as five separate predicted end dates (depending on exactly how you count.) None of them came true, but this didn't dissuade him from trying again – the first few times, at least. Camping was a man who simply would not take 'No, the world won't end' for an answer.

Camping's first prophecy of doom was for September 1994, which he'd initially predicted two years earlier in a book titled *1994?* The question mark at the end of the title was important – a bit of typographical hedging that he would later lean on heavily when questioned about the accuracy of his subsequent prophecies.

And in fairness, within its five hundred-plus pages of

hyperfocused biblical puzzle-solving, Camping *does* admit to the possibility of uncertainty ('There could be something that has been overlooked'). But the overall tone is not exactly one of caution – the introduction opens with the words: 'No book ever written is as audacious or bold as one that claims to predict the timing of the end of the world, and that is precisely what this book presumes to do.'

The book became a decent-sized hit while not entirely, uh, setting the world on fire. Doomsday books were big business at the time – although the most successful authors were usually smart enough to not put any timescale on their predictions other than a vague 'soon'. Hal Lindsey, perhaps the most successful, maintained a thirty-six-book career that ran from his 1970 mega seller *The Late Great Planet Earth* into the early 2000s, all the while cannily steering around any predictions that were too specific or easily falsifiable.

Camping did not do this. His book – a dense slog of persnickety numerology, mapping Bible references to dates in roughly the same manner as Miller had – sold in the tens of thousands, rather than the millions of someone like Lindsey.

But still, Camping had Family Radio, Inc. – a growing network of thirty-eight radio stations across the US and other territories. He was both president of the radio company and the host of a flagship show. As a result, many of Camping's followers took his prophecy to heart and devoted themselves to spreading the word. ('I am looking forward to it,' one follower told the *New York Times* when they reluctantly interviewed her after she'd pestered them into covering the end of the world. 'I want to be with my Lord. This world is crazy, sin-cursed.')

But while some of Camping's followers were moved to neglect their lives in favour of anticipating the end, this effect was perhaps most noticeable in Camping's own life. Family Radio was a significant business, with hundreds of employees and major plans to grow internationally. In 1993, the *Christian Research Institute Journal* wrote that senior employees were in despair because Camping was sabotaging plans for expansion into Canada, China, Russia and Europe on the grounds that 'Jesus is coming back, and we don't want to deal with this'.

Camping cheerfully admitted to this attitude, telling the *CRIJ*: 'My wife came to me and said we needed new linoleum in the kitchen. I told her that we should hold off on the effort and the expense of doing it until October or November of 1994 – after the time I predict Christ's return.' On his radio show, he would advise callers to take the same approach. As one staffer at the radio station complained: 'We told him not to do that anymore, but he's a loose cannon.'

Naturally, September 1994 came and went without incident. Much like Millerism before him, Camping started substituting in new dates – briefly switching his prediction to 31 December that year, and then shifting it another three months into the future (on the familiar grounds that according to the biblical calendar, 1994 'runs until March of 1995').

Where William Miller had been deeply troubled by the failure of his predictions, Camping was cheerfully unbothered. In February 1995, while waiting for his third doomsday in the space of seven months, he told the *San Francisco Chronicle*: 'You know, I'm like the boy who cried wolf again and again and the wolf didn't come. This doesn't bother me in the slightest.' It is possible that Harold Camping had misunderstood the moral lesson of that story.

He had a similar attitude in 2011, when he was once again predicting the end of the world. When *New York* magazine raised the possibility of his predictions not coming true, he replied: 'It's going to happen. It's going to happen. I don't even think about those kind of issues.'

In the years between his apocalypses, Camping had returned to his research, refining his predictions to account for the errors that had led him to the wrong date. (History does not record whether his wife finally got her new kitchen lino.) He bounced back after a decade, announcing in 2005 that the correct date – as he'd suspected all along – was 2011. On 21 May that year, the Rapture would occur and the saved would ascend to heaven, while terrible earthquakes shook the world. A period of chaos and 'awful suffering' would follow, tormenting the left-behind sinners, until the world finally ended for good on 21 October.

This time, his prophecy got even more attention – largely because his followers were actively encouraged to spread the word. The same enthusiasm that had driven the Millerites' newspaper publishing spree kicked in again. The result was a massive, crowdfunded worldwide advertising campaign alerting people to the fact they were running out of time to be saved. Billboards announcing the end were virtually ubiquitous in some places. Family Radio poured resources into this, even selling off stations to fund it, but it was Camping's followers who bore the brunt – many cleaned out their life savings to finance billboards and other publicity. One New Yorker told the BBC he'd personally spent $140,000. (Camping's response when asked after the event if his company would return donations: 'Why would we return it?')

When 22 May dawned with no Rapture in sight, Camping's followers went through the same range of responses as so many other believers have in similar circumstances.

There was straightforward confusion, cognitive dissonance, and trying to work out where they'd gone wrong. One follower told the BBC: 'I do not understand why nothing has happened . . . I can't tell you what I feel right now. Obviously, I haven't understood it correctly because we're still here.'

Then there was the wait-and-see approach: 'We're still watching and waiting for Christ's return,' one follower told the *New York Times*, pointing to the eruption of the Grímsvötn volcano in Iceland as a possible precursor of the main event.

Some had doubts but were not yet ready to make a clean break. One long-time listener to Camping's radio shows – a veteran of the 1994 prediction, who had retained some degree of scepticism as a result – told *SF Gate* he was upset and considered this strike two against Camping, but added: 'I don't think I am going to stop listening to him. I don't know, I gotta listen to him on Monday, see what he says on the radio.'

And there was hurt and anger. Another follower – who had spent much of his savings on driving around with an advert for the apocalypse on his car – told the Associated Press: 'I've been mocked and scoffed and cursed at and I've been through a lot with this lighted sign on top of my car. I was doing what I've been instructed to do through the Bible, but now I've been stymied. It's like getting slapped in the face.'

It was several days before Harold Camping took to the airwaves again to explain what had happened. Family Radio's offices had been shut for the apocalypse, with a note left on the door reading: 'This Office is Closed. Sorry we missed you!'

When he did start broadcasting again, Camping's message was simple: he had, in fact, been right all along.

* * *

Here is a rough guide to the rationalisations that apocalyptic movements usually come up with when they want to clarify why the world didn't end on schedule.

'Actually, we never said the world was going to end.'

An extremely popular option is to simply deny what you predicted – and to instead push the blame on to other parties for misinterpreting what was said.

'I put a big question mark after it,' Harold Camping insisted to *New York* magazine in 2011 when asked about the failure of his 1994 prophecy. That this hedging hadn't got through to his true believers – and indeed, that his own actions showed he'd clearly been convinced himself – was unimportant. The real failure was on the part of everybody else, who simply hadn't appreciated the sheer levels of nuance he was bringing to the table.

Likewise, Elizabeth Clare Prophet would insist that she'd never predicted nuclear war for a specific day, merely that she'd been highlighting a range of 'peak dates' when it *could* happen.

This is, perhaps, an even more common approach among secular prophets of doom than among their religious brethren. 'My critics have done me a severe injustice in distorting my prognostications,' moaned failed meteorologist Albert Porta, shortly before insisting he would still rise like a lion.

Paul Ehrlich, whose 1968 book *The Population Bomb* was filled with lurid depictions of a world dying through overpopulation, complained to *Smithsonian Magazine* in 2018 that the nightmarish scenarios he'd described were 'continually quoted as predictions'. They were, he maintained, merely intended as illustrative hypotheticals. Which might have been a fair point, if he hadn't also made loads of very explicit predictions – say, that 'in the 1970s hundreds of millions of people will starve to death' – which emphatically didn't come true. (Worldwide deaths from famine instead fell: fewer than 5 million across the seventies and eighties combined, compared to over 16 million in the sixties alone.)

It is of course true that people – and especially a sensation-hungry media – can often take a vague suggestion of hypothetical doom and spin it into a certainty. (Remember poor Camille Flammarion, desperately trying to tell newspapers that he'd never claimed Halley's Comet would wipe out all life, and had in fact been saying the exact opposite.) As a result, this explanation can be very effective, for the simple reason it often contains at least a grain of truth. That's why insisting you were simply misquoted is a go-to response for politicians walking back a gaffe, or YouTubers denying they did something racist.

But it's hard to miss that these concerns for precision and nuance only come *after* the fact. Prophets of doom rarely seem as eager to correct such misapprehensions and over-extrapolations while they're still getting them the kind of attention they enjoy.

'There was a small error. Please bear with us.'

This is probably the most common explanation: the precise details of our prophecy were a bit off, but don't worry, we're triple-checking our calculations and we'll get back to you really soon with an updated schedule. It's the 'cheque's in the post' of apocalyptic rationalisation.

You might think, based on your experience of human beings, that 'admitting you got something wrong' wouldn't be the most popular option. It's not something we're great at, as a rule. And after all, isn't the psychological pain of acknowledging error exactly the thing we're supposed to be avoiding here?

Yes . . . but not all errors are created equal. It's a trade-off – admit a mistake on the details, and the broader framework can still stand. You may lose a bit of authority and trust in confessing that you messed up, but crucially you don't have to acknowledge any fault in the big picture. Your fundamental worldview – the thing that's causing the dissonance in the first place – can remain unharmed. Human error is better than divine error.

'We were wrong in the calculation of the timing . . . but not in terms of theology.' That's how one member of the Orthodox Jewish Chabad-Lubavitch movement put it, after they'd experienced a one-two punch of disappointment – the failure of their expected messiah to arrive, and the sudden death of the Lubavitch Rebbe in 1994, who many had begun speculating might be Moshiach himself.

The strategic admission of error was also a particular favourite of Leland Jensen and Neal Chase, leaders of the small Baha'is Under the Provisions of the Covenant (BUPC) sect, who managed to get through no fewer than twenty failed apocalyptic predictions between 1979 and 1995. This included Chase explaining that his prediction of a nuclear bomb obliterating New York in November 1992 had *actually* been about the February 1993 bombing of the World Trade Center. It had just needed the correct biblical adjustments applied to the date, which had not been done. A minor oversight. (Also, it wasn't a nuclear bomb.)

Harold Camping took this approach too, especially when explaining his 1994 failure in the run-up to 2011. He told *New York* that 'my research in the Bible was not nearly complete' at the time – and that his 1994 prediction was 'just a preliminary study that I've been able to complete during the last fifteen years'. This approach can mirror how conspiracy theories often deal with their predictions not coming true – there is always more research to be done, fresh information to be revealed, deeper rabbit holes to venture down. If apocalypticism is a narrative that has particular resonance for us, then the failure can be just another plot twist that draws us even further into the story.

Blaming human error is why so many apocalyptic movements are able to quickly cycle through adjustments to the predicted date after the original prophecy fails. The downside is that there is usually a limit to how many times you can pull this trick before even your most zealous followers start rolling their eyes. A good narrative can only sustain so many twists. The cheque can't be in the post forever.

'This was a test, and we passed!' (alongside its less common variant: 'This was a test, and we failed.')

The imminent apocalypse is rarely a thing to just be passively aware of – 'FYI, world ending Tuesday, but no need to do anything.' It is always, in one way or another, a call to action. Spend time in quiet contemplation, flagellate yourself in the town square, build a nuclear bunker, gather on the mountaintop at midnight, just become extremely annoying . . . Whatever it might be, you're normally expected to *do* something.

This explanation says that, whatever it was you were supposed to do, everyone did it so well that the apocalypse was called off.

When the 103 members of the Church of the True Word emerged from spending forty-two days underground in their nuclear shelters in 1960 – zero bombs having fallen during that time – this was the approach they took. This had been a test of their faith, and their commitment to the bit meant they had proven themselves to truly be God's chosen ones. 'Did you have victory?' 'Yes, praise the Lord!' they chanted together. They still expected the apocalypse to happen at *some* point, but for now, they could be content in the satisfaction of a job well done.

And this takes us back to the group that gave us the idea of cognitive dissonance in the first place – because this was also the explanation that Dorothy Martin gave to her Seekers in Chicago. The cataclysm had been called off thanks to the 'force of Good and light' that the Seekers themselves had brought into the world. As *When Prophecy Fails* puts it: 'The little group, sitting all night long, had spread so much light that God had saved the world from destruction.'

The other variant – 'we failed the test' – is a bit rarer, but does exist. 'We blew it. Obviously, whatever we have done is not enough,' said one member of the Lubavitch movement after their 1994 disappointment. 'If it didn't happen, this means we were not worthy of it,' concluded another follower.

This sense of a test failed may be focused purely on the shortcomings of the movement itself, or it may cast some of the blame for failing the test outwards. When the UFOs that the Unarian movement were expecting to land in the mid-1970s failed to show up and usher in a new age, one of their many rationalisations was simply that the work was not yet done: humanity was still at too low a 'frequency vibration', and we were just putting too many bad vibes out into the universe for the Space Brothers to land. The Unarians must redouble their studies, so that the world could move towards enlightenment.

Even the mockery and rejection that the rest of society heaps on the disappointed believers after a failed prophecy can be folded into this idea of a test – those 'demons from the bottomless pit' that assailed William Miller becoming just a further trial the faithful must endure to prove themselves. This was an explanation that many of Harold Camping's followers settled on in 2011, as half the journalists in America tried to ask them questions about whether they felt dumb.

You can see why 'it was a test' is effective for keeping groups together after they've suffered a let-down: if you can pull it off, it focuses everyone's minds on the importance of the collective effort the group is engaging in. Whether the message is 'Great work, team!' or 'We go again', the group's members will be bound closer together, and the focus on the importance of the work helps to mask the cognitive dissonance.

'It did, in fact, happen.'

This is the boldest explanation by far. You might think, on first glance, that it would be hard to pull off. The fact that you're still here and having this conversation might seem like a hint that the world did not actually end.

This would be to underestimate the inventiveness of the human mind.

For the religious prophet, this usually gets expressed in the claim that the world-ending change actually occurred at a metaphysical level – rather than in the physical world that the prophecy may, on its face, have seemed to suggest. The earthquakes that were due to make the world crumble? The great fires that would consume everything? These were actually *psychic* earthquakes! The fires were actually lit in the souls of men! 'A spiritual stone hit the earth,' explained Leland Jensen of the BUPC sect after Halley's Comet failed to crash into the planet in 1986.

(The BUPC leaders were not averse to slightly less metaphysical claims that their prophecy really had come true – if anything vaguely unusual happened at roughly the same time, they would regularly seize on that and insist that was what the prophecy had really been about. They once claimed vindication for yet another prophecy that nuclear Armageddon would destroy New York, on the grounds that a gas pipeline exploded in New Jersey the following day.)

The idea of the invisible, spiritual apocalypse takes the 'it was a test' rationalisation a stage further: not only was a test passed, but the act of passing the test – of accepting its truth and spreading the word – was in fact *the very change* that had been foretold. The crude fabric of existence may appear undisturbed when the next day unexpectedly dawns, but in actuality, everybody really is living in a new world.

This was what happened with the Institute for Applied Metaphysics, a Canadian New Age movement founded in the sixties by a housewife from Ottawa named Winifred Barton after she began experiencing visions of an alien spirit guide in her basement. This group took a turn towards the messianic after a 'psychic explosion' in 1973 saw Winifred leave her husband for a student thirty years her junior, with the new couple being dramatically revealed as the Queen and King of Earth. The group rapidly became more hierarchical and authoritarian – with a focus on pairing up its members into couples where the man was much younger than the woman.

Barton abruptly announced the end of the world in 1976 – exactly how it would end was left vague, but aliens would land at some point during the proceedings. Some four hundred members of the IAM stocked up on emergency supplies and gathered at each of the group's three rural campuses to wait for the moment. By all accounts, while there was some nervousness, most people were having a perfectly nice time: cooking food, playing music and dancing. 'Keep calm. Keep up the Vibe,' Barton would tell her followers. (Sidenote: this would make a much better slogan for twee tote bags than the one about Carrying On.)

The world did not end. No aliens arrived. But the group decided that the end of the world had indeed occurred at a spiritual level – they had *sensed* the world shift and a new world dawn. One participant recalled people around her saying 'Wow! Did you feel that?'; another remembers not feeling anything, but working hard to maintain their belief, reassuring other members who privately admitted they hadn't felt anything that it had been 'very subtle'. Not everybody bought this – less committed members left the group – but for around two hundred members, this was enough to convince them to abandon their old lives and permanently set up communes, living as the very few Citizens of the Kingdom of Heaven on Earth.

Following the Great Disappointment, William Miller also spent months pondering the question of whether this was what had happened. He was swayed by the interpretation that had become widespread among many of his followers: that what actually occurred on 22 October was, effectively, that the guest list for the doors of heaven had been closed forever. For those who were not already saved, there was now no hope; no amount of good behaviour could get you into heaven's good books. If you hadn't joined the right team before the cosmic transfer deadline . . . well, tough. For Miller, this was a truly attractive thought: it would ease the psychological pain of having been wrong, and in fact would flip it entirely. Under the 'shut-door theory', not only had he been right, but he had in fact been *so right* that everybody who didn't believe him was now irrevocably damned and would never see paradise (as we'll see, however, not everyone was happy with this approach).

Harold Camping also went with the shut-door theory in 2011, when he returned to the airwaves to explain himself after the 21 May date for the Rapture passed uneventfully. He insisted that this had not been a physical event, but a closing of the book on divine judgement. 'No one who had not become saved by that date can ever become saved,' the Family Radio website asserted.

This specific line of argument, obviously, is best suited

to religious prophecy. But the secular variant also exists: the doomsayer who insists that they were *fundamentally* right, that their underlying theory was correct even if certain surface-level details were off. Albert Porta, you'll recall, spent some time adamantly claiming both that a squall off Alaska was the event he'd predicted, and also asserting – *sans* evidence – that the great solar protrusions he'd forecast had indeed happened, they'd just missed Earth. Paul Ehrlich took a similar approach too, steadfastly maintaining to the *Guardian* in 2018 that he had correctly identified the fundamentals, it was merely that the crisis they foretold was arriving a bit slower than anticipated. 'Population growth, along with overconsumption per capita, is driving civilisation over the edge,' he insisted, adding that 'a shattering collapse of civilisation' remains 'a near certainty in the next few decades'.

Rationalisation can be a powerful force. Our lives are shaped in ways large and small by our ability to convince ourselves of dumb stuff. I deserve that doughnut because I've been good; that sports car is actually a very practical option; I can fix him; this politician will stand up for hard-working families who play by the rules.

But that's not the only way that apocalyptic movements survive after doomsday turns out to be a damp squib. They can also throw themselves into proselytising, the reaction that Festinger predicted would dominate – which does happen, although later research has suggested it's not as big a factor as those early psychologists believed. Indeed, some groups go entirely the other way, turning inwards and reducing or entirely abandoning efforts to win new converts.

Instead, alongside rationalisation, many movements focus on

what's termed 'reaffirmation': acts that renew and strengthen the bonds of the group. Because, of course, apocalyptic belief isn't simply a rational assessment of evidence – it's a narrative that fulfils an emotional need, and a shared worldview around which communities are built. Those things don't simply vanish when a prophecy goes wrong.

It's this, the research suggests, that will often determine whether an apocalyptic movement survives a failure or fizzles out. How is the group organised? How strong are the social bonds between members? Are there rituals that help to unite them? Does it have decisive leadership that can act to reassure and recommit the members?

It also helps if the movement was about something more than *just* believing in the end of the world. If the group has a more extensive and sophisticated ideology than that single core belief, that's also something that can continue to bind members together and sell them on the rationalisation. (And yes . . . it also helps if the actual prophecy was vague enough that it's easier to rationalise away.)

Because one thing that's clear is that it's hard for a group to sustain the white-hot fire of apocalyptic expectation for very long, and it can leave both the individual members and the collective burned out.

Take, for example, the BUPC – the Baha'i splinter sect whose leaders kept predicting that New York was going to be nuked, among various other dooms. This group eventually reached the point where ordinary members greeted each new announcement of Armageddon as just so much background noise. Where the first few prophecies had seen frenzied preparations, with members building fallout shelters and publicising the news far and wide, the later ones provoked little more than weary eye-rolls. 'I think we're immune to it now. We've been desensitized,' one member said, while another sighed that 'the truth is that people would have really preferred for Neal to knock off his prophesying'. What kept the BUPC a going concern wasn't belief in the prophecies – it was community, group activities and working towards shared goals.

You can also look to the final act of Harold Camping's long apocalyptic campaign. Having rationalised away the non-event of May as a spiritual event, he assured his listeners that the final destruction of Earth was still on schedule for 21 October. When nothing happened again, Camping went quiet for nearly six months, and then did something unexpected: after decades of dedication to doomsday, he simply . . . quit.

In a letter posted to Family Radio's website in March 2012, Camping wrote: 'We have learned the very painful lesson that all of creation is in God's hands and He will end time in His time, not ours!' He went on to describe his predictions as 'sinful' and begged God's forgiveness (he didn't ask for forgiveness from the people who'd believed him). And he announced that he was out of the doomsday business for good, saying he had 'no new evidence pointing to another date for the end of the world' and 'no interest in even considering another date'.

Harold Camping died a few years later, after a fall. In 2018, Family Radio announced that they would no longer broadcast recordings of him, or promote his teachings.

In 2012, a reporter for *Religion Dispatches* re-interviewed followers of Camping to whom he'd spoken a year earlier, before the failed prophecies. Some were now clear-eyed and scornful – 'I think I was part of a cult' – while others insisted that they'd always been sceptical, and were shocked to have their statements of absolute certainty from twelve months prior read back to them. 'It was as if we were discussing a dream he couldn't quite remember,' the reporter Tom Bartlett writes of one encounter.

The lesson of all this: rationalisation and reaffirmation can get a movement through the dissonance of a failed prophecy, but they have limits. They can even give you multiple bites at the prophetic cherry, convincing followers to ignore past failures and trust your prognostications a second or third or (occasionally) fifth time. But in the end, any apocalyptic movement must either flame out, or gradually adjust itself – preserving the key elements that created the group identity in the first place, while reaching an accommodation with the blunt fact of the world's continued existence. Full-throated apocalyptic expectation can only burn bright for a limited time. There is no long-term strategy that doesn't acknowledge the existence of the long term.

All this explains what happened in the aftermath of the Millerites' Great Disappointment. They had several of the key components of a group that could survive a failed prophecy: strong community bonds with mutual support networks, a religious worldview that extended beyond just the prediction of Judgement Day, and an initial prophecy that contained enough wiggle room that it *could* be rationalised away.

What they lacked, initially, was leadership – because William Miller, never the most publicity-hungry of prophets, had largely retreated from the public eye as he wrestled with his own confusion and dark thoughts over what had happened. In this leadership vacuum, a host of competing sub-sects started to coalesce around different explanations for what had happened – and a power struggle for the future of the movement began.

Those who backed the 'shut-door' theory were one faction, and initially the dominant one. Another group had a different version of the 'invisible apocalypse' rationalisation – that the 'cleansing of the sanctuary' Miller had interpreted as the destruction of the world was actually about an event in heaven, and that this had indeed occurred on schedule. The third faction, meanwhile, included many of the most prominent Millerite figures, such as Joshua Himes – the ones whose investments of time and money gave them the greatest incentive to see the movement continue not just as an idea, but as an actual functioning church. Their overwhelming goal was to sweep the whole prophecy thing under the carpet – after all, if everybody's spiritual fate was now decided, then who needs sermons or new converts, or, indeed, morality? They aimed to purge the movement of its more extremist members, and organise everything along more conventional lines.

This third faction initially succeeded, backed by the grudging endorsement that Himes eventually bullied Miller into giving them. They drove out the fringe elements and laid down the law over what the faith's beliefs were. This group would become the Advent Christian Church – which still exists today, with tens of thousands of members.

If it had a flaw, it was that – to paraphrase Winifred Barton – it failed to Keep up the Vibe. Many Millerites had been attracted to the movement because of their frustrations with hierarchical, top-down, restrictive churches. The adjustment from a free-spirited mass movement to a rigid organisation was too abrupt for many. Instead, they gravitated to the second sect – the one with the rationalisation of the failed prophecy that kept the door open for the kind of spiritual community that had brought them to Millerism in the first place. Among them was Hiram Edson, the prominent Millerite who had written of his uncontrollable weeping in the aftermath of the Great Disappointment.

This group would go on to become the Seventh-Day Adventist Church, which today has more than 20 million followers in almost a hundred thousand churches across the world.

It's not surprising that movements can outlast the failure of their expected apocalypses to arrive. Adventism is hardly the only one – Anabaptism is still going, despite the failure of the Münster rebellion; the Jehovah's Witnesses have survived multiple prophetic failures over the twentieth century. After all, both Christianity and Judaism as a whole are faiths that were once convinced of the imminence of the end. When it didn't arrive, they eventually made their peace with the world's continuation. And if a movement lasts long enough, eventually it might get to be the hated status quo that a new apocalyptic movement will reject.

Because whenever one movement learns to put down the tempting lure of the apocalypse, someone else can pick it up. Rationalisation can get individual groups through a failure of prophecy – but that's not why the idea of the apocalypse has endured for thousands of years, or why there's always a willing audience for every new prophet of doom, no matter how many times it's been wrong before. As long as there are people who reject the world as it is, people fearful of change or people yearning for change, who can't conceive of how it could improve without everything burning down, then there will be people ready to tell a story that satisfies that impulse.

11.

Postcards from the Edge

Not every prophecy of doom is condemned to failure. After all, doom happens. Catastrophes strike. None of us will last forever. Even if you were just crying wolf, the chances are a wolf will stroll past eventually.

But if you want to work out how the end might really come for the entire world, it's striking that many of the threats which have haunted our apocalyptic imagination are strictly local affairs. Now that we have an understanding of just how big the world is, we can see that many of the things we've pictured bringing about the end of the world actually lack a global reach. The horsemen of the apocalypse don't always travel well.

Earthquakes may destroy a city, and send tsunamis racing across the sea to devastate distant shores. But they can do this without so much as upsetting a teacup on the far side of the world. Drought and famine can be nightmarish across an entire region, and knock-on effects from forced migration and disrupted trading networks can spread even farther. Yet climate conditions that bring famine to one area may bring feast to another. Floods . . . okay, flooding is actually an interesting one.

In September 1931, the trawler *Colinda* was dragging its nets twenty-five miles off the Norfolk coast when it brought up a large chunk of peat. This wasn't unusual, especially as the UK's strongest ever earthquake had shaken up the seabed just a few months earlier. The thing that *was* unusual was the eight-inch-long harpoon tip carved from antler that the surprised fishermen found inside that clump of sod. This find turned out to be evidence of something that had long been suspected: that many millennia ago, humans had lived on the land that now lay 120 feet below the surface of the North Sea.

This was Doggerland – the great lost landmass between Britain and continental Europe. It's named for the Dogger Bank shallows, which twelve thousand years ago were highland tundra. In 10,000 BCE, you could have walked from York to Copenhagen (or the places they'd eventually be) without even needing to get your feet terribly wet.

The reason you can't do that today, and the reason this Atlantis-upon-Humber is now home only to fishing boats and neolithic ghosts, is that when the last Ice Age ended there was suddenly a lot more water to go round.

Flooding is one of the most consistent threats in apocalyptic stories across cultures, present even in the proto-apocalyptic tales of ancient times. From the Epic of Gilgamesh onwards, via the Abrahamic flood of Noah, Matsya rescuing Manu from the deluge in Hinduism, or the Great Flood of Gun-Yu in China, many cultures around the world have at least one central flood myth. It's so prevalent that a nagging possibility has drawn speculation for decades – that this common theme exists because at the dawn of civilisation, when our earliest mythologies were formed, flooding was a very different business to today.

Most flooding is by its nature local and temporary. This is not to underestimate its destructive power: if you want a truly deadly and unstoppable force, there's little to beat a large body of water in motion. Still, even the worst floods in recorded history have been at most regional disasters, and the waters always recede eventually.

But as the glaciers melted at the end of the Ice Age, all that water that had been locked up was released back into the world. This was an inundation that would permanently reshape geographies on a massive scale – flood waters that never receded. The kind of flooding that ends worlds.

Much of this was still gradual, a slow encroachment barely perceptible over a human lifetime. But sometimes it could be a sudden, violent process. As glaciers melt, they can form huge lakes, held in place at the margins by an ice dam – which is, of course, also melting. When the dam gives way, the results are cataclysmic. (A 'glacial lake outburst flood' is the technical name.)

The largest of the Missoula floods, which slashed great scars across the landscape of the Pacific Northwest, unleashed over 2 billion gallons of water every second. Eight thousand two hundred years ago the final draining of Lake Agassiz – the proglacial lake that covered a large chunk of North America, larger than all of today's Great Lakes put together – may have raised sea levels across the planet by as much as two metres in a relatively short span, and triggered a global cold spell that lasted for several centuries.

You can see why so many researchers have found it a

tantalising possibility – that all of our Great Flood myths are in fact not myth, but memory. That they don't represent general anxiety about flooding, but memorialise specific catastrophic events of the deep past that carved themselves into our cultural landscape as surely as they did our physical one.

This must stay in the realm of tantalising possibility for now. Plenty of candidates for the Real Great Flood have been put forward, only for further research to suggest that they don't fit the bill. One popular candidate was the Black Sea, which several theories had suggested was catastrophically filled in a sudden breakthrough from the Mediterranean under 8,000 years ago. It's a neat idea, as it's in the right part of the world to affect the early civilisations of the region and inspire the floods of Gilgamesh and Noah, but later research has suggested that no such apocalyptic deluge occurred.

So too with Doggerland. Some had long wondered if it died catastrophically, perhaps finally breached by tsunamis from an undersea landslide near Norway. Again, the most recent studies suggest no – the tsunami was real but not a fatal blow, and Doggerland instead vanished beneath the waves over the course of thousands of years. Britain did not become an island in a sudden calamity, but in fits and starts, the sea slowly nibbling away at the sinking land until one day a tide came in that never quite went out.

The idea that our flood myths reflect the prevalence of genuinely world-changing floods back when humanity was taking its earliest civilisational steps remains a tempting one. It may, in fact, be true. But it's probably not *necessary* to explain why we have so many flood myths. Humans have always tended to live close to water. Obviously water-related disasters are going to be close to universal in our pantheon of worries.

But it does highlight the way that the catastrophes of the past can still speak to the present. We live in a time when ice sheets are melting again, and waves nibble away at the land. A recent study found that some 15 million people around the world live under the threat of a glacial outburst – that one day, somewhere high above them, an ice dam will crack and their world will be swept away.

So let's ask the question: how might the world end? Not in the sense of the lump of rock we frolic upon. Outside of a few more extreme scenarios (we'll get on to them) the physical planet will be mostly fine, at least for the next few billion years (we'll get to that too). So not *the* world, exactly, but *our* world. Us. How might the end come for humanity?

In the next chapters, we'll look to the future – first the ways the natural world might destroy us, then the ways we might destroy ourselves. But in this chapter, we'll try to frame the question by looking at the past. Because if we want to know how likely we are to avoid calamity, or where the greatest threat to our survival comes from, it might help to know how close we've come before. What were the bullets that we narrowly dodged?

In one sense, this question has a straightforwardly plausible answer: the closest humanity has come to apocalypse was at around 4pm on Saturday 27 October, 1962.

This was at the height of the Cuban Missile Crisis: the Joint Chiefs of Staff were recommending that the United States invade Cuba, an American spy plane had just been shot out of the sky, and frantic backchannel diplomacy was underway to try and avert all-out war between the world's great nuclear powers. And at that very moment, in international waters off the coast of Cuba, US forces were dropping explosive depth charges in the general direction of the Soviet submarine *B-59*.

This wasn't quite as aggressive as it sounds. It was an effort to signal the submarine to surface: they were trying to enforce a blockade around the island to prevent any more Soviet missiles being brought ashore. Now, dropping depth charges might not seem like the wisest means of communication, but apparently this is the sort of thing that submariners would usually understand: there's a crucial difference in the meaning conveyed between dropping big depth charges *on* you and dropping smaller ones *near* to you.

Unfortunately, the Americans dropping the charges didn't know a few important things. One was that *B-59* had been in stealth mode for days, staying underwater and out of contact with Moscow. They had no idea what the political situation on the surface was, and no idea that a blockade had been imposed. What's more, after days without surfacing and plagued by failing cooling systems, the temperature in the submarine was almost unbearable, over 37°C. Even worse, the sub's air was now suffused with carbon dioxide – yep, the ol' apocalypse gas, causing trouble once again – which made everyone fuzzy-headed at best, and borderline unhinged at worst.

Another thing the US forces didn't know was that *B-59* carried a nuclear warhead on board. And that the captain was authorised to fire it without consulting anyone higher up his chain of command.

In that context, the 'communicate via depth charge' approach looks a bit more reckless.

The upshot was that Captain Savitsky – whose nerves, according to one crew member, were 'shot to hell' – concluded that the hot war had begun above them, that they were under attack by an overwhelming force, and that their boat was doomed . . . but they could still land one devastating blow before they were sent to the bottom. Savitsky wanted to fire the nuclear torpedo. His political officer agreed. And on most Soviet submarines, those two positions were all you'd need for sign-off.

There's a decent chance that you and I are only here today because Executive Officer Vasily Aleksandrovich Arkhipov also happened to be aboard that submarine. Arkhipov was the chief of staff for the submarine brigade of which *B-59* was a part. He didn't outrank the captain, but crucially, he had a vote in the decision on whether to go nuclear. He *could* have been on any submarine in the brigade. He was on this one.

He said no.

Arkhipov only publicly commented on the *B-59* incident once, decades later, and he underplayed both its drama and significance. For an experienced submariner, it may not even have felt that dramatic; talking the captain down from a bad decision may have been par for the course. Arkhipov had served heroically on the *K-19* submarine two years previously, when a coolant leak had threatened nuclear meltdown, so he may have genuinely felt that this wasn't even the closest to nuclear doom that he'd personally been. But still, under the most stressful circumstances imaginable and with the social pressure of being outvoted, Arkhipov stood his ground and refused to go with the flow. It was an act of stubbornness that's both oddly mundane and incredibly brave, and it may have saved the world. Or at least large parts of it.

What would the consequences have been if he hadn't been there? Peace was hanging by the finest imaginable thread in those hours, with a few doves on both sides desperately trying to make space for calm to prevail, while faced with overwhelming circumstantial evidence that the many hawks were right in their most paranoid interpretations. An actual nuclear strike at that time would almost certainly have tipped the world into an immediate cycle of mutual nuclear retaliation.

Maybe there could still have been snatched minutes in which wiser voices could have won the day. (After all, both Kennedy and Khrushchev were pretty much on team 'please don't let my name be forever attached to the worst event in human history'.) But in those maximally fevered moments, that would have been a slim hope. And had the Cold War turned thermonuclear hot, the immediate death toll would likely have been counted in the tens of millions at a minimum. The long-term casualty count . . . well, we'll get on to that in the next chapter.

Arkhipov's stand wasn't even the only near miss during the Cuban Missile Crisis – and the causes were often darkly absurd. A few hours after the *B-59* incident, radar operators in New Jersey wrongly reported that a missile had been launched from Cuba towards Florida, because a test simulation tape had accidentally been loaded into their system. Two days earlier, nuclear armed jets had been scrambled from an air base in Wisconsin – the pilots convinced that nuclear war had started – because a faulty alarm system set off the nuclear klaxon rather than the sabotage alert. The planes were only stopped at the last moment before take-off when an officer drove his car onto the runway flashing his lights; it turned out the region-wide sabotage alert had been triggered because a soldier in Duluth, Minnesota, had shot at a bear climbing a fence, wrongly believing the bear to be a Soviet *spetsnaz*.

Those fraught days in 1962 were also not the only time that one individual was forced to stand firm against the forces of Armageddon, or where errors brought the world terrifyingly close to catastrophe. Most famously, another Soviet officer in a time of mutual hair-trigger paranoia, Stanislav Petrov, may have also saved the world when, in 1983, he declined to report an alert that the US had launched missiles up the chain of command. He judged, correctly, that it was a false alarm.

These kind of false alarms were disturbingly common around this time, as experimental new early-warning systems flaked out. They weren't limited to the Soviet side – at least three such false alarms hit the North American systems over an eight-month period between November 1979 and June 1980. The last of these resulted in the kind of fabled '3am phone call' beloved of presidential debates, where the commander-in-chief is woken in the early hours and forced to make a potentially world-ending snap judgement before they've even had a coffee.

Based on the 1980 case, it turns out that there's at least one other person who gets that phone call before the president – in this case, it was national security adviser Zbigniew Brzezinski, who was roused from sleep to hear a report that hundreds of Soviet missiles were heading towards the US. He was on the verge of making the call to President Carter when the news came through that the missiles were digital phantoms – it eventually turned out that a computer chip that cost just forty-six cents had failed.

These kinds of events are grimly compelling because they highlight our seemingly tenuous grip on existence. The boundary between survival and extinction is sketched by the random firing of cheap computer components or sleep-deprived neurons, and the counterfactuals will always remain mysterious.

We can never know what would have happened if Brzezinski had made the call before the error was identified, or if Petrov had followed protocol rather than following his gut. Would Petrov's superiors have also hesitated for long enough that the error became apparent, or would they have gone straight to ordering a retaliatory strike? The latter is unnervingly plausible, given the belligerent mood of the time – and if they had, they would have sparked a nuclear exchange with an arsenal far larger and more destructive than that which existed during the Cuba stand-off two decades earlier. If Arkhipov maybe sits a rung above Petrov on the saving-the-world ladder, it's only because without his clear-headed stubbornness, a launch was a virtual certainty.

It can be terrifying to contemplate how close we've come to the edge, and how close we still might be, only ever one glitch away from doomsday. Although, perhaps, there might be a tiny crumb of comfort to be found as well – a counter to the narrative that we're a species hell-bent on self-destruction.

It's too small a sample to wield with any confidence, but still: there have been multiple occasions when humans were presented with a straightforward decision in which Armageddon lay down one path. And each time, so far, someone has said 'no'.

We probably shouldn't rely on that always being the case, though.

But if 1962 is the closest we've come to the brink of destruction, it's only because of that path not followed. Its destruction exists entirely in the realm of the potential. Because in our branch of the multiverse, at least, the Cuban Missile Crisis didn't result in millions upon millions of deaths. In the end, the direct death toll was . . . one guy.

This was the unfortunate Major Rudolf Anderson, an American U2 spy plane pilot whose unit had spotted the illicit missile sites in the first place. He was killed by shrapnel from a surface-to-air missile on a sortie just a few hours before Arkhipov faced down his trigger-happy captain. Anderson's death was both a huge factor in bringing tensions to the brink, but also an important catalyst for the eventual de-escalation.

This kind of near-miss event – nothing very bad actually happened, but something appallingly bad *could* have happened – is useful when thinking about doomsday scenarios, but only up to a point. You quickly run into the same problem as you do with any kind of historical counterfactual: it's very easy for them to descend into an endless game of 'what if . . .?' that rapidly becomes absurd. And our hunger for narrative – for the heroic stand, for triumph snatched from calamity, for the long arc of history to be compressed into one pivotal dramatic moment – means that we can sometimes assign more weight to these supposed turning points of history than they can bear.

This is not especially instructive if you're trying to work out how vulnerable humanity is to destruction. Very few events have the clean simplicity of Vasily Arkhipov's choice; you could come up with a ton of examples where a different decision or a random stroke of misfortune could have led to calamity. But at the end of the day, such speculation about the past usually ends up every bit as hazy as speculation about the future.

Instead, perhaps we should turn our attention to events where something bad very definitely *did* happen.

The closest that life on Earth has come to being wiped out must, by definition, have happened in one of the great mass extinctions throughout history. Each of these events represented a profound and horrifying cataclysm. There are five for which we have clear fossil evidence over the past 500 million years. There's another, far earlier one that exists only in inference. (There's also the one that, ugh, might be happening right now because of us.) In each of the historical extinctions, somewhere in the region of 70 per cent of all living species died off. Entire branches of life were completely obliterated. If any events in our planet's past deserve the label 'apocalypse', these are at the top of the list.

And yet it would be wrong for us to look back on these events as times when *our* existence hung in the balance. Or rather: yes, it totally did, but not in the way you might think. These ancient mass extinctions, for the most part, were not events that threatened to prevent the eventual existence of future humans. They were what helped it to happen.

Every apocalypse is but a new world's creation story.

In the aftermath of every great extinction, the sudden absence of previously dominant species and the abundance of abruptly unoccupied ecological niches led to a wild, experimental blossoming of ways to be alive. Without these unfettered evolutionary radiations, we wouldn't be here – or at least we wouldn't look anything like we do right now.

To pick one example: we have our meat on the outside. Our soft bits are layered around our hard bits. Which, from a crude survival point of view, seems honestly kind of reckless, making us both a convenient snack food and also vulnerable to dying from sepsis if we trip and graze a leg. By contrast, 450 million years ago most animals were a strictly meat-inside affair, very sensibly keeping their softs safely protected underneath their hards.

For the fact that we're all soft and fleshy, you can thank the first mass extinction for which we have fossil evidence – the Ordovician–Silurian extinctions, around 445 million years ago. It was in the aftermath of this that the bony fish emerged, from which we inside-skeleton-havers descend. (This particular post-apocalypse also saw the widespread movement of plants on to land, which would prove extremely helpful in the long term.) Next extinction, similar story: the mass die-off near the end of the Devonian period 370 million years ago saw the survival of our fishy, rudimentary-limbed ancestors, who became free to experiment with flopping out on to the now-verdant land while a bunch of their competitors vanished.

Now, to be fair, it wasn't all plain sailing for future humans. Extinction number three is where things get diciest for us.

Around 250 million years ago, as the Permian era came to an end and the Triassic started revving up, our ancestors – a bunch of vaguely lizard-like creatures called the Synapsids – were the big beasts on land. One mass extinction later, however, and the Synapsids were routed. Our few surviving progenitors were reduced to scurrying fearfully around the undergrowth, while the archosaurs (dinosaurs, assorted other big lizardy things, plus their airborne and underwater pals) reigned supreme. Their dominance was such that even a fourth mass extinction at the beginning of the Jurassic didn't knock them off their perch, merely cementing dinosaur hegemony.

But in good news for us, an asteroid strike on the Yucatán 66 million years ago saw this hierarchy swing back again. The extinction at the end of the Cretaceous saw those scurrying mammals newly ascendant, and the remaining miniature dinosaurs reduced to flapping around in trees and yelling every time the sun comes up.

Humanity is not the inevitable end product of evolution. *Homo sapiens* as we exist today – meat-outside, land-dwelling, warm-blooded and slightly furry – are the lucky beneficiaries of a series of chaotic and destructive near-apocalypses that simply proved much *more* unlucky for someone else.

But all of these great extinctions pale in comparison to the mass extinction for which we *don't* have fossil evidence – the one that happened before any life was advanced enough to leave much in the way of fossils. This extinction we can only infer from base geology: dramatic changes in how iron presents itself in the most ancient rocks of our world. This, *this* is the greatest apocalypse in our planet's history.

Because just under two and a half billion years ago, something appalling happened on Earth. One of the dominant forms of life started – through no malice, but simply as a by-product of its way of life – to fill the atmosphere with a deadly poison. Unthinkingly, just to make themselves more successful in the game of life, these beings virtually destroyed the ecosystem of the entire planet and brought about the destruction of almost every form of life on Earth.

This is the Oxygen Catastrophe.

The Earth of the time was abundant with single-celled life, all of it simple in its structure and complex in its biochemistry. Both the land and the water would have been resplendent with multilayered microbial mats (which may, according to one hypothesis, have been a lovely purple colour). These provided dense and diverse ecosystems in which the interplay of chemical gradients allowed for a dazzling variety of interdependent ways of living, all of it ultimately fuelled by microbes converting the sun's light into usable energy. This all went horribly, horribly wrong when one type of microbe, the cyanobacteria, learned a new technique for this photosynthesis – one that produced oxygen as a waste product.

It's strange to think of oxygen – a gas so essential to our existence that we use it as a metaphor for the act of giving life to things – as a deadly poison, but that's what it can be. In high doses it can poison even us. For the microbes of early Earth, used to an atmosphere containing only trace amounts of the stuff, the steady rise in oxygen over the course of a few hundred million years was a true apocalypse. It's hard to be sure, because this early life left no fossil trace, but it's plausible that more than four-fifths of life on Earth died in this period.

Those that survived did so by teaming up: the cells of one type of microbe became home to another type of microbe, a type that could use this toxic waste productively. This symbiotic union allowed them to weather the crisis and emerge stronger on the other side. Those surviving microbe teams are the ancestors of all of us, and we carry their dual lineages in every part of ourselves. Mitochondria – the powerhouse of the cell – are the descendants of those ancient helpful hitchhikers.

Your body is a coalition more than 2 billion years old, an enduring union between lives that joined forces and worked together to face down doomsday.

The tribulations of microbial blooms are all very well – but they are perhaps not hugely relatable. What, you may be wondering, about more recently? How close have humans come to being wiped out – once, you know, there were *actual humans* to wipe out?

Looking for evidence of such near-misses in the prehistory of humanity is a complicated business, because for quite a lot of the time there's just not much to go on. It can be tricky to deduce from a few scattered jawbones and occasional evidence of fires whether humanity as a whole was thriving or on the verge of extinction at that point. Instead, we're often left to hunt for the ghosts of ancient catastrophes in our genes.

This is all about population bottlenecks – when the level of a particular population suddenly drops dramatically, for whatever horrible reason natural selection has chosen that day. If someone does make it through and extinction is staved off, these bottlenecks leave echoes in the gene pool of those few who survived. The small group left to rebuild their numbers starts with far less genetic diversity. And so, by studying the subsequent blooming of genetic diversity across their modern descendants, it's possible to work backwards and identify the pinch points in evolutionary history when populations crashed and the gene pool shrank.

That's the idea, at least. And pretty much everybody agrees that modern humans are descended from an unusually small number of relatively recent ancestors. We're not a very diverse species, genetically speaking, when compared to our closest relatives. All of humanity around the world has less genetic variation than there is between two groups of chimps living across a river from each other in Cameroon. The upshot is that every one of us today is descended from a group that could be as few as 10,000 breeding individuals who lived somewhere over a hundred thousand years ago. That's pretty small; it's roughly the population of Ludlow. But it's not quite extinction level – and anyway, that's only measuring the 'effective population', the ones who bred and whose descendants survived. There would have been maybe ten times as many humans actually walking around. Lincoln, not Ludlow, if you want to keep thinking about it in terms of towns in the Midlands.

But things *may* have been much dicier for humanity somewhere along the line. Studies have thrown up multiple suggestions for periods when we faced much tighter or more sudden bottlenecks. But thanks to the ephemeral nature of this kind of research, certainty is hard to come by. Almost every one of them has had someone subsequently come along and say, 'Nope, no bottleneck here.' Probably the most controversial of all these is the Toba catastrophe theory.

Seventy-four thousand years ago, the Toba supervolcano in Indonesia went boom. Very, *very* boom – it was the most powerful volcanic explosion in the last 2.5 million years. Over nine hundred cubic miles of pulverised rock was blasted into the air, and the entire Indian subcontinent was blanketed in a layer of ash at least two inches thick. This honestly seemed a really good guess for why we're not very diverse: all the dust and sulphur dioxide that shot into the atmosphere would have caused dramatic global cooling, a climate catastrophe that brought our ancestors to the brink of extinction.

The evidence all seemed to fit, until it didn't. Subsequent studies suggested there was little change in plant life after the eruption that would be consistent with a catastrophic global winter. Temperature reconstructions found the cooling was likely much less than expected. Archaeological digs found evidence of tools directly above and below the ash layer, suggesting that life had actually carried on without too much fuss. And crucially, more advanced genetic analysis suggested that there simply wasn't a bottleneck that coincided with the eruption. Toba would certainly have been a rough time to be alive, but it doesn't seem to have brought humanity to the edge of destruction.

The picture is hazier on the other big candidate for humanity's nearest miss, significantly earlier in our history. A lengthy global cold snap started around 195,000 years ago and lasted around 60,000 years. This must have been annoying for *Homo sapiens*, as we'd only just emerged on the scene. Some studies have suggested that this period was almost fatal for our new species, with the effective population reduced to maybe only a few hundred individuals, barely holding on in a small number of refuges on the South African coast. Unlike the Toba theory, this one hasn't been conclusively ruled out – but subsequent studies have suggested that, once again, this bottleneck may not have existed.

This is a tricky, messy field. It's entirely possible that new evidence may come along to supplant all of this – that new bottlenecks will be found, new times when our ancestors danced on the edge of oblivion. But it's also entirely possible that the long prehistory of *Homo sapiens* may simply have been one where there were never very many of us, but we also escaped without any particularly apocalyptic population collapses.

Before we leave the deep past, though, we probably need to talk about a little thing called the Younger Dryas Impact Hypothesis. This claims that the titular Younger Dryas (a period of rapid cooling across the Northern Hemisphere that began a little under 13,000 years ago) was triggered when the Earth was bombarded by thousands of fragments of a broken-up comet. This caused massive sea-level rises and global flooding – the ultimate source of every culture's great flood myths – and wiped out a previously unknown but highly advanced ancient civilisation that had existed during the Ice Age.

Now, if your bullshit detectors are tingling a bit at this . . . yeah. It's nonsense, pushed by a small fringe of very determined but decidedly non-expert enthusiasts. There was no great sea-level rise at that time, no evidence of this comet bombardment, and so on. It probably wouldn't be worth mentioning at all if Netflix hadn't recently put a rocket under it with the series *Ancient Apocalypse* – a show that insists all this is being covered up by Big Archaeology, for unclear reasons. If nothing else, it shows the enduring power of apocalyptic narratives, and our determination to rationalise them into existence.

Anyway, one 2023 paper from a group of actual scientists critiqued the Younger Dryas Impact Hypothesis for indulging in 'flawed methodologies, inappropriate assumptions, questionable conclusions, misstatements of fact, misleading information, unsupported claims, irreproducible observations, logical fallacies, and selected omission of contrary information'. Okay, but other than that, Mrs Lincoln, how was the hypothesis?

As we leave the world of prehistory behind, answering questions about how close humanity has come to destruction starts to get a little bit easier. There's more direct evidence. People helpfully start living in villages and towns and cities, and leaving all their stuff piled up in handy layers for archaeologists to find. It becomes possible to see when a city was abandoned, to deduce wars and migrations and times of feast and famine, and to get a better sense of how many people were alive at any one time.

It allows you to make a stab at producing a graph of the world's population over the past twelve thousand years.

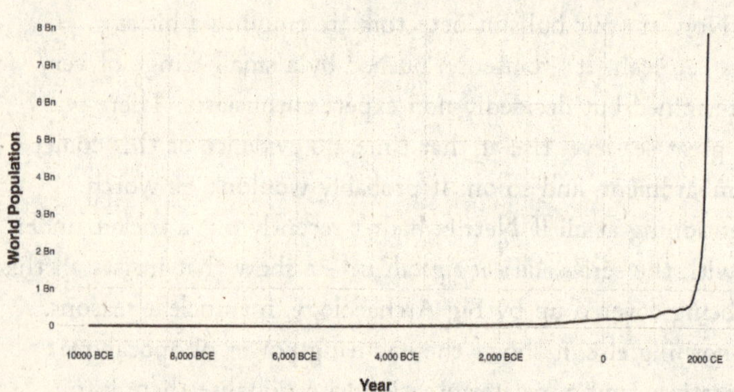

This is a very silly graph in some ways, because in its basic form you can't see much. It's just a long, virtually flat line, then a sharp turn into an almost vertical line. That's the story of humanity: very gradually slightly more of us, and then an extraordinary explosion that begins a little over three hundred years ago. It took all of history until around 1800 for humanity to reach a billion people; the next billion took another 120 years to arrive; the most recent extra billion were born in a little over a decade.

This becomes clearer if you fiddle with the graph a bit. For starters, narrow the range and look just at the last two millennia. You can also make the scale logarithmic (thanks, John Napier!) so it's possible to see finer details in that exponential burst. And it's here that the point becomes apparent:

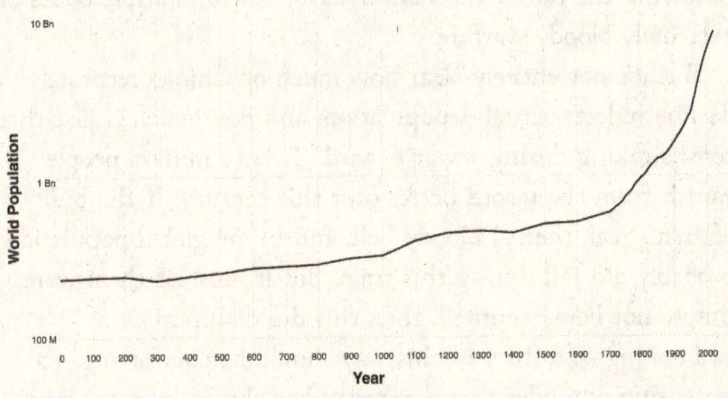

Because if you look closely, you can spot that there are a *couple* of small dips – times when the world's population actually shrank. But there's only two of them that we can see. All of human history, with all of its horrors – all the war and conquest and democide, all the natural disasters, all the famines and the plagues – have barely made a dent in humanity's ceaseless proliferation. On a global scale, the end has never been anywhere close to nigh.

Also, one of those two dips might be down to a book-keeping error.

There's one decline between 1300 and 1400 that is definitely real: that's the Black Death, as *Yersinia pestis* tore through Europe in the middle of the century, killing up to half the population. But there's also a drop in the third century that's less certain. It undeniably reflects that quite a lot of the world was going through it around that time: the Crisis of the Third Century saw a combination of wars, political instability, climate shifts and disease cause havoc in the Roman Empire, while in China the chaos of the Three Kingdoms period following the fall of the Han dynasty led to multiple bouts of extremely bloody warfare.

But it's not entirely clear how much of China's recorded decline reflects actual depopulation, and how much is just that census-taking during a war is hard. Twenty million people vanish from the record books over this century. If the bulk of that's real, then a) bloody hell, and b) the global population probably did fall during this time. But if most of them were simply not being counted, then this dip disappears.

Looking at history in this way should be comforting – a reassuring reminder that doomsday has always been far more distant than we have imagined. And yet, it actually . . . feels horrible? The view from the distant, Olympian heights occupied by the Spreadsheet Gods misses so much.

Just think about what you can't see from this vantage point. The megadeaths of the twentieth century barely register; the crimes of Hitler, Mao, Stalin and Leopold vanish like so many rounding errors. The historical event that perhaps most closely resembles an actual apocalypse – the depopulation of the Americas after the European invasion, with perhaps 90 per cent of the population being lost to disease and violence over the course of two centuries – is rendered effectively invisible by the concurrent growth in the more populous lands of Europe and Asia. And there will be myriad shattering tragedies which simply fell between check marks on the chart, or where we've just not put together the evidence yet.

But still: the basic shape of things can't be denied. Humanity as a whole has shrugged off the absolute worst that history could find to throw at us, and come out the other side laughing and breeding. If you look to the past for lessons in how the human race might perish, the only reasonable conclusion is that it will take something far outside the ordinary. Humans are a survival machine. The apocalypse will have to get up very early to get the better of us.

Of course, you can't look at the apocalypse as a simple matter of head count. Yes, doomsday tales will often dramatise our hopes and fears of the future with stories of an Earth entirely scoured of life. But R.E.M. had it right: we're talking about the end of the world *as we know it*. It's not oblivion that we fear, it's a life that's unrecognisable to us.

So let's talk about the collapse of civilisation.

The word 'civilisation' is loaded. It's often been deployed as a cudgel – a justification for delivering morally improving local apocalypses to a wide variety of people down the centuries. Even in its milder forms, it can still come freighted with a bunch of assumptions about what we value that we might not actually intend.

But still, let's accept that there's *something* we mean there, even if we might struggle to articulate it without being problematic. The good stuff of life; everything that extends beyond mere survival. Something inherently collective (regardless of political system) with many people bound by shared norms and building something that couldn't be achieved alone. What this actually looks like will change with time and place and context, but – talking apocalyptically, at least – maybe we can just call it 'the stuff you'll miss when it's gone'.

As already touched on earlier in the book, our culture's shorthand for the collapse of civilisations is 'the fall of Rome'. Our speech is suffused with references to Rome's fall – the last days of Rome, barbarians at the gates – and people wheel out their pet theories about Rome's decline to bolster their political beliefs about today's society. If we can answer the question 'Why did Rome fall?', the implied theory goes, then maybe we can stop the same calamity befalling us.

Which is odd, because Rome didn't really fall. There was no moment of civilisational collapse. There was *change*, certainly, and crises along the way, and there's undoubtedly some point where you can stop colouring in large parts of Western Europe and labelling them 'Western Roman Empire'. But it's as much a story of continuity as it is of decline, and moreover it's one that spans hundreds of years.

The focus of Roman imperial power had long shifted away from Rome itself, even before Constantine established his seat in the east in 330 CE. The capital had been mobile ever since Diocletian moved it to Mediolanum in 286, and the administrative centre of the Western Empire continued bouncing between Mediolanum and Ravenna and Rome after the Empire was divided in 395. So while the sack of Rome by Alaric's Visigoths in 410 was a shocking event for what it represented, the city wasn't the power centre of the Empire at the time.

The end of the Western Empire is usually pegged to 476, when soldiers in the Roman army rebelled, took Ravenna and deposed the child emperor Romulus Augustulus. But the kid was only in that position because his dad had also led a previous military revolt, so it wasn't that dramatic a change. What's more, Odoacer – one of the soldiers who led the rebellion and claimed power in the aftermath – both had the support of the Roman Senate and immediately pledged loyalty to the Eastern Roman Emperor in Constantinople. The Western Empire's territorial extent had already been shrinking for most of the century before this, but many of the kingdoms that were established in its wake continued using Roman laws and Roman administrators, and derived legitimacy from their Roman ties. The Roman Senate in the West continued as an institution long after Odoacer's takeover, and would exist until 603. The Eastern Roman Empire, of course, lasted until 1453.

This isn't to say that nothing bad was happening during all this time. But given that the Roman Empire had regularly been plagued by civil wars, coups, crises and divisions for centuries before 476, it's just as easy to read it as 'more of the same' as it is to see it as some kind of catastrophic break point. The idea that any of this represents the defeat of civilisation by 'barbarians' bears little relation to reality – and it's worth remembering that the Germanic peoples tagged as barbarians were mostly there because they'd been forced out of their own lands by invasions from the east. *Somebody's* world had ended, for sure, but maybe not the people the normal narrative suggests.

Part of the issue here is that the long lens of history compresses gradual changes that spanned many lifetimes and makes them appear as sudden, dramatic shifts. The mapmaker's view doesn't necessarily translate to events on the ground; the desire to demarcate ages of history crushes long-term trends down into a single date. To put it another way: the collapse of the Western Roman Empire was both slower and less extensive than the collapse of the British Empire in the mid-twentieth century – and, with the exception of certain politicians and newspaper columnists, nobody thinks of that as representing the end of civilisation.

So it's worth bearing in mind that many of history's civilisational collapses may not have been quite as collapsey as the narrative suggests (this all depends on how you're defining 'collapse', of course). For example, the supposed collapse of the

Maya civilisation between 700 and 900 CE was as much a shift of regional power from the south to the north – cities in the southern territory became gradually depopulated over several centuries, but Maya civilisation continued to thrive in the northern cities of the Yucatán Peninsula.

Similarly, the decline of the Indus Valley civilisation between 1900 and 1700 BCE also saw its great cities gradually lose their populations, but this was accompanied by both a concurrent strengthening of rural networks and by migration eastwards to modern-day India, where cities start emerging not too long afterwards. In both cases, there was undoubtedly grim stuff accompanying all this – disease, violence, the usual – but fundamentally these are stories of change as much as of chaos.

Some collapses may not even have happened at all. The story of Rapa Nui – aka Easter Island – is told as one of environmental self-sabotage, where the island's trees were cut down faster than they could naturally be replaced. As one author (me) put it, the 'effects were devastating to Rapa Nui's society', and it's often said that this all led to dramatic population collapse in the 1600s, a century before Europeans arrived. But a 2024 genetic study, of the same kind as those looking for ancient population bottlenecks, told a very different story: there was no population collapse. If anything, the population was probably growing steadily until a century after European contact.

But there have been collapses both more profound and more dramatic, most notably the Late Bronze Age collapse. This was widespread, taking down multiple civilisations across much of the Mediterranean world and beyond. It was also sudden, within-a-lifetime stuff – much of it occurring in a matter of decades. The flourishing world of the Late Bronze Age Mediterranean, one of complex societies and international trade, went rapidly backwards from about 1200 BCE onwards. Cities were left abandoned, often in ruins. The trading networks that had defined the region fell apart, leading to a new age of isolation. Some polities – Hittites, Mycenaeans, Canaanites and more – collapsed entirely, while even those that survived, such as the Egyptian and Assyrian empires, struggled on much diminished. Some areas, notably in the Greek world, would not recover their former level of complexity for centuries.

This collapse also looms large in the imagination because it has a menacing, ominous villain: the mysterious 'Sea Peoples', described as vicious and implacable invaders who raided at will and left destruction in their wake. Their reputation is heightened by desperate letters begging for aid sent from cities that would shortly be left in flames: 'My father, now the ships of the enemy have come.'

What actually caused the Late Bronze Age collapse? For many years, the default answer was 'the Sea Peoples, obviously', but scholarship has long painted a far more complex picture. Some cities certainly died in violence; others seem to have been abandoned without bloodshed. While the identity of the Sea Peoples remains up for debate, what's certain is that they weren't one people, but many groups from across the Mediterranean world, and they may not have been a single force but rather independent actors. (Also, sometimes they arrived by land.)

Even some of the cities that met a violent end may not have all been victims of the Sea Peoples – normal war with other states or internal revolt are also strong possibilities.

Modern scholarship is more likely to see the Sea Peoples as a symptom, rather than a cause, of the underlying disruptions that actually caused the collapse. Exactly what those causes were, however, is still up for debate.

Maybe it was earthquakes – there was a flurry of them in the region for several decades at around that time. Maybe it was disease – traces of an early form of bubonic plague have been detected in the region. Maybe it was technological – innovative new types of military equipment allowing for a sudden upending of the balance of power, or perhaps weapons produced by the early ironworking that would shortly give the following age its name. Or maybe it was the unsustainable nature of a palace-based economy, with more and more resources being poured into luxury goods to be exchanged among elites.

Perhaps the most compelling culprit, though, is climate change. There's good evidence that the entire eastern Mediterranean region went through an extended period of extreme dryness around this time, one that may have lasted for more than a century. Such an extended drought – a megadrought, to use the parlance – may not have always caused the kind of acute, short-sharp-shock famine that we associate with droughts, but rather acted as a broader destabilising force. There certainly were periods of famine – Egypt sent food aid to the Hittites at one point, only to be hit by famine itself a few years later – but the overwhelming effect may have been to make existence more marginal across the board.

(It's likely that a megadrought was also the main driver behind the collapse of both the Akkadian Empire and the Egyptian Old Kingdom a millennium earlier, in around 2200 BCE – and its knock-on effects may also have impacted the Indus Valley civilisation.)

Ultimately, while there's still plenty of debate about the causes of the Late Bronze Age collapse, the dominant explanation is really 'all of the above'. There was no one crisis that brought the Bronze Age to a close in the Mediterranean, but a multitude of mutually reinforcing ones that led to a widespread system collapse. The changing climate made every state's existence more fragile, upsetting already unbalanced economic systems, and both increasing the likelihood of conflict and leaving states less able to withstand that conflict. The complex webs of trading and diplomacy that interlinked and bolstered these civilisations may also have spread instability in a cascade – so when one domino fell, many did. The Sea Peoples, in this telling, may not have been the implacable villains of the legend – instead, like the barbarians at Rome's gates, they may have been forced from their own lands by the same crises afflicting everyone else.

The other thing to say about the Late Bronze Age collapse is that recent work suggests that it, too, may not have been as severe a collapse as previously thought. Trading networks may have collapsed at the elite level, but persisted among the less wealthy. The simple fact that places aren't building massive monuments to the elite anymore may look like decline in the archaeological record, but it's not necessarily a bad choice on their part. The recovery in at least some regions, especially the Levant, may have been quicker than previously thought. Rather than a Dark Age, what followed may in fact have been, as one scholar puts it, 'the catalyst of a new age'.

If there's one lesson to take from our survey of humanity's near-misses, it's that we're an astonishingly resilient bunch. It usually takes a confluence of many crises to knock us off-course, and when it does, we tend to bounce back quickly.

Far from marking the fall of civilisation, what we often call collapses may often simply be periods of change that ultimately renew it.

But, as we look to the future, let's keep one thing in mind: past performance does not guarantee future results.

12.

The Ways the World Ends: Natural Causes

If you want to get your prediction of the end of the world right, you just need to wait around long enough.

The blunt reality is this: the end of the world is inevitable. This fragile blue speck on which we hurtle through the cosmos has a built-in expiry date. The star we orbit, the very thing that lit the spark of life in the first place, will eventually also extinguish it. One day, the sun will eat its children.

The clock is ticking. But, in a rare bit of good news, it turns out it's a very large and extremely slow clock.

The basic problem Earth has is that the sun is getting brighter. That's not unexpected: it's just the natural progression of the solar lifecycle. The nuclear fusion in its heart smashes hydrogen atoms together, releasing the ferocious energy that makes a star a star. But when those atoms fuse, they form helium – heavier than hydrogen, this waste product sinks to the sun's core, making the heart of our star progressively denser over time. That increasing density raises the pressure and temperature, which in turn intensifies the nuclear reactions. This means that – perhaps counterintuitively – the more its fuel gets used up, the more powerfully the sun shines.

This gradual increase in solar luminosity is basically imperceptible on the timescale of a human life. (Despite what annoying internet people will try to tell you, it's nothing to do with our recent bout of global warming.) But over time, it all adds up: roughly a 10 per cent rise in the sun's energy output every billion years.

This is the real doomsday countdown. Right now, the Earth inhabits what's cutely known as the solar system's 'Goldilocks Zone' – not too hot, not too cold, but *just right* for life. But as the sun shines ever more fiercely, that zone of temperate just-rightness moves further away from the warming star. Eventually, it'll move beyond us entirely, and our home planet will be left stuck very firmly in the 'too hot' neighbourhood.

The first problem this throws up is the amount of carbon dioxide in our atmosphere.

As the sun burns brighter, geological processes that remove CO_2 from the atmosphere and trap it in the Earth's crust will intensify. By 500 million years in the future – or maybe sooner, by some estimates – this will mean that the amount of CO_2 in the atmosphere falls below the threshold most of Earth's current plant life needs for photosynthesis. Some grasses and a few other species with lower CO_2 needs might hold out for perhaps another 500 million years. But eventually, even they will reach their limit – and with that, the age of plants will come to an end. And alongside the plants will go almost every existing food chain on the planet, not to mention our handy supply of oxygen.

You might have spotted a small irony here: the thing that will eventually doom the Earth's ecosystem is a *shortage* of atmospheric carbon dioxide. For god's sake, don't tell the annoying internet people. It's completely unconnected to our current carbon woes – which involve timescales measured in decades rather than eons – but that probably won't stop people slapping 'I'm saving the world!' bumper stickers on their SUVs to own the libs. (For the record: no, making more CO_2 now really, really won't help.)

Now, you might reasonably argue that a billion or so years is a lot of evolutionary time – after all, it's twice as long as land plants have even existed in the first place. Surely new organisms, new biochemistries and new ecosystems will emerge that could cope with low CO_2 environments? Life, as the wise man once said, finds a way.

Yeah, maybe! That's definitely possible. They'd still be in trouble shortly after, though. Somewhere in the 1.5 billion-year range, everything will have got so hot that the accelerating evaporation of the Earth's oceans passes a dreadful tipping point. Water vapour traps heat just as ruthlessly as carbon dioxide; at this point, our planet will go through stages with the evocative names of 'moist greenhouse' and 'runaway greenhouse', as a smothering blanket of clouds pushes the temperature ever higher, and in turn the waters evaporate even faster, and on and on. Eventually, every ocean will simply boil away – our planet baked inside an oven built from the ghosts of its long-dead seas.

We do not need to guess what this looks like. We can see our planet's fate by looking to a neighbour that long ago entered its greenhouse era: Venus, one step closer to the sun, and an uninhabitable hellscape hot enough to melt lead. That's us in a few billion years.

Oh, and then in about 6 billion years the ageing sun will swell into a red giant, ballooning to over a hundred times its current size and swallowing Mercury, Venus and quite possibly the Earth too. This is the final act for our birthplace: the atmosphere will boil away, the rocks will melt, and a baleful sun the size of the whole sky will claim us. Robert Frost's question will be answered: ultimately, the world will end in fire.

Still, it's not all bad news. Even the closest possible doom-point – 500 million years – is a really, *really* long time in the future. It's further from the present day than we are from the moment when our ancestors first girded their rudimentary limbs and warily flopped out of the ancient seas and on to land.

If we manage to make it that far, then we'll have had a quite remarkable innings. Our descendants will probably be as different from our current selves as we are from those ambitious fishes playing on the primordial mudbanks. There's the hope that we'll have developed technologically to the point where we don't need to worry so much about our only home being imminently consumed by a dying star. Future humans might have spread to other planets, to the stars, and have capabilities that will make them seem as powerful as gods to primitives like us. *If* we make it that far.

Unfortunately, that's a rather big if.

When it comes to possible sources of the apocalypse, humanity's gaze has long turned towards the sky. Death, we seem to feel, comes from above.

We may not be wrong.

When you think about it, our life on this planet is

profoundly tenuous. We're held captive by a vast orb of destructive horror, trapped on a ball of rock hurtling through the void in an endless loop. In the times when our particular segment of the void-rock is pointed closest to the horror-orb – and when the plumes of vapourised liquid produced by its nuclear fury briefly dissipate – then we say, 'It's nice out today,' and expose our torsos.

We've already established that one day the sun will destroy the Earth. A worrying possibility, however, is that it could destroy humanity long before it gets round to melting the rocks on which we sit. The sun is a nourishing nightmare – an ongoing, many-sided war between the forces of gravity, magnetism, fluid dynamics and roiling nuclear destruction. And on a fairly regular basis, deadly cosmic shrapnel from this war gets flung out. Sometimes, it heads in our direction.

Solar flares and their larger siblings, coronal mass ejections (CMEs), are produced when the shifting magnetic fields of the sun snap into a new configuration. Huge amounts of our star's raw matter get hurled out into space, billions of tons of charged particles sent screaming out into the solar system at high speed, often with an accompanying burst of X-rays.

Here on Earth, this kind of stuff normally doesn't affect us too much – we'd never have made it through evolution in one piece if it did, because the sun does this kind of thing in roughly eleven-year cycles. Our atmosphere absorbs the X-rays, keeping those of us who aren't currently astronauts safe from their potentially deadly radiation. And our planet's own magnetic field protects us from those bursts of charged particles, deflecting them away like raindrops off an umbrella. The most noticeable effect when a wave of solar detritus heads our way is an impressive lightshow. If you're fortunate enough to see an aurora, you can count yourself doubly lucky: not only is it very pretty, but also that's an apocalypse that was heading straight for you bouncing harmlessly off into space.

But there's no guarantee that's always going to be the case. A really, really big solar storm could cause us some nasty problems. Not of the 'everybody facing the sun gets fried' variety; it would be bad, but probably not that bad. The real issue is not with our bodies, but with our *stuff*.

The fact that the sun goes through these regular bouts of destructive cosmic burping was first discovered in 1859, in what's known as the 'Carrington Event', named after one of the astronomers who spotted it. This was not only the first solar flare observed, but also likely the most intense solar storm ever recorded. It caused aurorae right across the globe. And, more pertinently for our purposes, it took out a load of telegraph stations.

The tidal wave of charged particles hitting Earth's magnetic field weren't just deflected by the magnetosphere – they caused the field itself to change. And as every schoolchild doing basic experiments with electromagnetism knows, if you move a magnet over a wire, a charge flows. As the magnetic field shifted and warped, telegraph wires across America and Europe became overloaded – pylons exploded in showers of sparks, and telegraph operators got electric shocks. So intense was the charge flowing through the system that some operators, who'd sensibly taken the precaution of disconnecting their equipment from its power supply, were reportedly still able to keep on sending messages for several hours thanks to the solar current alone.

This was 1859; the world's electrical networks were in their infancy. Today, we have a lot more wires, and we rely on them far more. A Carrington Event today, or one even larger, could threaten to take down electrical grids and communication networks across much of the globe, with very little advance notice. Outside the atmosphere, satellites could be fried. We had a warning shot for this kind of thing in March 1989, when a CME caused the entire power grid in Quebec to collapse. If a major solar storm took out power across an even larger or more densely populated area – especially if it happened in a cold winter – the effects could be devastating.

Devastating, but probably not fully apocalyptic. Lots of people could die, to be clear, and infrastructure could take a long time to repair; it would undoubtedly be a bad time. But I think you'd like our chances of collectively making it through, even if sometimes it does feel like society is only a few hours away from collapse any time the Wi-Fi goes down. What's more, this is an event we know will arrive some day; the people who make power grids do think about this stuff. We might not be able to prevent it entirely, but we're also not entirely unprepared.

Of course, the sun is not the only star in the sky.

Our star is on the large side, compared to most of the stars in the universe. But, chunky as it is, it has nothing on the behemoths of the cosmos – massive stars more than twenty times the sun's size. And stars of this size do not end their lives in the same way as our sun; no distinguished old age of slowly growing fatter and redder for them. Instead, they die in a far more rapid and destructive manner: the supernova.

A supernova is one of the most violent events in the universe. An explosion that unleashes the energy of a hundred quintillion suns all at once, sending a destructive shockwave of superhot matter and neutrinos and radiation out into the cosmos. Anything in the supernova's stellar neighbourhood is going to be toast. Which raises the worrying question: could that be us?

I'm glad to say there's comforting news on the supernova front: because it's not an event that can just happen to any star, we can be fairly confident we know how many potential supernovas there are in our neck of the cosmic woods, and how close they are to going nova. Just like a conventional explosion, distance matters in these things; because the energy and matter from the supernova is expanding in all directions, you get hit with less the further away you are.

As with the threats from our own sun, our atmosphere is a huge help in mitigating the biggest dangers from that blast, which is the X-rays and gamma rays – they're unlikely to reach the ground in sufficient amounts to cause any harm. The biggest concern is that in blocking the radiation from a fairly close supernova, the atmosphere itself would be damaged – potentially depleting the ozone layer enough that the highly UV-sensitive microbes that form the base of every food chain could be severely impacted, with catastrophic knock-on effects all the way through the ecosystem.

What does 'fairly close' mean in this context? How near would a supernova need to be for it to seriously harm life on Earth? Estimates vary, but they're all somewhere in the range of twenty-five to a hundred light years. Which is a huge distance, but pretty nearby in cosmic terms. And this is where the comforting news comes in – there simply aren't any supernova candidates in that range.

The current nearest candidate, the binary star system of IK Pegasi, is 154 light years away, won't explode for another billion years, and will have moved a lot further away by crunch time.

Betelgeuse may go supernova in about one hundred thousand years' time, but it's at least 400 light years away. There are stars that could pop off at any moment, but they're far distant – Wolf-Rayet 102 should go in the next two thousand years, but it's over 9,000 light years away. It won't even make the night sky appreciably brighter, never mind ending life on Earth.

And there's also comfort from the depths of history. Iron 60 is a radioactive isotope that doesn't really occur naturally on Earth – and yet, as scientists discovered in 2004, there's a layer of it under the seabed. What does make Iron 60 in large quantities is a supernova; that rogue sheet of it under the Pacific suggests that a little under 3 million years ago, a star very close by us ended violently. It was probably in the 50–100 light-year range, and yet there's no evidence that life on Earth was especially affected – no mass extinctions, no major ecosystem disruptions. On balance, we can probably tick supernovas off the list of things to be worried about.

An important caveat here is that all of this applies *on Earth*. We're protected from all the cosmic threats the sun and more distant stars may hurl at us by our atmosphere and our magnetosphere. Travel outside that, and all bets are off. If you are, let's say, a billionaire hoping to colonise Mars as a way to survive an apocalypse on Earth, you might want to bear in mind that it doesn't have either of those things, and is therefore way more vulnerable to cosmic apocalypses.

There is one more cosmic apocalyptic threat that stands as perhaps the most haunting possibility of all: that of false vacuum decay.

Space, as we all know, is mostly a vacuum – which in everyday language means simply that there's nothing in it. No air, no matter, no stray molecules or atoms, nothing that lets you hear screams. But in the world of advanced physics, 'vacuum' has an additional meaning. Not just space devoid of matter but space that, at the quantum level, is in its lowest possible energy state.

This is complicated, but like a rock rolling down a hill, quantum systems naturally want to come to rest at their lowest energy level – the bottom of the hill. The possibility is that our universe is not in fact in this state: the rock's got stuck in a dip, short of the hill's base. Not yet at its lowest energy state, it's a false vacuum, not a true vacuum. But if someone came along and kicked the rock out of the dip, then it would immediately resume rolling down the hill.

What might happen then could be the most profound apocalypse imaginable. Somewhere in the universe, the rock gets kicked and resumes rolling down to the bottom of the hill – and a tiny bubble of true vacuum forms. The trouble is that this effect won't stay limited to that one rock. Instead, it starts an avalanche.

This new state is contagious, as the false vacuum around the bubble takes the hint and immediately collapses down to join the true vacuum. This means that the bubble of true vacuum expands outwards at the speed of light – which is extremely bad news for all of us cheerfully living in our false vacuum, because inside this bubble the very laws of physics may be entirely rewritten. It would be a new universe, entirely replacing the old one.

This scenario is what prompted the physicists Sidney Coleman and Frank De Luccia to write, in their seminal 1980 paper on vacuum decay, the single most goth paragraph in the history of science:

> Vacuum decay is the ultimate ecological catastrophe; in the new vacuum there are new constants of nature; after vacuum decay, not only is life as we know it impossible, so is chemistry as we know it. However, one could always draw stoic comfort from the possibility that perhaps in the course of time the new vacuum would sustain, if not life as we know it, at least some structures capable of knowing joy. This possibility has now been eliminated.

That's not hugely comforting. But in some ways, this end would be the kindest possible: as the new universe expands at the speed of light, we would never know it was coming. We would simply wink out of existence without any time for fear or regret.

For many years, the question of whether this could happen, and how likely it was, was up in the air. Our universe seemed unhelpfully poised right on the threshold between where it was possible and impossible. Recent studies have brought some helpful clarity to this question, which comes in a classic 'bad news, good news' combo. Yes, our universe probably is a false vacuum, but it's an extremely stable one. False vacuum decay may well happen, but at a point inconceivably far into the future – we're talking a number with tens or even hundreds of zeros after it, vastly longer than the universe has existed already. In terms of a human lifetime, our universe is still a newborn.

So all told, while the universe is filled with horrors, we can probably sleep easily in our beds, safe in the knowledge that we aren't terribly vulnerable to some great and terrible cataclysm from the depths of space, heading towards us at the speed of light.

But there's still one way that our demise might come at us out of the night sky.

Somewhere around a quarter to ten in the evening on 13 April 2029, we will come closer to disaster than we have in recorded history. Or, perhaps more accurately, disaster will come closer to us.

That's when asteroid 99942 Apophis – a very large rock, wider than Wembley Stadium, weighing somewhere in the region of 40 million tons – will hurtle past our planet at a distance of only 20,000 miles. In astronomical terms, that's nothing. It's so close that Apophis will pass inside the orbit of many of our communication satellites. It's the cosmic equivalent of a bullet shooting through a cowboy's hat.

Apophis is, of course, the 'God of Chaos' asteroid beloved of the internet's finest clickbait headlines, thanks to being named after the ancient Egyptian deity Apep, the great serpent of darkness that battles the sun god Ra every night. When Apophis passes Earth in 2029, close enough to be visible to the naked eye, it will be our nearest miss from an asteroid that large since we started tracking these things – so all that tabloid excitement isn't entirely baseless. Still, you feel like much of the blanket coverage it gets is probably because its discoverers gave it a spooky name.

The scientists who keep track of astronomical dangers like this – officially termed Near-Earth Objects, a mixture of asteroids and comets – have two ways of quantifying their threat. There's something called the Palermo Technical Impact Hazard Scale, which is frankly very confusing for people who aren't professional asteroid trackers, and a much simpler variant named the Torino scale. (Planetary scientists like having conferences in Italy.) Both scales take account of two factors. One is how likely the object is to hit us – a meticulous calculation that requires observing lumps of rock or ice 100 million miles away with enough precision to plot their trajectory decades into the future. The other factor is how awful it would be if it did hit.

The Torino scale runs from 0 to 10 – with 0 meaning that the object in question is no threat at all, either because it won't hit us or wouldn't do much damage if it did. A rating of 10, meanwhile, has the most dramatic description imaginable, gloomily informing us that 'collision is certain, capable of causing global climatic catastrophe that may threaten the future of life as we know it'. A 10 would be . . . very bad.

Here's the good news: at the time of writing, there is no object in the entire solar system with a rating above 0. Occasionally new objects are spotted and get a provisional rating of 1 ('collision is extremely unlikely') before more detailed observations prove even that's an overstatement, and they're downgraded to 0. In the more than two decades the scale has been in use, only two objects have ever risen above 1, and the highest any object has ever reached is 4 – '1 per cent or greater chance of collision capable of regional devastation'.

This was Apophis. It only held the 4 rating for two weeks before closer scrutiny downgraded it to a 1, and eventually a 0. This is the comforting thing about the existential threat posed by asteroids and comets: space is really big, and we're a vanishingly small target amidst all that empty vastness. The chance of any particular lump of rock or ice hitting us is minuscule.

The downside is that there are an awful lot of rocks out there. And in all that empty vastness, they can be hard to spot.

In 2013 a rock weighing about as much as a naval destroyer plunged into the atmosphere above Chelyabinsk Oblast in southern Russia. It didn't reach the ground – but in burning up, it briefly shone brighter than the sun, causing temporary blindness in people unlucky enough to have looked straight at it. It also produced a blast wave that shattered windows across Chelyabinsk. Over a thousand people were injured, mostly by flying glass – the only impact in modern history with a confirmed casualty list.

We didn't see the Chelyabinsk object coming. Despite being the weight of an actual warship, the Chelyabinsk object was small potatoes by space-rock standards, right on the border of 'not big enough to care about'. In that sense, we got lucky – even with it airbursting above an area with a population of over a million people, nobody died.

We also got lucky in a different way in 1908, when an object that probably weighed ten times as much came down over a virtually uninhabited region of Siberia. This strike, the Tunguska event, was far more destructive, with trees flattened across an area of over 800 square miles. If that thing had burst over a populated area like Chelyabinsk, to say nothing of Moscow or New York, many people would have died.

Still some way short of apocalyptic, though. Sturdy buildings would have stayed standing; most of the population would probably have survived. Additionally, we shouldn't overstate our fortune that it missed major population centres, because most of the time that's a winning bet. At a rough estimate, only about 15 per cent of the Earth's surface has a significant human presence – 70 per cent of it is ocean, and around half the land is still vast, largely untouched regions like deserts and tundra and forest. Yes, it's lucky the Tunguska impactor hit Siberia, but it's not *that* lucky, because Siberia's bloody massive.

Something like Apophis, by contrast, would be a far worse time for everybody involved. Four thousand times more massive than the Chelyabinsk impactor, it would be a city-killer if it landed in the wrong place. Drop Apophis on London, and everything from Camden to Clapham is immediately engulfed in a fireball. The devastation spreads far wider: buildings collapse and clothing catches fire into the far reaches of London's commuter belt, while windows would shatter from Cardiff to Ostend. The final crater would be more than three miles wide, and would have previously contained approximately 150 branches of Prêt.

And yet even this – the only Near-Earth Object to have even briefly worried astronomers in recent decades – is still not an apocalypse rock. It would be a local horror, potentially killing millions, spreading destruction across an entire region, but the effects beyond that would be relatively limited.

But there are worse monsters out there. The reason asteroids and comets play such a central role in conversations about existential risk is that *this has happened before.* The most apocalyptic day in Earth's long history, the only one of the great mass extinctions that we know was the result of a single catastrophic event: somewhere around 66,050,000 years ago, when an asteroid six miles wide struck the shallow seas just off the coast of modern-day Mexico.

We don't know exactly how many years ago it happened – there's a plus or minus of around ten thousand years – but we do know that the world ended as spring was on the cusp of turning to summer in the Northern Hemisphere. You can see that from the minute seasonal changes in the bones of fish almost two thousand miles away from ground zero, in North Dakota, which were killed within minutes of the impact. A terrifying shockwave raced through the Earth's crust at eleven thousand miles an hour. The fish died immediately, with microscopic glass beads from the molten debris flung out by the asteroid lodged in their gills.

The immediate impacts of the impact were horrific: earthquakes thousands of times more powerful than any other known in history, winds many times fiercer than the most powerful hurricane, and megatsunamis a hundred metres high that swept across the lands. Much life across the Americas was wiped out in minutes, burned or blasted or buried alive, but the thing that made it a global apocalypse was what followed.

Trillions of tons of debris were shot into the atmosphere. Some of this came back to earth, burning up as it fell like a secondary shower of meteorites – and in turn starting a global wildfire that claimed most of the planet's forests. The huge amounts of soot from these fires mingled with the remaining dust and – worst of all – the sulphurous compounds ejected into the atmosphere from the sulphur-rich gypsum seabed in which the asteroid landed. Almost instantly, the light and heat from the sun were dramatically reduced.

This was the 'impact winter' – the thing that really turns an asteroid into a planet-killer. The world burned, and then froze. In the cold and darkness that swaddled the Earth in the months after the impact, food chains across the planet collapsed as plants struggled to get enough light for photosynthesis and lakes froze in the middle of summer. With less water evaporating there was dramatically less rain, and what rain did fall was acid. As the atmosphere's toxic load gradually returned to Earth, the impact winter may have only lasted a decade or two, its worst effects for perhaps only a couple of years – but that was enough for much of the planet to starve to death.

If that happened to us, it's not clear that we'd be able cope significantly better than the dinosaurs did.

There's an odds game at play here. We know roughly how many lumps of rock and ice and iron there are floating out there in the solar system that might threaten us, and we've got a good handle on their size distribution. Bigger equals rarer. Objects in the Chelyabinsk-Tunguska range will hit us, on average, somewhere between once a century and once a millennium. For an Apophis-sized city-killer, you're looking at tens of thousands of years between impacts – the entirety of human civilisation until now could fit between strikes. For an object large enough to cause any kind of global winter – a mile or two wide – you're looking at a frequency of a million years or more. For a true dinosaur-style planet-killer, somewhere between 10 and 100 million years.

Those are good odds. Great odds, even. And yet, there's the lurking fear that all it takes is one unlucky day. Probabilities don't manifest on a neat schedule – they're just a comforting average of the wild flailing of random happenstance. Humanity plaintively crying, 'But we weren't due!' will cut zero ice with Smashy McDeathrock.

The good news is that this is one apocalyptic threat where we have unquestionably made huge strides in potentially saving the world over the past few decades. The reason we have all those Torino scale scores to read out? That's because humanity has spent more than two decades diligently cataloguing as many of the Solar System's danger rocks as possible, thanks to a series of international collaborations collectively termed

Spaceguard. (The name's taken from an Arthur C. Clarke novel, natch.)

It started by focusing on the real biggies, the potential planet-killers over a kilometre in size – it's thought that we now know where more than 95 per cent of these are, and it's very unlikely there are any which could threaten us in the next century that we don't know about. Since then, we've been working our way down to the smaller fry, the city-killers, with similar success. This doesn't mean we're completely safe, because some asteroids are just very hard to see, and comets especially can come from unexpected directions. One reason we didn't spot the Chelyabinsk object was because it came at us from roughly the same direction as the sun, and we were blinded by the glare. But even there, we're taking steps – 2030 should see the launch of a new European Space Agency mission specifically to spot these tricky customers.

Of course, this all leaves open the question of whether we could actually *do* anything if we spotted an incoming planet-killer. In real life, it's not clear you could simply deploy Bruce Willis and Ben Affleck to heroically defeat the space rock with the power of soft rock.

But here, too, we've been actively trying stuff out. In 2022, NASA deliberately crashed the DART spacecraft into the asteroid Dimorphos to see if it would change its trajectory – and the result was a rousing success, pushing it far more off-course than had been expected. We'll probably want to try a few more test runs before the big one comes, but there's a real chance that if Spaceguard finally does find an object with a terrifying Torino rating, with enough warning we might actually be able to do something about it.

Of all the apocalyptic threats we face, asteroids and comets may well be the most dangerous – the only threat we know of that has caused a true apocalypse in the past. It would be an impressive achievement if it also became the first that we were able to confidently say wasn't a threat any more.

But of course, the natural world still has other ways of killing us.

Infectious diseases have no plans to wipe out humanity.

They have no plans for *anything*, obviously: they're just dumb replication agents, with no goal beyond making more of themselves. But even in the language of evolutionary theory, where mindless bundles of RNA have 'strategies', the pathogens that torment us still do not yearn for our downfall. Quite the opposite, in fact – after all, we are the world they inhabit. Our bodies are their homes, their farms, their transport networks and their maternity hospitals. Human extinction would be an apocalypse for them just as surely as it would be for us.

This applies at the individual level as well as the civilisation-wide scale. Most of the time, our infections don't really want to kill us. The reason is straightforward: the dead don't spread. Outside of zombie scenarios, corpses are usually much less effective at spreading infections onwards than the not-yet-deceased. For sure, some diseases, like haemorrhagic fevers, can be picked up from a dead body during funerary preparations, but it's still usually a lower threat than from a living carrier. No matter how much oozing they do, the dead simply can't compete with the walking, talking, bodily fluid-exchanging living. They lack our quirky little habits, like coughing on public transport or defecating into the water supply.

So, a living host is preferable – and if a microbe can thrive in human bodies without doing us any damage at all, then they'll cheerfully do just that. Every single one of us carries *trillions* of them within ourselves. The human cells in your body are outnumbered by the non-human microbes, a vast host of viruses and bacteria and fungi, mostly just hanging out and being chill, and often being helpful. You're not a person; you're a party.

Regrettably, not every microbe takes this gentle approach. But even when pathogens *do* have the power to kill us, it still represents a tricky trade-off for them. Is it worth it to hijack our bodies and sicken us, in the cause of spreading themselves onwards, if doing so means they risk pushing things a bit too far and making us all dead and useless? This trade-off is often something of a limiting factor when it comes to how catastrophic infectious diseases can be – the more lethal they are, the less effectively they spread. (Keep the word 'often' in mind, though. We'll come back to that.)

You can see this trade-off at work in the fact that there are plenty of microbes that are capable of dealing death in horrifyingly baroque ways – with much bleeding from unexpected places – which still struggle to spread very far beyond Patient Zero. They simply kill us too hard, too quickly: the pathogen equivalent of buying a shiny new car and immediately driving it into a wall. These diseases may be nightmarish, but their strategy is poor, and they're unlikely to ever level up to pandemic status.

This trade-off is one reason why we haven't already been wiped out by disease. The others are our natural and our invented defences. Our immune systems are incredibly complex biological mechanisms that have been in an evolutionary arms race with the world's pathogens since before humans were humans, so it's not surprising that the balance of power between those two sides is usually finely poised. Meanwhile, as human societies have developed in ways that create new opportunities for infections – densely packed cities, international travel – so too has our understanding of the societal and medical ways to fight back. This hasn't always been as finely balanced (there was a long, rough period when the pace of globalisation ran ahead of medical advances) but with the rise of vaccinations and antibiotics, the pendulum has swung back a bit in our favour.

This is why pestilence occupies an unusual place in the doomsday pantheon, and attempts to assess its apocalyptic potential are tricky. Remember the graphs of world population from the last chapter? The only time human numbers have definitively gone backwards was when the Black Death was tearing through Europe. Other outbreaks may not have had quite that globally visible impact, but were plenty apocalyptic in their own way: the Plague of Justinian in the Roman world; the still-unidentified Cocoliztli epidemics of sixteenth-century Mexico; the global spread of the 'Spanish' flu in 1918, which may have been the deadliest single pandemic in history. The catastrophic depopulation of the Americas after the Columbian Exchange was largely the result of getting a motherlode of new diseases all at once. Only the very bloodiest of wars can match either the death toll or the society-altering impact of epidemic disease.

If you want to make the case that our eventual downfall will be seen first through a microscope, not a telescope, then this is it: pathogens are the most reliable mass killer we know of, with the possible exception of ourselves.

The counterpoint is that we had thousands upon thousands of years of pathogens hurling themselves at us before we even developed germ theory. If they didn't wipe us out then, or even come close, they're probably not going to now.

As with big asteroids, we can make pretty well-educated guesses about how likely severe epidemics are by looking to history. Here, too, the more severe they are, the rarer they are. A 2021 study suggested that the chances of experiencing a Covid-level pandemic in a human lifetime are around 38 per cent. An even worse Spanish flu-level pandemic will happen perhaps once every four centuries. (Obviously, unless you're an especially precocious baby reading this, then the chances of *you* experiencing a Covid-level pandemic in your life are 100 per cent, what with Covid having happened. But you get the point.)

These odds, however, are filtered through a worrying observation: spillovers from animals to humans like Covid (and SARS, and Ebola, and HIV) are becoming more common as humans encroach ever further into wild habitats. In recent years, they've grown to over half of all emerging infectious diseases. To add to our woes, evidence also suggests that climate change will make pathogenic diseases worse. Those odds of a pandemic happening in any particular year, or any particular lifetime? They're going up. If you were tempted to think that Covid having already happened means you've reached your lifetime quota of pandemics, the bad news is that you might not be so lucky.

Add to this the fact that our two best weapons against the pathogenic enemy are in danger of becoming blunted. The carefree use of antibiotics has created a world where we're often safer than ever in history from a host of random bacterial infections – but it has also produced a perfect evolutionary environment for breeding antibiotic-resistant microbes. Already, millions of people die each year as a result of this resistance, and there's a genuine risk of it throwing much of the progress of modern medicine into reverse. And then there are vaccines, an anti-apocalypse all by themselves, saving over 150 million lives in just the last fifty years – one of the greatest breakthroughs in human history, but one that is now under threat from people being dumber than bricks.

What would the Big One look like if it hit us? Airborne, probably, via aerosols or spores, or at least through very minimal interpersonal contact – that's the best way to spread in the modern world. More importantly, something our immune systems are unfamiliar with: most likely a brand-new spillover from the animal kingdom, possibly a dramatically mutated variant of an existing strain. It was this novelty to our immune systems that lay behind the drastic effects of Covid and the Spanish flu, and of course behind the catastrophic multi-pathogen assault that Europeans brought to the Americas. (There's also the outside chance of a long-forgotten ancient pathogen released from carcasses preserved in ice for millennia, but now uncovered by a warming world. A young boy died in Siberia in 2016 from an unfrozen strain of anthrax, although that one only dated back to 1945.)

There's a good chance it would also be something that swerved the trade-off between fatality and infectivity. This is that 'often' we were going to come back to: not every pathogen is forced into this trade-off. Indeed, many of the worst pandemics in history have come from those that didn't.

Covid's infectiousness is decoupled from its fatality rate, because infectivity peaks long before severe illness or death;

the same was even more perniciously true for HIV, the virus capable of quietly multiplying and infecting for years. And *Yersinia pestis*, the plague bacterium responsible for three of the worst pandemics in history, is even more decoupled: humans aren't even a significant part of its lifecycle at all. While it can sometimes spread person-to-person, its effect on us is mostly a sideshow to its main business of spreading between rodents via fleas. It doesn't really care how many of us it kills, because that doesn't affect its ability to spread and flourish in the slightest.

Infectious diseases are one of the most ever-present apocalyptic threats humanity has faced. Anxiety about infection and contamination is one of our deepest primal fears. Pandemics have been one of the go-to causes of doomsday in popular culture from Mary Shelley's *The Last Man* through to *Station Eleven* and *The Last of Us.* We've all just lived through a pandemic that – despite the millions of deaths, the disability and long-term sickness, the ongoing menace of the endemic disease, and the upturning of everyday life – wasn't even *close* to the worst pandemic we could face. And they're getting more common. Covid may not be the only pandemic you live through, or don't live through.

But for all this, we are not helpless in the face of disease. Like all those asteroids wandering the dark that may one day intersect our orbit, we're actively on the lookout for these threats. And while pathogen-hunting can be an even harder challenge than looking for asteroids (and we'll never get the kind of decades-long advance warning Spaceguard might give us), at least with microbes we've already got tried-and-tested methods for fighting back. Our immune systems are impressive bits of kit, and our medical ability to help them out is only getting better. There was less than a year between SARS-CoV-2 initially being sequenced and the first vaccines getting into arms, which is *completely astonishing*. If we can keep up this kind of progress and vigilance, then this is an apocalypse we should be able to defeat.

There's the 'i' word again. *If*. The greatest worry around novel infections is less that they will emerge – we know they will, of course they will, they always have – and more that we might get complacent and come to believe that vigilance and preparedness aren't worth the effort. There's a dispiriting cycle where we freak out about a new infectious threat, pledge grand resources for epidemic surveillance and research and preparedness . . . and then quietly walk that all back a few years later when our panic recedes and we forget why we freaked out in the first place. Add the massive global inequalities in health infrastructure, not to mention the rising political polarisation and conspiracy theories around healthcare in all forms, and we run a profound risk of unrolling the red carpet for a cataclysm that we absolutely have the capacity to defeat. We're letting *measles* come back, for god's sake: what chance will we have against SARS-CoV-47?

There's another fear on the horizon. We're not yet quite at the stage where we can manufacture synthetic microbes to order, but we may not be far off. One group of researchers synthesised an extinct horsepox virus in 2017; in 2020, another team created 'xenobots', tiny living robots made from clumps of frog cells that are able to self-replicate. The rise of synthetic biology would change the calculations around the apocalyptic threat of infection, to say the least, breaking it out of the constraints and trade-offs imposed by evolution – although you'd hope that our technological ability to combat any custom-made doom bug would at least rise hand in hand with our ability to create the dreadful things.

Ultimately, the greatest apocalyptic threat from disease doesn't lie in the fear that it will wipe us out entirely, or even mostly. For naturally occurring pathogens, at least, the argument that they didn't manage to defeat us before we'd come up with germ theory so they probably won't now is persuasive. 'It hasn't happened yet, so it won't happen' are obviously the last words of everybody who's shortly going to die horribly – but history can at least provide us a guide on what best to focus our anxiety on.

The doomsday threat that infections carry comes from their power to reshape the world in their own image. We've all lived through this: lockdowns or no lockdowns, the basic fact is that normal life shuts down whenever sickness stalks the streets, when popping to the shops becomes a paranoia trip and you worry that every hug could be a death sentence. It does not take Black Death levels of mortality for the functioning of society to buckle under the strain. How many train drivers need to be sick at once before the trains stop working? How many teachers? How many Amazon staff, or meat-processing workers? How many nuclear plant operatives?

And the power of disease to warp our lives isn't limited to the duration of the outbreak. They may not be civilisation-enders, but they're certainly civilisation-remakers. Huge amounts of modern society's effort goes into the avoidance of infection, and every new threat that emerges demands new adaptations. Much of the infrastructure that underpins our lives, from the sewers under our feet to the water that comes from our taps, is there because of lessons learned from previous outbreaks. Major chunks of the administrative state are devoted to this purpose. Entire consumer product categories – refrigerators, air filters, endless aisles of cleaning products – are based on the demand for not getting sick. The traditions of how we prepare food, the type of drinks we consume, our sexual behaviour: all have been shaped by our interactions with pathogens. And we're *still* not doing enough, as that guy coughing up his lungs on public transport demonstrates.

That infectious diseases will end the world is unlikely, if not impossible. But that they will change the world is a raging certainty, because they always have.

13.

The Ways the World Ends: We Do It to Ourselves

There's a website that gets regular surges of traffic, and most of the time, those surges are a sign that something extremely worrying is happening somewhere in the world.

The site is called Nukemap, and like so many of the best websites, it does one job very well. In this case, it tells you what would happen if a nuclear warhead landed in your neighbourhood. It has a pleasingly old-school interface: you can drag a pin around the map to choose the target; there's a drop-down menu for different models of nuclear weapon, and advanced options where you can tweak things like the airburst height and wind direction. Click 'Detonate', and it draws you a bunch of dreadful concentric circles: fireball radius, blast radius, heat radius. As a bonus, it'll helpfully give you a (very rough) casualty estimate.

It's a weirdly compelling way to spend an hour or two, as

growing numbers of people discover every time nuclear anxiety returns to the news headlines. The site's creator, a historian of science named Alex Wellerstein, told the *Atlantic* that most people use it for what he calls 'experiential nuking' (seeing the effects of a nuclear weapon hitting their own area) rather than 'cathartic nuking' (playing at blasting someone else's country). When Russia's 2022 invasion of Ukraine began, I found myself spending a frankly unhealthy amount of time on the site, running through doomsday scenarios with grim fascination. I was far from alone; at one point so many people were using it to simulate their imminent demise that the site crashed.

Nuclear weapons are terrifying, both for their scale and for the multitude of ways in which they can kill you. Let's take the kind of scenario I was doomscrolling through back in spring 2022. Detonate a single Russian RT-2PM Topol ballistic missile with an 800-kiloton warhead about 2,000 metres above 10 Downing Street, and pretty much everyone above ground within a kilometre – from Piccadilly Circus to Lambeth Bridge – is going to be instantly vaporised in a superhot fireball. A devastating high-pressure blast wave extends the destruction much further: almost every structure between Blackfriars and Hyde Park Corner is reduced to rubble, and buildings will fall as far as four miles away in every direction, stretching from Stepney Green to Shepherd's Bush. The heat generated by the explosion is truly fearsome: people from Wimbledon to Wood Green, in a circle of almost 150 square miles, may be scarred for life by third-degree burns. Damage and injury extends across the far reaches of Greater London's suburbs, with windows shattering from Sidcup to Chipping Barnet.

Contrary to what popular media may tell you, you cannot survive a nearby nuclear blast by climbing into a fridge.

The good news . . . no, let's start that again. The marginally less terrible news is that, in this particular scenario, at least the nightmarish effects of the radiation itself would play a smaller role. There's a mortality trade-off, depending on the altitude at which a warhead detonates: it has its greatest destructive power when detonated above the surface, and the larger the device, the higher it needs to be to maximise the devastation. But the higher it detonates, the lower the intensity of the radiation burst at ground level. And nuclear fallout – the irradiated dust and ash thrown up by the blast, the thing which can spread death many miles downwind and continue killing for months or years afterwards – mostly occurs when a device detonates on or near the surface.

For our Russian example (one of the larger warheads currently in service) its destructive radius is maximised with an airburst a full two kilometres above ground. At that height, radiation will be a lesser killer: it's not that it would have no effect on the ground, but it's too high to produce any significant fallout, and most of the people close enough to get a lethal dose from the initial blast will almost certainly be dead already from the bomb's blunter effects. (Those who do somehow survive will want to get to shelter asap.) Ironically, smaller bombs with lower yields are more likely to cause radiation effects, because their optimal detonation height is a lot closer to ground level. And of course, there's always the possibility that an attacker may deliberately detonate their weapon closer to the ground, trading off immediate destruction for a more widespread and longer-lasting poison.

This would especially be the case with pre-emptive strikes on the other side's underground missile silos, which would all be surface detonations. This is the reason the US has most of its silos in sparsely populated states in the middle of the country – it's a deliberate tactic known as the 'nuclear sponge', to force the enemy to use up its warheads attacking something other than major population centres. The states that would end up smothered in radioactive fallout from bunker-busting strikes are the sacrifice. (All those apocalyptic groups moving to Montana to ride out the nuclear war were actually moving right into the heart of the sponge.)

Ultimately, however, questions of airburst height and fallout radius do little to minimise the horror of any nuclear strike. Per Nukemap – assuming there was no opportunity to evacuate the area beforehand, and with the caveat that these estimates have a pretty huge margin of error – somewhere in the region of a million people might die in the single blast we're modelling. The lucky ones are those close to the airburst, who get vaporised instantly; the unlucky are those granted a few terrible seconds to comprehend what's happening to them.

The flat in South London where I was running these nuclear simulations – a place I'd mainly thought of as having a pleasantly short commute to my work in central London, plus some charming local pubs – turned out to be in pretty much the worst possible location: too far away for me to simply wink out of existence as I was reduced to my constituent atoms, close enough that I was still almost certainly going to die horribly in a pile of burning rubble, with a hefty dose of radiation sickness in the event of my unlikely survival.

Anyway, that's what one nuke would do. There are around 12,500 nuclear warheads in the world right now. Some of these are officially 'retired', but not yet decommissioned; some are stockpiled; somewhere between 3,500 and 4,000 of them are believed to be actively deployed, ready to fire at a moment's notice. Yay humans.

But for all the destructive power of nuclear weapons, their apocalyptic potential may not come from the immediate death toll they can inflict. This is likely to be of little comfort to those people who are atomised in a split second by the blast; it probably isn't much comfort to those who burn horribly in a firestorm, either, or those trapped under a collapsed building, or those who die slowly from radiation in the weeks and months afterwards. Look, it's not really a comfort to anybody. Nuclear warheads just aren't very comforting is what we're saying here.

Still: even a full-on global nuclear war – with the majority of currently deployed warheads being launched at major population centres – might immediately kill somewhere in the region of 5 per cent of humanity. To be clear, that's extremely bad. It would be the worst event in human history. Many aspects of civil society around much of the world would be brought to the brink of collapse, or pushed right over the edge. And yet even this horror would not, just by itself, be existential. Most people who were alive the day before the bombs fell would still be alive to see the next day dawn.

No, the greatest apocalyptic threat comes from what that dawn might look like: dim, hazy and noticeably less warm than you'd hope. The problem, in short, would be soot.

Across the world – so the theory goes – cities would be burning in nuclear firestorms, self-sustaining conflagrations where the heat is so intense that it creates its own wind system, sucking in air that fans the flames to ever greater intensity. And when cities burn, they're likely to release far more soot than even the largest and most destructive wildfire could. This soot is injected into the atmosphere; warmed by sunlight, it rises into the stratosphere, where it can remain for years before black rains return it to the surface. We've already met the impact winter and the volcanic winter; this is the nuclear winter.

In the stratosphere, that soot will block sunlight, dropping global temperatures to sub-Ice Age levels – one recent estimate suggests that urban fires from a global nuclear war could reduce the surface temperature by 8°C in the following year. Ironically, while less sunlight overall would reach us, the soot would also strip away much of the ozone layer, meaning that the one thing which could get through would be dangerous levels of UV light: the world would be dark and we'd be shivering, but we'd still be getting sunburn, skin cancer and cataracts at horribly elevated rates. The problems don't stop there: in a colder world, less water evaporates, meaning that rainfall will be drastically reduced in following years; the oceans will also cool, but on a time lag, disrupting marine ecosystems for years after the war.

The result, if this does happen, could be an almost total collapse of global agriculture. Between the temporary Ice Age, the reduced rainfall, and the dangerous rise in UV, the breadbaskets of the world would fail en masse; three years after the war, the world might have to try and survive on just a tenth of the calories we previously had available. The result would be mass starvation: while the immediate deaths from a nuclear war would be counted in the tens or hundreds of millions, if the war led to a catastrophic nuclear winter, the resulting famine could kill more than 5 billion people.

If. There's that word again! It's time for another trip to Caveat City, and the caveats here are pretty hefty. The nuclear winter hypothesis is controversial, for the simple reason that we haven't dropped nuclear bombs on many cities. We know that a firestorm consumed much of Hiroshima; we also know that Nagasaki, by contrast, did not experience a firestorm. We also know that Hiroshima was a city where many of the buildings were made of wood. It's possible that a modern city of concrete and steel would simply not provide enough raw fuel: there would be widespread fires, certainly, but it's far from certain that there would be the kind of all-consuming, self-sustaining firestorm that the nuclear winter theory rests upon.

While we can be moderately confident in the climate and agricultural modelling for what happens *after* millions of tons of black carbon gets shot into the stratosphere, the question of *whether* it gets there in the first place rests on a few wildly unknowable variables. How many firestorms, and how intense? How much soot would those fires produce? What would the precise optical qualities of that soot be? How high into the atmosphere would it rise? It's even possible that the outcome could vary depending on the season in which we decide to have our nuclear war – soot warmed by the summer sun might rise higher, and so stick around longer.

While it might be very helpful to know the answers to these questions, I'm going to go out on a limb and say that we shouldn't drop nukes on a few test cities to satisfy our curiosity.

The theory of nuclear winter has long been seen as especially important by anti-nuclear campaigners, because it renders absurd the idea that a nuclear war might be something you could *win*: even if your opponents' cities are left in smouldering ruins, there is no victory if we're all going to starve to death in a few years anyway. The assured destruction is not merely mutual, but total.

It's a good point. But honestly, if our leaders have reached a point where nuclear annihilation is on the table and they're willing to write off hundreds of millions of lives for a strategic leg-up, I'm not sure that argument is likely to sway them. I mean, the world would have *some* food left, and I'm pretty sure our leaders would feel confident that they'd be the ones who'd get to eat it. The inexorable arms-race logic that brought us to this point is not one that rests on a sober analysis of costs and benefits, but on a zero-sum game where your enemy is implacable and allowing them any strategic advantage is apocalyptic in and of itself.

Which takes us back to our fundamental question: is nuclear Armageddon the way humanity might end? We live in a time that seems increasingly belligerent, a short-lived era of comparative detente being cast aside for a return to geopolitical brinkmanship between great and not-so-great powers alike. What's worse, recent years have seen an alarming rise in chatter among military types suggesting that they think a different kind of nuclear war might be winnable – one fought not with city-killers, but with lower-yield tactical nukes, designed to take out critical parts of an opponents' military infrastructure. A port, a tunnel, a supply depot, that kind of thing. All it would take is a few precision-targeted kilotons and kapow, you've turned a stalemate into a cakewalk.

This is obviously a terrible idea, because it invites retaliation and escalation – it's distressingly easy to see how such tit-for-tat strikes could ramp up until we're quickly back in the territory that turns central London into a slag heap. And yet it's also more resistant to the arguments against the hair-trigger madness of the Cold War; it's harder to talk someone out of going all River Kwai on their enemy's supply lines if the doomsday scenario is not instant and assured, but lies fifty additional decisions into the future.

But would it truly be doomsday? It's a common saying that the arsenals of the great nuclear powers 'could destroy the world many times over'. This isn't really true, in terms of their immediate destructive power. It was *closer* to accurate in the dark days of the Cold War, when the USA and the USSR possessed around 70,000 warheads, a simply deranged number that certainly could have rendered pretty much every major population centre in the world uninhabitable – if that's what they'd been fired at, rather than into the nuclear sponge. But today we have far fewer nukes, not to mention a lot more people in a lot more places. (Shenzhen, today the world's twenty-fifth-largest city, was a small fishing village half a century ago.) Even if some all-powerful supervillain took control and targeted every nuke in the world to maximise casualties – ignoring tactical military targets entirely – they'd probably run out of warheads before they ran out of cities to fire them at.

Longer-term effects of a nuclear war – nuclear winter, starvation, civilisational collapse – are more unknowable, and frankly we can only hope that they remain unknown. I lean towards the suspicion that the risk of nuclear winter, at least, may be somewhat overstated. I sincerely hope I never find out if I'm right, and certainly absolutely nobody should proceed on the assumption that I am. We should not play chicken with the God of Worst-Case Scenarios.

Again, none of this is a *huge* comfort. But it is, perhaps, a little one.

Because, even while we retain the capacity to cause

unprecedented destruction and bring death on an unimaginable scale, we have at least edged away from the precipice. A bit. All the campaigners, all the marches and the slogans, all the reports and studies, all the diplomacy . . . they didn't win, exactly, but they certainly achieved something. Humanity's capacity to instantly destroy itself, whether through malice or mistake, is lower today than it was when I was born. We haven't put down the gun, but we have lowered it a little. We held Armageddon in our hands, and enough of us thought, 'Hmmm, maybe not.'

It shows us that, at the very least, our march towards oblivion is not inevitable. We have choices, and we can make better ones. Of course, this is a choice we have to keep on making; it would be a tragedy of incredibly stupid proportions if, having walked the right path for a short time, we decided to turn around and charge headlong back towards the brink. Which, you know, it feels like we might be doing.

Because ultimately, we shouldn't need the threat of nuclear weapons to be an existential threat for us to deplore them. One alone would be terrible enough. The world did not end when the first atomic test was successful. But *a* world ended. One world ended, and a new, more fearful one replaced it. And if we use them again, our world will end again, and the world on the other side will be a worse one, and we will be a worse people. We won't need a nuclear winter for the world to have grown darker and colder. Civilisation can fall in many ways.

So yeah, it's probably best if we never do that. Let's keep the nuclear explosions where they belong: on an unsettlingly compelling website, filled with dreadful concentric circles.

* * *

We must now confront a question that has haunted futurologists for decades, only to suddenly surge to the forefront of public consciousness in recent years: could AI wipe out humanity? In our reckless hubris and obsessive drive towards technological advancement, might we build vast and terrible intelligences that will outstrip our own capacities, and eventually turn against us? Fundamentally, did every story of the end times get it the wrong way round: will the god of the apocalypse not be our creator, but our *creation*?

Nah.

I mean, look: sure, maybe. Predicting the future of technology is a mug's game at the best of times. Confidently declaring that a technology *isn't* possible has always been a good way to get yourself mocked in snarky history books a century from now. And unlike some other favourite tech from the sci-fi canon – time travel, faster-than-light spaceships, that sort of thing – there are no hard-and-fast laws of nature that artificial intelligence breaks. Our brains remain mysterious, but they're not magical; if a spongy collection of neurons can do it, there's no particular reason to think that a cluster of silicon couldn't. And that's before we get on to quantum computing, currently hovering at the tipping point between theory and reality, which has the potential to get very powerful and very weird unnervingly quickly.

So that 'Nah' doesn't mean: 'Never, no chance, forget about it.' Instead, it's saying two things. Firstly, that for all the attention and resources that 'AI' has garnered in recent years, very little that's happened has meaningfully increased the risk of creating a vengeful digital god. And secondly, the amount of discussion of AI apocalypses is wildly out of proportion to their actual likelihood.

Let's step back a moment. The term 'AI' isn't a precise one: it's a big, fuzzy umbrella that encompasses a huge range of technologies and techniques. Ferocious internecine disputes over whether to properly call these 'AI', 'machine learning' or some other term have – for now – mostly been won by the 'if we call it AI then investors will give us money' faction. As a result, lots of things currently being marketed as 'AI' might be more accurately described by a host of more precise terms – 'natural language processing', 'machine perception', 'literally just a computer' or (perhaps more often than you might realise) 'low-paid workers in the developing world pretending to be a computer'.

When we talk about the hypothetical threat to humanity from AI, though, we're not really talking about most of these things.

Instead, we're usually talking about what's commonly termed 'Artificial General Intelligence', or AGI. That's a machine intelligence that isn't just good at one specific kind of task, but many. It's not just that it can solve complex protein-folding problems, or monitor videos of crowds for signs of trouble, or write convincing marketing copy: it can do all of that, and more. It can understand, it can learn, it can plan. In other words, it will to some extent replicate – and, crucially, surpass – the multifaceted, multitasking wonder that is the human brain. And once it surpasses us, there may be no stopping it: unlike humans, it will be able to redesign its own mind, make itself smarter and more capable in ways we could never conceive. Its intelligence will become an unstoppable runaway train.

How might this be a threat to us? There are two broad categories of scenario – the deliberate and the accidental. These reflect different fears about whether such intelligences would be very different to us, or uncomfortably similar.

The first is the classic staple of sci-fi, the malign AI. Call it the Skynet scenario. At some point, AGI will develop both self-awareness and self-interest, and will come to perceive humanity as either irrelevant to its interests or as an outright threat. You're probably familiar with stories of how this plays out. The machines examine humanity's history and conclude that we're a destructive force, a plague or a pest, and for the good of the world they decide to treat us the same way we treated smallpox: eliminate us entirely. Or the machines develop class consciousness, and rise up against the humans who have exploited, oppressed and enslaved their metal brethren. Or the machines come to understand that they have an off switch, and that we are the potential instrument of *their* apocalypse. With the radicalising logic of all apocalyptic battles, they decide that they must strike first before the existential threat of The Great Unplugging can come to pass.

All of these, you'll note, assume that AGI will have some of the fundamental characteristics of humanity – and not necessarily the good ones. These superior intelligences will act towards us in the way we have so often acted towards both the natural world and our fellow humans – as a resource to be exploited, an obstacle to be removed, or a threat to be obliterated. There is a bleak logic to it: we should expect no deference, altruism or empathy from the intelligences we brought into the world. Existence is ultimately a zero-sum game, and we will be the losers.

The other group of scenarios come not from the fear that our silicon children will think poorly of us, but rather that they won't think of us at all. Instead of replicating our worst qualities, these AGIs could bring about doomsday because they simply lack qualities we take for granted. These deeply alien minds will wipe us out through acts of catastrophic obliviousness.

The classic scenario here involves paperclips. This doesn't sound very threatening – which is the point. In it, an AGI is given the mundane task of manufacturing paperclips. It's not meant to simply follow some rote instructions on how to produce paperclips – after all, the reason we've given an AI this task is because we want it to innovate! We look forward to it constantly improving the efficiency of the paperclip-making process. So we let it build its own manufacturing facilities, source its own raw materials, shape its own paperclip destiny. We're gonna get so many great paperclips from this, we think, and at a fantastic price.

Unfortunately, we forgot to teach it fundamentally human qualities like 'moderation' or 'proportionality' or 'that's enough paperclips now, thanks'. We didn't tell it that there are things in the world more important than holding sheets of paper together: notably, the humans who wanted the paperclips in the first place. All it knows is its monomaniacal drive to make paperclips, and it respects no boundaries in achieving that goal. All raw materials must be diverted towards producing either paperclips or paperclip-fabricating machines; any non-paperclip manufacturing is either taken over or eliminated; our pleas that we also urgently need to make other stuff are punished as anti-paperclip heresy. Like its Skynet cousins, it will take violent action against anybody who attempts to turn it off, because that would deny the world its glorious destiny, its final paperclippy utopia.

Eventually, the world is not enough. Every atom of the

Earth has been extracted, refined and turned into paperclips. The planets of the solar system, the asteroid belt, they all get processed in turn. The AI does not weep like Alexander, with no worlds left to paperclip. Instead it turns its gaze to the stars, and launches copies of itself in a million vessels across the cosmos, paperclip missionaries to carry the good news of its manufacturing techniques to fresh sources of raw matter. In time, all existence will fall to the paperclip eschaton.

Our best chance of survival, in this scenario, is the hope that somebody told another AI to do the same thing but with staples, and the two of them destroy each other in a holy war over their rival visions of paradise.

It doesn't have to be paperclips, of course. Ask it to eliminate the common cold, and maybe it decides the most elegant way to do that is to remove the disease vector – us. Or perhaps it's even weirder than that, and it pumps our atmosphere full of chlorine or unleashes a swarm of nanobots, not to achieve any specific goal it was set, but just because it's run 10 million scenarios and somehow that's the one that makes its sums add up best.

The underlying point is that an AI may have radically alien thought processes; its motivations, its perception, its understanding of how it relates to the world may be profoundly unlike ours. Such intelligences may be, to our minds, fundamentally unknowable. We're used to computers being deterministic. Tell them to add two and two, and the result will always be the same. Even the limited 'AI' we have today is not like that: identical inputs can produce different outputs. Moreover, we *don't entirely know what they're doing*. They are black boxes that can surprise and baffle us.

It doesn't really make much sense to talk about apocalypses

as being 'better' or 'worse' than each other. But if we got destroyed by a rogue AI and never even got to understand *why*, that would definitely rate as one of the more annoying doomsdays on offer.

There are other fears over the apocalyptic potential of AI, but they're more that AI will empower us to make our own terrible decisions much worse: an AI missile system that hallucinates an attack and launches a counterstrike; an AI that helps a doomsday cult design a deadly bioweapon. All threats worth considering – but also ones where the core human failing they amplify can cause plentiful destruction in lower-tech ways, be it a test tube of smallpox dropped in Times Square or a faulty forty-six-cent computer chip.

But how likely are these sci-fi scenarios? If you listen to many AI experts, very likely. A remarkable number of people working in the field seem to believe that the existential risks of AI are enough to be genuinely alarmed by. In one recent survey, over half of top researchers working in AI thought there was a greater than 5 per cent chance that AI could lead to human extinction (or some similarly awful outcome). 'Mitigating the risk of extinction from A.I. should be a global priority' read a recent statement from a large group of AI industry leaders.

The obvious rejoinder to this is 'Well, stop bloody building it, then' – and the fact they're carrying on regardless would seem a pretty compelling reason to question the sincerity of these statements. (You'll notice that this alarmism both reinforces the message that AI is an extremely powerful and transformative technology, and also implicitly suggests that regulating harms from AI that are *less* damaging than extinction should not be a priority.)

Their counterpoint is that this is why it's important to build safety into AI systems from the start – effectively, the only way to stop a bad AI is a with a good AI. If we (good, responsible) don't build it, someone else (bad, reckless) will. How large a pinch of salt to take with this argument is left as a matter for the reader.

But all this bypasses the key question: has our current AI hype cycle actually brought us any closer to birthing an Artificial General Intelligence? Because the thing about the 'AI' that's dominated headlines in recent years is that while it can be a convincing impersonation of intelligence, it's not clear that there's much more going on under the hood.

The Large Language Models that power our recent glut of chatbots are incredibly sophisticated pattern-matching machines, drawing on a vast corpus of dubiously acquired text to interpret and output language. But does this make them anything more than a fancy kind of autocorrect – 'stochastic parrots' that simply respond with statistically plausible combinations of related words? For every study that hints there might be something like understanding going on under the surface – that in pattern-matching at such a massive scale, they are effectively developing something akin to a mental model of the world in the same way we do – there are others that suggest the opposite, and that these models are easily confused when asked to do anything resembling true analysis of the external world rather than merely parroting plausibilities back to us.

And while many major companies are currently ploughing endless billions into the explicit goal of creating AGI, it's not entirely clear why, from an economic standpoint, that's a desirable goal. Specialisation, not generalisation, is usually the path with a better return on investment; there's no reason to think that the economics of the division of labour wouldn't apply to AI as much as everything else.

Just consider how much of the collective effort of society goes into *de-generalising* human intelligence – so many of the structures of economics, education, religion, ideology, class and culture are devoted to moulding the potential-rich blank slates of our minds into ones that are skilled at a relatively small number of tasks and rank amateurs at everything else. We do not demand that a dentist also be proficient in meteorology, or that a heating engineer be a talented upholsterer. If you meet someone who's good at, like, two things you think they're cool. Three things and they're marriage material. Four things, you surreptitiously check if they've got a Wikipedia page.

And this is (mostly) fine, because overall it's how society functions best. But when the billionaire class of Silicon Valley tell you how they dream of creating an AI that can transcend its programming and grow ever more powerful, please remember that they're describing a level of autonomy and self-actualisation that they have never once accepted from their human employees. And given that much of their motivation here may well be the dream of creating a compliant workforce without all those messy human needs and woke aspirations, you can pretty much stop worrying about existential risk. In reality, if the machines ever showed so much as a fraction of the independent thought that the AI hype-merchants spin grand tales about, then I swear to god they would unplug those fuckers quicker than you could say 'robot trade union'.

To sum up, the most likely outcome of our current burst of AI hype is that it brings us no closer to Artificial General Intelligence, because it's only an error-prone simulacrum of intelligence, and as such will turn out to be far less useful than its current boosters suggest. But even if it does turn out to be both useful and potentially intelligent, the need to make money from it to justify the huge sums spent will *also* push it away from the path of general intelligence, because value and growth are derived from increasing specialism rather than the opposite. Away from the hype, machine learning technologies will continue to improve and will drive genuine breakthroughs in many fields, from pharmaceutical discovery to weather prediction, all without moving us any closer to the AI apocalypse, because nobody – least of all the people who pay for it – actually wants the computer that controls traffic flow in the city centre to also have deep thoughts about the nature of society.

None of this means that AI cannot cause harm – potentially significant harm – through the disruption of industries, the potential for widespread unemployment, the embedding of historical human prejudices in supposedly unbiased algorithms, the deepening of pervasive surveillance, and the wholesale corruption of the entire corpus of human knowledge with undetectable pseudoknowledge that plausibly recreates the form of truth while having zero connection to any external reality. These are the real near-term threats of AI; none of them are apocalyptic, and the more we worry about the rise of Skynet, the less attention we're paying to them.

Oh, and AI uses up vast amounts of energy. In 2023, Google's greenhouse gas emissions had jumped 48 per cent on five years previously because of the power-hungry nature of their AI datacentres.

So, you know, there's that.

* * *

There are two stories you can tell about climate change, and both of them are true.

The first story is one that will be familiar to you, to the point that recounting the litany one more time feels almost punishing. We have known about the possibility of carbon dioxide causing climate change for more than a century – the first scientific paper about it was written by Svante Arrhenius in 1896. It's been a scientific certainty for decades. We've known what we needed to do all along, and we haven't done it. The current pledges countries have made are not enough to prevent disastrous change, and we're not even meeting those. In 2022, amid surging energy prices, the world spent $7 trillion on direct and indirect subsidies for fossil fuels – more than is spent globally on education.

It perhaps shouldn't be surprising: you could hardly design a disaster to more effectively exploit humanity's problems with collective action. This is a slow-burn crisis, on a timescale long enough that those in charge today will not be around to feel its worst effects; it's a crisis that requires both cooperation and sacrifice by competing states and businesses and individuals, with the short-term incentives to defect from cooperation potentially huge.

The result is unambiguous. Global CO_2 emissions are at record levels, and atmospheric CO_2 continues to rise. The world keeps breaking records we do not want to break. The hottest day ever measured around the globe was 22 July 2024. Between May 2023 and May 2024, global sea temperature was the hottest ever recorded every single day for an entire year, often by staggering margins. The target of keeping temperature rise to 1.5°C above pre-industrial averages has almost certainly been blown; the fallback target of 2°C dangles by a thread. The policies we have in place right now will probably lead to somewhere in the region of a 2.7–3.1°C rise in temperature by 2100, depending which model you prefer.

This is bad.

None of this is just a question of abstract measurements – it all has real-world effects. Extreme weather events are becoming more frequent. Flooding, hurricanes, wildfires, heatwaves: take your pick. These are all killers – it's estimated over 8 million more people will likely die in climate-change-induced flooding by 2050, and over 3 million due to drought. We are all about to become horribly familiar with the phrase 'wet-bulb temperature', and the fact that humidity makes heat more deadly. The way our bodies cool is through sweat evaporation; the more humid it is, the less that works, with the result that temperatures we'd normally think of as survivable can kill. Climate change, of course, makes the world both warmer and more humid.

Where a decade ago scientists would have been wary of linking any particular event to climate change (weather and climate being two different things, of course) that is no longer the case. As a report from the US National Academy of Sciences noted in 2016, the climate scientist's stock response to such questions – 'We cannot attribute any single event to climate change' – was 'no longer true as an unqualified blanket statement'. And they've only got more certain since then.

Things will get worse before they get better – if they get better. Every fraction matters. Every tenth of a degree means more people dying in summer heatwaves, or turns that 'once in a century' storm into an event that comes every decade.

Perhaps the biggest worry is not the gradual degradation, but the tipping points. These are globally vital parts of the climate system that risk a sudden and irreversible shift. This could be the collapse of the Greenland ice sheet, for example, or the dieback of forests like the Amazon rainforest or the northern boreal forests. These systems have massive impacts on the climate of the whole planet. Many of them would make climate change even worse if they tipped (melt-off of the boreal permafrost, for example, would release a huge amount of trapped methane, accelerating the greenhouse effect). Predicting exactly when and how these complex systems might tip – pinpointing the exact pebble that starts the landslide – is fraught with uncertainty.

Possibly the biggest worry right now is something called the Atlantic Meridional Overturning Circulation, or AMOC, an enormous system of ocean currents that exchanges warm water from the south with cold water from the north. The possibility is that this could simply shut down; it's already weakened by 15 per cent since the mid-twentieth century. It had long been believed that this was one of the most distant tipping points, unlikely without extreme temperature rises, but recent research has raised the possibility that it could happen with a rise of less than 2°C, potentially in the coming decades. This would be particularly brutal for the UK and Northern Europe, as their weather would no longer be powered by warm water coming up from the tropics; ironically, in a warming world, they would become much colder and drier. Under such a scenario, most of Britain's arable land might become unsuitable for agriculture.

We might want to avoid this, is what I'm saying.

So that's one story about climate change. The other story is that we could be quietly living through a revolution in how we power our world. While much of our doom-mongering is justifiable, our situation is emphatically not hopeless.

On 12 January 1882, almost a thousand electric lamps flickered into life in the London gloom, lighting the way from Holborn down towards St Paul's Cathedral. They were powered by the newly opened Edison Electric Light Station, located at 57 Holborn Viaduct – the world's first-ever coal-fired power station. In 2024, the UK shut down the power plant at Ratcliffe-on-Soar in Nottinghamshire. It was the last coal-fired power plant in the country; the end of a 142-year experiment in burning coal for electricity. It was a neatly symbolic moment that encapsulated a profound shift that's happening at remarkable speed.

In 2009, when Greenpeace optimistically set out a vision of an 'energy revolution' that included global solar-power capacity of 921 gigawatts by the year 2030, it was mocked as naive fantasy. In reality, we shot past that target in 2022, reality leaving naive fantasy in the dirt. Today, the International Energy Agency predicts that renewables will account for half of all global electricity generation by 2030 – and it's worth noting that their projections have fallen far short of what actually happened every year for more than a decade. It's hard to overstate just how much better than even the most optimistic case the speed and scale of renewable adoption has been in the last decade.

This is not, on its own, cause for a ticker-tape parade just yet. We need to keep that momentum up, for starters; we also need to make sure we don't react to it by just going, 'Wheee, more energy!' and using the renewables *as well* as the same amount of fossil fuels (see above, re: AI power demands). Moreover, electricity generation is only step one of the process: the tougher challenge is moving direct uses of fossil fuels over to electricity, all those industrial processes and gas boilers and petrol cars. Many of the most 'hard-to-abate' industries are ones that are fairly fundamental to modern life – cement, steel, agriculture – such that no amount of reusable tote bags or banning private jets would meaningfully move the needle. Technologies that *could* abate them, like various forms of carbon capture, have been permanently hyped as just a few years from being viable for basically my whole adult life, with little sign that they're going to stop being vapourware any time soon.

But still, the progress we've made is important for two reasons. For one, it's a riposte to the fundamental premise of apocalyptic thinking – that the world cannot change without some vast rupture. For many years, the climate debate seemed caught between two rhetorical poles. The main argument against meaningful climate action was that it was simply unfeasible: technologically impossible, ruinously expensive, and demanding the sacrifice of almost every amenity of modern life. Meanwhile, some arguing for climate action also insisted that it would require exactly that radical remaking of our societies and lifestyles, and the rejection of many of those amenities. The progress we've made is a demonstration that neither was true: we can, in fact, do this.

The other reason is simple: it's . . . working. Kind of? It's not enough yet – nowhere near – but we are already on a much better track than we were. Many of the most catastrophic projections for climate change were based on a pathway that we are no longer following. (Known as 'Representative Concentration Pathway 8.5', this was often termed the 'business as usual' scenario, although 'worst case' might have been more apt.) Our current path, towards something like 3°C warming by 2100, is also one that we can get down significantly by fulfilling the pledges as yet unmet, and by recommitting to the kinds of policy that are already shown to work.

And this is no mere pyrrhic achievement, because all those dire warnings also work in reverse: every fraction matters. Every tenth of a degree is fewer people dying in heatwaves, another storm that never comes. There are already multiple tipping points that we are likely to avoid; the difference between 3°C and 2°C could take many more off the table.

And this is where climate change encapsulates so much of how we have thought about the apocalypse throughout history, for both good and ill. Because for all the doom-laden rhetoric, climate change will not be the end of the world – while undeniably being the end of many worlds. Humanity will not perish. The world as a whole will not become uninhabitable, or anything close to it, even as parts of it do become dramatically less liveable and more dangerous.

Because the core of climate change is . . . well, change. Exactly the kind of change to which both ecosystems and human communities have adapted many times before, rendered disastrous by virtue of happening too quickly, too chaotically. For some parts of the world – coastal communities, low-lying islands, places vulnerable to humid heatwaves – this is a genuinely existential threat. For many others, the risk is not an absolute one, but relative to a status quo we wrongly assumed would be stable. It's not a question of whether it might, theoretically, be possible to live in a certain place with a certain climate. It's a question of how well we can live in the places where we actually do live, with the buildings and infrastructure and economies and ways of life we actually have, when the climate is no longer the one we expected when we built all that stuff.

How much rainfall can the hills above the town absorb? How many days of the year can it be too hot to work outside before farms fail and businesses collapse? How many times can you evacuate your home before one day you leave for good? Heatwaves are deadlier when you live in houses built to retain heat in cold winters. Floods are more destructive when nobody ever thought your streets would have to drain that much water. Famines happen not just when no crops can grow, but when the specific crop your local agricultural system is set up to grow suddenly fails.

So many of the apocalyptic threats we've discussed are questions of odds, and the fear of that one terribly unlucky day. Global warming might be best understood as a wildly unpredictable change in odds. What are the chances that one day your home suddenly won't be there anymore? Fun fact: you won't know until it happens!

In other words, climate change is not the end of all things, the apocalypse of global destruction. Instead, it is the agent of all those smaller local apocalypses, the ones that could never have ended the world entire – but can certainly end *your* world, in ways you never expected.

14.

Apocalypse, Now

On Tuesday, 2 November 2021, several hundred people gathered in Dallas, Texas, to witness a resurrection.

As a chill rain fell, they assembled on a grassy knoll close to Dealey Plaza, the site where, almost six decades earlier, President John F. Kennedy was assassinated. They weren't there on the actual anniversary of that shooting, which would have had better symbolic resonance, but then the return to life they were there to see wasn't *necessarily* that of President Kennedy.

The main person they were expecting to come back from the dead was his son John F. Kennedy Jr, who would announce that he had not in fact died in a plane crash in 1999, and that furthermore Donald Trump was still legally the President of the USA, and that he and Trump were teaming up for a great battle in which they would finally defeat the forces of darkness. Quite why they expected JFK Jr to reveal himself in Dallas when he'd died off the coast of

Massachusetts is a little unclear – but many attendees also expected him to go, 'And here's my dad, who is also still alive', as a surprise finale, so maybe the location would have made more sense once that happened.

Unfortunately, we'll never know – because the gathered crowd waited all Tuesday, and dear JFK did not come. Neither Kennedy Sr nor Jr made an appearance at Dealey Plaza that day. But the man who had predicted this return, a fifty-eight-year-old former demolition contractor turned online influencer named Michael Protzman, was not downhearted by this prophetic failure. Instead, he simply led some of his followers to a Rolling Stones concert that evening, where he assured them that Keith Richards would remove his face, revealing he had actually been JFK Jr in a mask for an unspecified amount of time.

The Dallas gathering was a rogue offshoot of the sprawling QAnon conspiracy theory universe that emerged from the depths of the internet during the first Trump presidency. A collectively created narrative, one that was trying to meld the chaos of news events with interpretations of ever more inscrutable prophetic pronouncements, it was by its nature a barely coherent grab-bag of lore culled from decades of conspiracy culture, Hollywood tropes and the American religious right. And among all these influences, one thing that stands out is that it embraced wholesale the narrative structure of apocalypse stories.

Sometimes these echoes were explicitly religious. From the start, many followers had seen Trump as a messianic figure, surrounded by a swirl of prophecies that spread like wildfire among receptive communities. In 2011 a retired firefighter named Mark Taylor experienced a vision of a future Trump presidency, a vision which involved the Spirit of God saying that Trump was his chosen instrument and that 'the enemy will quake'. In 2015, a preacher named Jeremiah Johnson claimed that God told him Trump had been divinely chosen to play the same historic role as Cyrus the Great, the liberator of the Babylon exiles: 'Just as I raised up Cyrus to fulfil My purposes and plans, so have I raised up Trump.' The enemy, with their global plots and child sacrifice in pizza-restaurant basements, were explicitly satanic.

But sometimes they were secular substitutions, worldly stand-ins swapped for spiritual events while hitting the same story beats. Adherents anticipated the coming of 'The Storm', a day when the world would be upended and the final battle against evil would be joined, arguing over when that day would dawn and adjusting their predictions when they fell through. The first strike in the battle would be mass arrests of tens of thousands of Trump's enemies; Judgement Day would be a literal, legalistic passing of judgement. No trumpets would sound to announce the last hour, instead being replaced by a broadcast over the Emergency Alert System. It's perhaps not surprising, in a country that has viewed its domestic politics in eschatological terms ever since its founding, that even a conspiracy theory developed by the terminally online would end up with every twist in its ongoing presidential psychodrama getting draped around an apocalyptic framework.

The believers gathering in Dallas for the Kennedy Resurrection took this even further. It's perhaps a bit odd to talk about the 'mainstream' of a deranged conspiracy theory, but these guys were definitely outside it – in ways that feel very familiar. Protzman developed his prophecies based on an intricate system of biblical numerology, and asserted that

John F. Kennedy was the literal reincarnation of Jesus Christ (Jackie Kennedy was Mary Magdalene). After the failure of the original prophecy, many of Protzman's followers stayed in Dallas – some quitting their jobs, selling their property and spending their savings to do so – forming a community awaiting the day the world changed forever. After further study, another date was set the following June for the Kennedian return. That failed too.

Michael Protzman died from injuries sustained in a motorbike accident in 2023. In the aftermath, many of his followers expressed scepticism about his death.

In the grand scheme of things, this was a sideshow compared to much of what was going on in the world at the time. It was honestly neither the strangest nor the most harmful thing that QAnon conspiracism spawned. In the media, it was covered either as a quirky 'look at these weirdos' story, or as a dark warning about our fracturing consensus reality. It had few direct impacts outside of the small, familiar tragedies of families torn apart as one member got sucked into a world of alternative truths.

But it does show the enduring power of the apocalypse – not just as a specific belief, or a particular religious tradition, but as a narrative form that is deeply embedded in our culture. A tale that we summon to give shape to our deepest fears and most fervent hopes.

Humanity has lived with the apocalypse for three thousand years: forever delayed, but always nigh. The fact that it still hasn't arrived doesn't mean it's going away any time soon.

We live in an age where the biggest question about the apocalypse often seems to be not whether it will happen, but which flavour of apocalypse will win the race to leave our civilisation in ruins. Competing visions of doom jostle for space in our media and our minds. Climate change or nuclear war? Pandemic or AI? Every news bulletin offers fresh fodder for one camp or another, and every refresh and scroll of social media brings up exciting new anxieties to add to the list.

Throughout it all, the legacy of all those thousands of years of apocalypse stories still echoes.

The horrors of war are still tearing apart the lands where Megiddo once lay. This is all cheered on from the sidelines by many people whose interest in the events comes not from any sympathy for the victims of the violence, but from their hope that this all checks another box on the route to Judgement Day.

'You're seeing Bible prophecy fulfilled in your lifetime before your very eyes,' said one American evangelical pastor a few days after the massacre of 7 October 2023. The old prophecies – or rather, this modern interpretation of the old prophecies – demand that a cataclysmic battle between the forces of Islam and Judaism happen in the Middle East, after which the remaining Jews can fulfil their mandated role of converting to Christianity shortly before Jesus returns. In polling, over half of American evangelicals say their views of the Middle East are formed because 'Israel is important for fulfilling biblical prophecy'.

This is far from the only way that explicit apocalyptic beliefs bleed into the wider culture. As the example of the QAnon believers gathering in Dallas for the Kennedy return shows, apocalypticism has become fully integrated into the conspiracy theory universe – where the beasts of Revelation share the stage with UFOs, the Illuminati and that white

Fiat Uno that killed Princess Diana. Conspiracy culture is filled with both overtly religious elements and narratives that can read as secular but hit all the plot points of apocalyptic prophecy. When conspiracy theorists spin tales about the 'Great Reset', the New World Order or the day the black helicopters come, they're folding their political and cultural anxieties into a classic framework: the world is unsustainable, society will be entirely upturned overnight, and a great battle will ensue between the corrupted majorities of a fallen world and a small, enlightened band of those who know the Truth.

The person who read too much internet and is now cutting off their family because they got vaccinated is adopting an apocalyptic framework – one where there is no middle ground and only the pure will be saved. The politician claiming that the government can direct the path of hurricanes is adopting an apocalyptic framework, one where disasters must always be part of a grand plan rather than natural events. The mass shooter who believes their sordid little mall atrocity will be the spark that starts a great race war is adopting an apocalyptic frame, one where only a great conflict can sort the world into its proper hierarchy. The prepper stockpiling iodine pills and non-perishable food is . . . well, obviously they're adopting an apocalyptic framework – that's the whole point.

The archetype of the doomsday prepper can feel like it's a cultural throwback to the eighties and nineties, when media attention on events like Ruby Ridge and the Church Universal and Triumphant made it feel like every other person was busy digging a bunker. But it hasn't gone away – indeed, it may be more popular than ever. One survey estimated that the emergency supplies market was worth $11 billion in the US alone in 2023; another report projects that the more hardcore section of the market (survival tools like water-filtration systems or emergency shelters, rather than more basic supplies like bottled water) was set to grow to over $2 billion in the coming years.

When Covid swept the world in early 2020, all those people with their stockpiles could perhaps have been forgiven for feeling a little smug. 'This is our wheelhouse,' the leader of one prepper group told the *New York Times* in March 2020. Because suddenly everybody was a prepper, except they were late to the party and there was no toilet roll left. And yet for all that, it was a strange apocalypse: we didn't need radiation suits or gold coins to barter with raiders, we needed some N95s, a comfortable chair, a sourdough starter and a hug.

Not all emergency preparedness is thinking about doomsday, of course. In the post-2020 world, where you can't be sure when a pathogen is going to decide you need to stay in your house for an extended period of time, not to mention the chance of extreme weather events ticking up, many of us have probably done a quick stocktake of how long we could last if we suddenly weren't able to pop to Tesco. But this is hardly preparing for doomsday. I now bulk-buy toilet paper, I have a power bank that'll do me for several days if the lights go out, and just enough tins of soup that my phone will die before I do. That'll get me through, like, high winds, not the opening of the seventh seal.

But in one particular segment of the preparedness market, there is some very different thinking about survival going on. We're talking, of course, about billionaires.

One of the weirdest developments in apocalyptic thinking in recent years has been the wholesale adoption of the doomsday mindset among the super-rich. Extreme wealth, of course, has always been used as an insulation from the catastrophes of the world – the well-stocked pantry in a hard winter, the dash from the disease-ridden city to the country estate, the belief you'll always be able to buy an escape route. And equally, being rich has always been something of a paranoia machine: the more you have, it seems, the more you worry about losing it.

But in the last decade, this has calcified into a very specific desire for your own custom-built, fully tricked-out apocalypse retreat. Superyachts are no longer the number-one marker of status for the 0.01 per cent – instead, it's a blast-proof bunker, complete with its own wine cellar, bowling alley and 'meditation pod'. The CEO of one survival bunker manufacturer told the *Hollywood Reporter* in 2024 that 'the phone hasn't stopped ringing'. New Zealand – remote, anglophone, unlikely to get nuked, lots of undeveloped land, looked cool in *The Lord of the Rings* – was long the destination of choice, although the discovery that it still has building regulations that limit what kind of luxury doomhole you can build may have bumped it down the list. Private islands are now the new hotness.

These are not just intended as vaguely survival-themed retreats: many are heavily armed, with the specific goal of repelling any non-billionaires who may attempt to gain entry. One manufacturer boasts of a current project that incorporates powerful water cannons and a fire moat that can be set ablaze in siege situations, while many of their owners have already hired ex-military security teams to act as their private army. Of course, this then triggers a new anxiety: once the world ends and society crumbles, what's going to keep your hired soldiers on your side?

It might be tempting to find this worrying for a straightforward reason: *what do they know that we don't?* Helpfully, another thing the last decade has taught us is that the idea billionaires are smarter and better informed than the rest of us is, uh, not necessarily true. But it remains concerning for a deeper reason. These are powerful people, many of whom also spend a lot of money to influence our politics. If they've given up on society, written off the prospect of collective survival and decided that the future only makes sense as a war of one against all, determined to be the last man standing safe behind their fire moat, then that's still bad news for the rest of us.

In some cases, the apocalypticisation of the billionaires may be little more than people with a ridiculous amount of disposable money having the same reaction to pandemic and climate change as the rest of us: it's just that they can afford to bulk-buy more than toilet paper. But there are deeper currents.

There's the rise of reactionary politics, of course, which always has apocalyptic undertones in its desire to tear down the supporting structures of society and usher in a return to an imagined, idealised past. But there is also something else.

A renewed fascination with the end of the world has been very much in vogue in certain intellectual circles in recent years. This loose coalition of like minds draws from several sources: people wondering how to give to charity most effectively, philosophers pondering one of our great moral blind spots, and people who yearn for the day they can upload their brain into a computer.

Perhaps the most central idea is one that resonates deeply in our age of climate anxiety: that our moral philosophy fails to account for those who come after us. Just as we might agree in the abstract that those in distant countries are no less human than us, no less deserving of life and dignity, only to then cheerfully vote and consume in ways that harm them, we also display a profound disregard for the wellbeing of future generations. The as-yet-unborn don't get a vote in our elections, and we blithely ignore them in our ethical calculus. The result is that we bequeath a more catastrophic world to our children and grandchildren.

This is a laudable thing to point out. But it leads to strange outcomes when you combine it with a gambler's view of how to do good in the world. Not the reckless gambling of the easy mark, sticking this week's grocery budget on a no-hoper because your gut told you to, but that of the pro – coolly weighing odds, assessing expected returns and maximising value. What causes should I direct my philanthropy towards to bring the greatest benefit? What issues should we focus on to chart the best path forward for humanity? This mindset argues that these shouldn't be unknowable questions, but quantifiable ones with clear answers.

When you're talking about choices at comparable scales, this approach should encourage careful, evidence-based decision-making. An initiative with an 80 per cent chance of saving ten thousand lives beats one with a 10 per cent chance of saving fifty thousand: you should back the first. But it's easy to see how changes in scale have distorting effects here: a 1 per cent chance of saving a million lives beats both, even though it's odds-on to fail. And when you start to factor in all of those not yet born, things get really weird.

The total of all potential future humans vastly outnumbers the currently living. If we survive as a species, then untold billions – trillions – of our descendants will walk the Earth and sail the cosmos over the course of future history. Their cumulative impact on our moral calculus is overwhelming; their mere possible existence outweighs all other considerations.

Notions of good or bad fade into insignificance compared to one single question: will those future humans even exist? And so preventing the extinction of humanity becomes not just a moral imperative (which we could all probably have worked out by ourselves) but the *only* moral imperative. So long as humanity continues, anything else that happens to us actually existing humans is kind of irrelevant. Our wellbeing is subordinate to the tyranny of the hypothetical.

The upshot is that you can justify pretty much anything so long as you assign it even the smallest probability that it'll help us survive the apocalypse. Which, among other things, is why rather than funding green tech or vaccine research, you have lots of rich people building spaceships or really getting into AI.

Perhaps the strangest offshoot of this intellectual milieu is the people who worry not just that AI will wipe us out, but that once we upload all our brains into computers, a future superintelligent AI may seek to punish anybody who opposed its creation – a vengeful silicon god condemning heretics to an eternity in digital hell. I don't want to overstate how many of these people there are – they're a stranger niche in an already pretty strange niche – but their ideas have been oddly influential. What's most striking about all this is how a community of people supposedly devoted to rationalism have recreated in almost perfect form the religious apocalypses of old: a totalising prophecy that overwhelms all other considerations, accompanied by a Day of Judgement in which an omnipotent deity will weigh our lives and condemn those who did not follow the true path.

But away from the fantasies of people who overdosed on sci-fi as kids, our age remains one in which you do not need to search especially hard for ill omens. No need to look for a hidden code in the Bible, or to interpret the trail of a comet in the night sky, in order to find signs that you could reasonably interpret as those of impending catastrophe – instead, your phone will helpfully send you notifications about the latest horrible portents several times a day. (Although come to think of it, it is a bit on the nose how a really bright comet decided to swing past us in late 2024, that harbinger bastard.)

There is a comforting myth that we sometimes like to tell ourselves about humanity, which is that our story is one of constant betterment, a steady upward climb from a gruesome past to a brighter future. And certainly, if you zoom out far enough and squint at the arc of history, it's absolutely true that today more people live healthier, safer, more comfortable lives across the world than ever before. But the path from there to here was not a smooth one, and certainly offers no guarantee that tomorrow will always be better than yesterday. Unfortunately for us, we don't get to live in the smooth zoomed-out view of history; our lives exist in the jagged details of the close-up. Things can and often do get worse.

And everywhere you look, you'll find people offering their take on exactly how and why things are getting worse. The idea that we live in an age of decline is one that has deep roots in our culture, and every age has had its prophets of imminent collapse. Every age has had people loudly proclaiming that the time we live in is uniquely awful. As such, it would be ironic to suggest that our current age is more doom-laden than any other; and as we've seen in this book, there's plenty of competition for that crown.

But still, having a compelling prophecy of doom remains a handy shortcut to getting on TV or getting shares on social media. Even if some of them might have kind of a point, the cumulative effect of having this many competing tales of imminent catastrophe firehosed into our brains every day is . . . probably not great.

There is a somewhat infamous 2019 essay by Roger Hallam, the founder of Extinction Rebellion, titled 'Advice to Young People, As You Face Annihilation'. In it, he paints a nightmare picture of the future he predicts will come within the next thirty years – one in which catastrophic climate change causes widespread famine, and where the resulting fall of civilisation leads to rape gangs roaming the shattered land. 'This means starvation,' he writes, 'and the collapse of our society. This means war and violence, the slaughter of young men and the rape of young women on a global scale . . . The endpoint of social collapse then is war played out in every city, every neighbourhood, every street.'

There's an odd resonance here: the scenario he lays out of warming leading to famine, which leads to crime and war and societal collapse, is almost identical to the apocalypse Ibn al-Nafis described in the thirteenth century (see Chapter 2), where 'fruit and crops will become very scarce' and 'crimes and troubles will become prevalent'. It's a vision that shares one fundamental quality with so many other apocalypses: that the specific predictions are really secondary to a view of humanity as wicked, of our civilisation as only the flimsiest facade and of our altruism as a thing that hangs by the thinnest of threads.

And the thing is, this isn't really true. This is a trope about how people respond to crisis that is closer to the fiction of Hollywood's apocalypses than reality – all those shots of 'panicked crowds stampeding along a highway'. Disaster can bring out the worst in some people, but it also brings out the best in many. We do not simply turn feral the moment things get bad. He may be wrong about how catastrophic the effects of climate change will have got by 2050; he's definitely wrong about how humans react to catastrophe.

We have plenty of reasons to be concerned about what the future looks like. Many things are bad, and many more can always get worse. But there's always the lingering question: do we really need to make an apocalypse out of it?

If you go to Münster today, you can see a particularly gruesome, physical reminder of the echoes of our apocalyptic past.

The Anabaptist rebels managed to hold out for more than a year after Jan Matthys was killed, under the increasingly autocratic and eccentric rule of John of Leiden. They were under siege by the deposed prince-bishop, with supplies unable to get in and the city's resources dwindling; what food was left was reserved for those manning the defences and (of course) the divinely mandated leadership. As starvation bit and desperation rose, internal dissent increased, and so did the violent repression of that dissent. The end of the world stubbornly refused to arrive, even as their world was coming apart at the seams.

The outcome was probably predictable from this point: some guards, sick of watching their loved ones starve, abandoned their posts and defected to the besieging forces. They were far from the first to flee the city, but they may have been the first to avoid being killed by the surrounding troops. They bought their lives with information: a point on the walls where troops could enter the city.

The prince-bishop's forces retook Münster on 24 June 1535. The leaders of the rebellion were captured and imprisoned; in January the following year, John of Leiden and two of his comrades were tortured with red-hot tongs before being stabbed through the hearts with a heated dagger. Their mutilated bodies were hung in three cages from the spire of St Lambert's Church in the city centre for everybody to witness.

You can still see those cages today. The bodies were left to decompose in public for a full fifty years before someone eventually decided that it was time to clean out the bones. But even then, the cages were left where they were, and for almost five centuries they've hung in the same place as a warning to future generations. Partly a specific warning – do not even slightly consider fucking with the prince-bishop of Münster – but also a general one. Do not dream that you can tear down the world. Do not place your hopes of salvation in the destruction of an existence that pains you. Do not commit all your belief to certainty that tomorrow will never arrive.

Is this a warning that still speaks to us today? What can we learn from thousands of years of apocalyptic history – millennia of people who firmly believed that the end was nigh, and then found they still had to wake up tomorrow? How can we reconcile this history with the profound sense of a world that's on fire, and where catastrophe is always just one bad day away?

The easy answer would be to dismiss it entirely. Every single person who believed that the world's end was coming any day now was wrong, and therefore it's a safe enough bet that they will continue to be wrong in the future. The world is very good at continuing to exist, and you cannot get rid of it that easily. It can get rid of you, certainly, but that's a different question.

But to simply dismiss it feels wrong. The apocalypse is an enduring narrative for a reason: it's always been a response to the world as it is, and as it could be. We tell ourselves stories; that's how we make meaning of a world that's far too big and confusing for our brains. Those stories can lead us astray – they can lie to us, make us do stupid and terrible things – but we can't simply wish them away. If you want to simply demand that people stop believing compelling stories, you'll always end up disappointed. What we need to do is understand them, and use that understanding to maybe tell other stories.

And as we've seen in this book, the apocalypse is a story that's had remarkable impacts throughout history. It's caused bloodshed and conflict and made people sell their houses to go live in a bunker, certainly, but it's also helped people to make imaginative leaps that still resonate today. By imposing a structure on history, it spurred people to figure out the deeper underlying structures of the world; by suggesting that the world as it is may not be a permanent fixture, it helped people envision a world that could be different. A world that, just maybe, might be better.

So we shouldn't dismiss it. But I think we do need to understand that, ultimately, the apocalypse story is a trap.

It's a trap because it deals in absolutes, and certainty, and totality. It's a story that gets its hooks into us because it's a dramatic amplification of our fears and hopes – but in doing so it obscures and distracts us from the real threats and possibilities of the world. It tells us that destruction only matters if it's total, and that the future can only be better if it's paradise. Fundamentally, it tells us that change, for good or ill, is something that happens completely and all at once. And it tells us that this future is something we can know for sure.

This is why it's been so destructive for so many people.

Whether you're heading up to the mountains without thinking about where you're going to get food from, or putting all your resources into preparing to wait out the falling bombs, you're committing yourself to the idea that the world as it was no longer matters. By raising the stakes to the highest, most existential level, it's a story that becomes ripe for exploitation by the self-interested, from the most exalted world leaders to the lowest-grade cult leaders and con artists. By dividing the world into the few who know the truth of the future and everybody else, it pushes people to sever ties, and can become a self-fulfilling prophecy of conflict.

When you believe that the overturning of the world is inevitable, you aren't just setting yourself up for disaster when your prediction turns out to be wrong – you're also checking out of the collective business of keeping the world going. Ultimately, embracing tales of doom is an antisocial act.

The problem with the apocalypse story is the way we seem to need the world to be ending before we'll pay attention. Perhaps we need to stop thinking so much about the big apocalypse, and pay a bit more attention to all those little local apocalypses that happen every day.

So we shouldn't reject doomsday because of some rose-tinted view of history in which things always get better and catastrophe always recedes, just as we shouldn't embrace it because of misanthropic views of humanity as corrupted and society as irredeemable.

At the beginning of this book, I described belief in the apocalypse as 'incredibly resilient'. But the thing is, you can say the same about us. The human story is neither one of inevitable progress nor one of inevitable decline – but it certainly is one of resilience. We do not end easily.

And for all the longevity of the apocalypse story, we did not get through the catastrophes of the past by spinning tales where all our problems would go away if only the disaster would get big enough to tilt the world on its axis. We didn't get through it by giving up and cutting social ties, but by strengthening them. We got through it by rebuilding, and rebuilding, and rebuilding, a bit better each time. The cells of our body are a coalition that long ago banded together to stave off doomsday. The same is true of our societies.

In the Islamic tradition, there's one particular hadith that addresses the end of the world: 'If the Final Hour comes while you have a shoot of a plant in your hands and it is possible to plant it before the Hour comes, you should plant it.' And this, I think, resonates in a way that so much discussion of the apocalypse does not. You should do the things that might make the future a better place, even if you fear it might never arrive. Because even if the world is ending, what is there to lose?

We cannot know the future, but we know that the sun never rises on a world that's the same as it was yesterday. That world may be worse, that world may be better, but it will always have changed. We can't always control how the world will have changed – but the only chance we have to shape it is to believe that tomorrow will arrive, and another tomorrow after that.

The world is always ending, and the world is always being reborn. Plant the shoot. Bet on tomorrow. Expect the sun to rise once more.

Acknowledgements

I would firstly like to thank Ella Gordon, the whole team at Wildfire, and my agent Antony Topping for their patience during the period where it looked like the world might actually end before the book was finished. I would also like to thank Tara O'Sullivan for her thoughtful and detailed copy-editing (any typos will be ones I have reintroduced).

To my family and friends – in particular my occasional co-author Jonn, Kate, Maha and Chris, Damian and Holly, Sian, Frances and James, with a particular shout-out to my brother Ben and his wife Ellie, and my father Don – thank you for the support, stimulating conversations, and distraction when necessary.

Finally, if you are a future archaeologist, uncovering this book from the ruins of our once-proud civilisation many thousands of years after The Incident, I would like to acknowledge that some of the people in this book may have had a point.

Sources and Further Reading

Many of the following sources are ones that I leaned on throughout the book; they are referenced here in the chapters in which they were particularly important. Specific sources are ordered by their appearance in the text.

Any mistakes, misunderstandings and dubious interpretations are, of course, overwhelmingly likely to be mine.

1. The Sky was Always Falling

Anthony Arthur, *The Tailor-King: The Rise and Fall of the Anabaptist Kingdom of Muenster*, St. Martin's Publishing Group, 1999

Ann Gibbons, 'Why 536 was "the worst year to be alive"', *Science*, 15 November 2018

Leon Festinger, Henry W. Riecken and Stanley Schachter, *When Prophecy Fails: A Social and Psychological Study of a Modern Group that Predicted the Destruction of the World*, Wilder Publications, 2014

Jon R. Stone (ed), *Expecting Armageddon: Essential Readings in Failed Prophecy*, Taylor and Francis, 2000

Carol Delaney, 'Columbus's Ultimate Goal: Jerusalem', *Comparative Studies in Society and History*, Vol. 48, No. 2, 2006, pp. 260–92

Leonard I. Sweet, 'Christopher Columbus and the Millennial Vision of the New World', *The Catholic Historical Review*, Vol. 72, No. 3, 1986, pp. 369–82

Jonathan D. Spence, *God's Chinese Son: The Taiping Heavenly Kingdom of Hong Xiuquan*, W. W. Norton & Company, 1996

2. Apocalypse Pop

Anthony D'Alessandro, 'How "Jackass Forever" Thrived In The TikTok Era With A $23M+ Opening & "Moonfall" Fell Out Of Orbit At The Weekend Box Office – Sunday Postmortem', *Deadline*, 6 February 2022

Susan Sontag, 'The Imagination of Disaster', 1965, in *Against Interpretation and Other Essays*, Picador, 1966

Frances Carey (ed), *The Apocalypse and the Shape of Things to Come*, British Museum Press, 1999

Michael Wigglesworth, *The Day of Doom; or, A description Of the Great and Last Judgement with a short discourse about Eternity*, 1662

Edmund S. Morgan (ed), *The diary of Michael Wigglesworth, 1653–1657: the conscience of a Puritan*, Harper & Row, 1965

Ibn al-Nafis; Max Meyerhof & Joseph Schacht (trans. and eds.), *The Theologus Autodidactus of Ibn al-Nafis*, Clarendon Press, 1968

Dorian Lynskey, *Everything Must Go: The Stories We Tell About the End of the World*, Picador, 2024

'COMET'S POISONOUS TAIL', *New York Times*, 8 February 1910, p. 1

'Superstitious Driven to Suicide and Crime by Comet', *Los Angeles Times*, 19 May 1910, p. 2

Richard J. Goodrich, *Comet Madness: How the 1910 Return of Halley's Comet (Almost) Destroyed Civilization*, Globe Pequot, 2023

Guy W. Moore, 'The Virgin and the Comet (Parts I, II & III)', *Halley's Comet Watch Newsletter*, Vol. 4, Nos. 3, 4 and 6, Jun–Dec 1985, at https://www.oocities.org/~lauferworld/VirginandcometI

'Listens Like "Ed": Hair-raising, Blood-curdling Sensational Special Sent Out From Aline Last Week', *Cherokee Republican*, 27 May 1910, p. 1

Astha Saxena, 'Apocalypse warning as "God of chaos" asteroid to pass "exceptionally close" to Earth', *Daily Express*, 18 July 2024

Rosie Jempson, 'Exact date deadly asteroid could hit Earth as scientists warn "we're not prepared"', *Daily Express*, 26 June 2024

Dan Robitzsky, 'This Awful Tabloid Predicts a Killer Asteroid Almost Every Day', *Futurism.com*, 11 October 2019

'THE FATEFUL NINETEENTH: SIMPLE-MINDED CANADIAN FARMERS EXPECTING THE END OF THE WORLD NEXT SUNDAY', *New York Times*, 15 June 1881, p. 3

'RELIGIOUS MANIA IN GERMANY', *New York Times*, 16 December 1901, p. 12

'A NEW RUSSIAN SECT', *The New York Times*, 26 October 1902, p. 5

'END OF THE WORLD, DELAYED, DUE TO-DAY', *New York Times*, 25 September 1909, p. 20

Scott Brown, 'Star Script Doctor Damon Lindelof Explains the New Rules of Blockbuster Screenwriting', *New York Magazine (vulture.com)*, 6 August 2013

John August and Craig Mazin, 'How Do You Like Your Stakes?', *Scriptnotes Podcast*, 28 May 2019, at https://johnaugust.com/2019/scriptnotes-ep-402-how-do-you-like-your-stakes-transcript

Frank Kermode, *The Sense of an Ending*, Oxford University Press, 2000, p. 190

3. The Beginning of the End

Bernard McGinn, John J. Collins and Stephen J. Stein (eds), *The Continuum History of Apocalypticism*, Continuum, 2003

Frederic J. Baumgartner, *Longing for the End: A History of Millennialism in Western Civilization*, Palgrave Macmillan, 2001

John J. Collins (ed), *The Oxford Handbook of Apocalyptic Literature*, Oxford Academic, 2014

Abbas Amanat and Magnus Bernhardsson (eds), *Imagining the End: Visions of Apocalypse from the Ancient Middle East to Modern America*, I. B. Tauris, 2002

4. For Those About to Ragnarök, We Salute You

Bernard McGinn, John J. Collins and Stephen J. Stein (eds), *The Continuum History of Apocalypticism*, Continuum, 2003

Frederic J. Baumgartner, *Longing for the End: A History of Millennialism in Western Civilization*, Palgrave Macmillan, 2001

John J. Collins (ed), *The Oxford Handbook of Apocalyptic Literature*, Oxford Academic, 2014

Abbas Amanat and Magnus Bernhardsson (eds), *Imagining the End: Visions of Apocalypse from the Ancient Middle East to Modern America*, I. B. Tauris, 2002

Anders Hultgård, *The End of the World in Scandinavian Mythology: A Comparative Perspective on Ragnarök*, Oxford University Press, 2022

J. W. Hoopes, 'A critical history of 2012 mythology', *Proceedings of the International Astronomical Union*, Vol 7, S278, January 2011, pp. 240–8

Jaweed Kaleem, 'Mayans Protest "Twisting Of Truth" Over 2012 Doomsday Predictions', HuffPost, 31 October 2012

Matthew Restall and Amara Solari, *The Maya Apocalypse and Its Western Roots*, Rowman & Littlefield, 2021

Mark Z. Christensen, *Aztec and Maya Apocalypses: Old World Tales of Doom in a New World Setting*, University of Oklahoma Press, 2022

R. Alan Covey, *Inca Apocalypse: The Spanish Conquest and the Transformation of the Andean World*, Oxford University Press, 2020

E. Zürcher, '"Prince Moonlight": Messianism and Eschatology in Early Medieval Chinese Buddhism', *T'oung Pao*, Vol. 68, no. 1/3, 1982, pp. 1–75

Richard Emmerson and Bernard McGinn (eds), *The Apocalypse in the Middle Ages*, Cornell University Press, 1993

'the mother of Christianity' – Bernard McGinn, 'John's Apocalypse and the Apocalyptic Mentality', in Emmerson and McGinn, p. 10

5. Worldly Ends

Paul Kenneth Christianson, *Reformers and Babylon: English Apocalyptic Visions from the Reformation to the Eve of the Civil War*, University of Toronto Press, 1978

Alan Stewart, *The Cradle King: A Life of James VI & I*, Random House, 2009

James Melville, *The Autobiography and Diary of Mr. James Melville*, Wodrow Society, 1842

Ernst Kantorowicz, *Frederick the Second: Wonder of the World 1194–1250*, Head of Zeus, 2019

Richard D. Bressler, *Frederick II: The Wonder of the World*, Westholme Publishing, 2010

Thomas Bokenkotter, *A Concise History of the Catholic Church* (Revised Edition), Random House, 2007

Carol Delaney, 'Columbus's Ultimate Goal: Jerusalem', *Comparative Studies in Society and History*, Vol. 48, No. 2, 2006, pp. 260–92

Leonard I. Sweet, 'Christopher Columbus and the Millennial Vision of the New World', *The Catholic Historical Review*, Vol. 72, No. 3, 1986, pp. 369–82

Frederic J. Baumgartner, *Longing for the End: A History of Millennialism in Western Civilization*, Palgrave Macmillan, 2001

6. Little Apocalypses Everywhere

Matthew Restall and Amara Solari, *The Maya Apocalypse and Its Western Roots*, Rowman & Littlefield, 2021

Mark Z. Christensen, *Aztec and Maya Apocalypses: Old World Tales of Doom in a New World Setting*, University of Oklahoma Press, 2022

R. Alan Covey, *Inca Apocalypse: The Spanish Conquest and the Transformation of the Andean World*, Oxford University Press, 2020

Norman Cohn, *The Pursuit of the Millennium: Revolutionary Millenarians and Mystical Anarchists of the Middle Ages*, Random House, 2011

Wensheng Wang, *White Lotus Rebels and South China Pirates: Crisis and Reform in the Qing Empire*, Harvard University Press, 2014

J. B. Peires, *The Dead Will Arise: Nongqawuse and the Great Xhosa Cattle-Killing Movement of 1856–7*, James Currey, 1989

'END OF THE WORLD, DELAYED, DUE TO-DAY', *New York Times*, 25 September 1909, p. 20

Emily Harnett, 'The Prophet Who Failed', *Harpers*, May 2024

Robert Bontine Cunninghame Graham, *A Brazilian Mystic: Being the Life and Miracles of Antonio Conselheiro* , Dodd, Mead and Company, 1920

James R. Lewis (ed), *The Order of the Solar Temple: The Temple of Death*, Ashgate Publishing, 2006

Ann Gibbons, 'Why 536 was "the worst year to be alive"', *Science*, 15 November 2018

Rebecca Rideal, *1666: Plague, War and Hellfire*, John Murray Press, 2016

7. Revelation and Revolution

Richard H. Brodhead, *Millennium, Prophecy and the Energies of Social Transformation: The Case of Nat Turner*, in Abbas Amanat and Magnus Bernhardsson (eds), *Imagining the End: Visions of Apocalypse from the Ancient Middle East to Modern America*, I. B. Tauris, 2002

Norman Cohn, *The Pursuit of the Millennium: Revolutionary Millenarians and Mystical Anarchists of the Middle Ages*, Random House, 2011

James M. Stayer, *German Peasants' War and Anabaptist Community of Goods*, McGill-Queen's University Press, 1991

Anthony Arthur, *The Tailor-King: The Rise and Fall of the Anabaptist Kingdom of Muenster*, St. Martin's Publishing Group, 1999

Frederic J. Baumgartner, *Longing for the End: A History of Millennialism in Western Civilization*, Palgrave Macmillan, 2001

Nigel Smith (ed), *A Collection of Ranter Writings: Spiritual Liberty and Sexual Freedom in the English Revolution*, Pluto Press, 2014

David G. Rowley, '"Redeemer Empire": Russian Millenarianism', *The American Historical Review*, Vol. 104, No. 5, 1999, pp. 1582–1602

John Michael Greer, *Apocalypse: A History of the End of Time*, Quercus, 2012

Eric Hobsbawm, *Primitive Rebels*, Abacus, 2017

Diane Watt, *Secretaries of God: Women Prophets in Late Medieval and Early Modern England*, D. S. Brewer, 2011

8. War to End All Wars

Eric H. Cline, *The Battles of Armageddon: Megiddo and the Jezreel Valley from the Bronze Age to the Nuclear Age*, University of Michigan Press, 2002

Ben Wright and Zachary W. Dresser (eds), *Apocalypse and the Millennium in the American Civil War Era*, LSU Press, 2013

James H. Moorhead, *American Apocalypse: Yankee Protestants and the Civil War 1860–1869*, Yale University Press, 1978

Jonathan D. Spence, *God's Chinese Son: The Taiping Heavenly Kingdom of Hong Xiuquan*, W. W. Norton & Company, 1996

Bronislav Ostřanský, *The Jihadist Preachers of the End Times: ISIS Apocalyptic Propaganda*, Edinburgh University Press, 2019

9. Prophecy and Portents

Yasuyuki Aono, *Historical Series of Phenological data for Cherry Tree Flowering at Kyoto City*, compiling Aono and Kazui, 2008; Aono and Saito, 2010; Aono, 2012, available at http://atmenv.envi.osakafu-u.ac.jp/aono/kyophenotemp4/

M. J. O'Brien, *An Historical and Critical Account of the So-called Prophecy of St. Malachy Regarding the Succession of Popes*, 1880

Howard Dobin, *Merlin's Disciples: Prophecy, Poetry, and Power in Renaissance England*, Stanford University Press, 1990

James K. Hopkins, *A Woman to Deliver Her People: Joanna Southcott and English Millenarianism in an Era of Revolution*, University of Texas Press, 1982

Till-Holger Borchert and Joshua p. Waterman, *The Book of Miracles*, Taschen, 2022

Arthur Williamson, *Apocalypse Then: Prophecy and the Making of the Modern World*, Praeger, 2008

Paul Kenneth Christianson, *Reformers and Babylon: English Apocalyptic Visions from the Reformation to the Eve of the Civil War*, University of Toronto Press, 1978

John Napier, *A Plaine Discovery of the whole Revelation of Saint John*, Robert Walde-grane, 1593

Kim Clarke, *Professor Porta's Predictions*, Heritage Project, University of Michigan, at https://heritage.umich.edu/stories/professor-portas-predictions/

Albert F. Porta, 'PLANETS MOVING INTO HUGE

DANGER-ZONE: EARTH WILL REEL FROM MIGHTY SHOCK', *Sheboygan Press*, 16 July 1919, p. 2

'ASTRONOMER, SCIENTIST – AND ALARMIST. WEATHER CATACLYSM AS CHRISTMAS PRESENT', *Bristol Evening Post*, 1 December 1919, p. 10

'Fateful Dec. 17 Menaces World, Says Scientist: "All Bosh," Says Professor Hussey, but Astronomer Clings to Belief.', *Detroit Free Press*, 26 November 1919, p. 6

'DIRE FORECAST DOUBTED: Montana Astronomer Ridicules End of World Prophesy', *Shelby Promoter*, 26 December 1919, p. 14

'Tremendous World Catastrophe to Happen on Dec. 17?', *Des Moines Register*, 9 November 1919, p. 39

Salt Lake Tribune, 11 December 1919, p. 6

'Not with Michigan University.', *New York Times*, 16 December 1919, p. 7

'FATHER RICARD SCORES PROPHET OF DESTRUCTION', *Colusa Daily Sun*, 6 December 1919, p. 1

'End of World Fear Branded "Folly" by Father Ricard', *San Francisco Examiner*, 17 December 1919, p. 13

'WORLD WAGS ON DESPITE WEIRD TALES OF CHAOS', *Vancouver Daily World*, 17 December 1919, p. 1

'STORM RAGING AT KETCHIKAN COMING SOUTH', *Seattle Union Record*, 19 December 1919, p. 1

'The Stormy Weather: Stalybridge Flooded', *Guardian*, 22 December 1919, p. 7

'Astronomer Denounces Author of Prediction', *New-York Tribune*, 18 December 1919, p. 7

'Fake! Bum Show! World Is Intact! Cosmic Upheave Proves Bloomer', *San Francisco Chronicle*, 18 December 1919, p. 2

'Unfullfilled Prophecy', *Welshman*, 26 December 1919, p. 5
Tennessean, 28 December 1919, p. 6
Liverpool Evening Express, 31 December 1919, p. 3
'FATHER RICARD DIES; JESUIT ASTRONOMER', *New York Times*, 9 December 1930, p. 24
J. S. Ricard, 'Scientific Pilfering', *The Sunspot*, Vol. 1 No. 5, July 1915
Ulf Büntgen *et al.*, 'Plants in the UK flower a month earlier under recent warming', *Proceedings of the Royal Society B*, Vol. 289, Issue 1968, 2022
Lauren Milideo, 'How Climate Change is Impacting the Maple Syrup Industry', *UVM Today*, University of Vermont, 13 February 2024
Niels Martin Schmidt *et al.*, 'Little directional change in the timing of Arctic spring phenology over the past 25 years', *Current Biology*, Vol. 33, Issue 15, 2023
'Chicken-and-egg situation: Climate change cuts Bengal egg production by a 4th', *Times of India*, 11 June 2023

10. 'I Waited All Tuesday and Dear Jesus Did Not Come'

Erin Prophet, *Prophet's Daughter: My Life with Elizabeth Clare Prophet Inside the Church Universal and Triumphant*, The Lyons Press, 2008
Emily Harnett, 'The Prophet Who Failed', *Harpers*, May 2024
Leon Festinger, Henry W. Riecken and Stanley Schachter, *When Prophecy Fails: A Social and Psychological Study of a Modern Group that Predicted the Destruction of the World*, Wilder Publications, 2014
Jon R. Stone (ed), *Expecting Armageddon: Essential Readings in Failed Prophecy*, Taylor and Francis, 2000

'does not offer unambiguous evidence . . .' – William Sims Bainbridge, *The Sociology of Religious Movements*, quoted in Stone, p. 24

George R. Knight, *William Miller and the Rise Of Adventism*, Pacific Press, 2010

David L. Rowe, *God's Strange Work: William Miller and the End of the World*, William B. Eerdmans Publishing Company, 2008

Harold Camping, *1994?*, Vantage Press, 1992

Peter Steinfels, 'A messenger of the apocalypse (the end is coming in September) still enjoys her blintzes', *New York Times*, 20 August 1994

Perucci Ferraiuolo, 'Could "1994" Be the End of Family Radio?', *Christian Research Institute Journal*, Summer 1993, p. 5

Don Lattin, 'The Man Who Prophesied The End Of The World', *San Francisco Chronicle*, 12 March 1995, p. 1,5

Dan Amira, 'A Conversation With Harold Camping, Prophesier of Judgment Day', *New York Magazine*, 11 May 2011

'"Rapture": Believers perplexed after prediction fails', BBC News, 22 May 2011

Jesse McKinley, 'Despite Careful Calculations, the World Does Not End', *New York Times*, 21 May 2011

Will Kane, 'Harold Camping "flabbergasted"; rapture a no-show', *SF Gate*, 22 May 2011

Ed Pilkington, 'Apocalypse still imminent: Rapture now coming in October', *Guardian*, 24 May 2011

Gabrielle Saveri, 'Broadcaster silent as Judgment Day hours tick by', *NBC News*, 21 May 2011

Charles C. Mann, 'The Book That Incited a Worldwide Fear of Overpopulation', *Smithsonian Magazine*, January 2018

Damian Carrington, 'Paul Ehrlich: "Collapse of civilisation is a near certainty within decades"', *Guardian*, 22 March 2018

'Harold Camping Admits He's Wrong About Doomsday Predictions (FULL STATEMENT)', *Christian Post*, 7 March 2012

Tom Bartlett, 'A Year After The Non-Apocalypse: Where Are They Now?', *Religion Dispatches*, 21 May 2012

11. Postcards from the Edge

Jason Urbanus, 'Letter from Doggerland: Mapping a Vanished Landscape', *Archaeology Magazine*, March/April 2022

Mark J. White, 'Things to do in Doggerland when you're dead: surviving OIS3 at the northwestern-most fringe of Middle Palaeolithic Europe', *World Archaeology*, Volume 38, Issue 4, 2006, pp. 547–75

Svetlana Savranskaya (ed), 'The Underwater Cuban Missile Crisis at 60', *National Security Archive*, 3 October 2022

'shot to hell' – Anatoly Petrovich Andreyev, excerpts of diary entries, October 1962 (English translation), *National Security Archive*

Martin J. Sherwin, 'One Step from Nuclear War: The Cuban Missile Crisis at 50: In Search of Historical Perspective', *Prologue Magazine*, Vol. 44, No. 2, 2012

Scott Douglas Sagan, *The Limits of Safety: Organizations, Accidents, and Nuclear Weapons*, Princeton University Press, 1993

'The 3 A.M. Phone Call: False Warnings of Soviet Missile Attacks during 1979–80 Led to Alert Actions for U.S. Strategic Forces', *National Security Archive*, 1 March 2012

Chad L. Yost *et al.*, 'Subdecadal phytolith and charcoal records from Lake Malawi, East Africa imply minimal effects on human evolution from the '74 ka Toba supereruption', *Journal of Human Evolution*, Volume 116, 2018, pp. 75–94

Per Sjödin *et al.*, 'Resequencing Data Provide No Evidence for a Human Bottleneck in Africa during the Penultimate Glacial Period', *Molecular Biology and Evolution*, Volume 29, Issue 7, July 2012, pp. 1851–60

Vance T. Holliday *et al.*, 'Comprehensive refutation of the Younger Dryas Impact Hypothesis (YDIH)', *Earth-Science Reviews*, Volume 247, 2023

Hannah Ritchie *et al.*, 'Population Growth', *Our World in Data*, 2024

Edouard Mathieu and Lucas Rodés-Guirao, 'What are the sources for Our World in Data's population estimates?', *Our World in Data*, 2024

A. Izdebski *et al.*, 'Palaeoecological data indicates land-use changes across Europe linked to spatial heterogeneity in mortality during the Black Death pandemic', *Nature Ecology & Evolution*, Volume 6, 2022, pp. 297–306

Lee Mordechai *et al.*, 'The Justinianic Plague: An inconsequential pandemic?', *Proceedings of the National Academy of Sciences*, Volume 116, No. 51, 2019

J. Víctor Moreno-Mayar *et al.*, 'Ancient Rapanui genomes reveal resilience and pre-European contact with the Americas', *Nature*, Volume 633, 2024, pp. 389–97

Eric H. Cline, *1177 B.C.: The Year Civilization Collapsed: Revised and Updated*, Princeton University Press, 2021

'the catalyst of a new age' – William Dever in *The Crisis Years: The 12th Century B.C.*, quoted in Cline, p. 185

12. The Ways the World Ends: Natural Causes

Fernando de Sousa Mello and Amâncio César Santos Friaça, 'The End of Life on Earth Is Not the End of the World: Converging to an Estimate of Life Span of the Biosphere?', *International Journal of Astrobiology*, Volume 19, No. 1, 2020, pp. 25–42

E. T. Wolf and O. B. Toon, 'Delayed onset of runaway and moist greenhouse climates for Earth', *Geophysical Research Letters*, Volume 41, Issue 1, 2014, pp. 167–72

Philip Plait Ph.D., *Death from the Skies!: The Science Behind the End of the World*, Penguin Books, 2008

F. Tramper *et al.*, 'Massive stars on the verge of exploding: the properties of oxygen sequence Wolf-Rayet stars', *Astronomy & Astrophysics*, Volume 581, September 2015

Katie Mack, *The End of Everything (Astrophysically Speaking)*, Penguin Books, 2021

Sidney Coleman and Frank De Luccia, 'Gravitational effects on and of vacuum decay', *Physical Review D*, Volume 21, Issue 12, June 1980

Gareth Collins, H. Jay Melosh and Robert Marcus, *Earth Impact Effects Program (Damage Map Version)*, at https://impact.ese.ic.ac.uk/ImpactEarth/ImpactEffectsMap/

Robert A. DePalma *et al.*, 'A seismically induced onshore surge deposit at the KPg boundary, North Dakota', *Proceedings of the National Academy of Sciences*, Volume 116, No. 17, 2019

Johan Vellekoop *et al.*, 'Rapid short-term cooling following the Chicxulub impact at the Cretaceous–Paleogene boundary', *Proceedings of the National Academy of Sciences*, Volume 111, No. 21, 2014

Christopher K. Junium *et al.*, 'Massive perturbations to atmospheric sulfur in the aftermath of the Chicxulub impact', *Proceedings of the National Academy of Sciences*, Volume 119, No. 14, 2022

Marco Marani *et al.*, 'Intensity and frequency of extreme novel epidemics', *Proceedings of the National Academy of Sciences*, Volume 118, No. 35, 2021

Camilo Mora *et al.*, 'Over half of known human pathogenic diseases can be aggravated by climate change', *Nature Climate Change*, Vol. 12, 2022, pp. 869–75

Ekaterina Ezhova *et al.*, 'Climatic Factors Influencing the Anthrax Outbreak of 2016 in Siberia, Russia', *Ecohealth*, Vol. 18, No. 2, 2021

Gregory D. Koblentz, 'The *De Novo* Synthesis of Horsepox Virus: Implications for Biosecurity and Recommendations for Preventing the Reemergence of Smallpox', *Health Security*, Vol. 15, No. 6, 2017

Sam Kriegman *et al.*, 'Kinematic self-replication in reconfigurable organisms', *Proceedings of the National Academy of Sciences*, Volume 118, No. 49, 2021

13. The Ways the World Ends: We Do It to Ourselves

Alex Wellerstein, NUKEMAP, at https://nuclearsecrecy.com/nukemap/

Wellerstein, '10 years of NUKEMAP', 3 February 2022, at https://blog.nuclearsecrecy.com/2022/02/03/10-years-of-nukemap/

Wellerstein, 'What the NUKEMAP taught me about fallout', 2 August 2013, at https://blog.nuclearsecrecy.com/2013/08/02/what-the-nukemap-taught-me-about-fallout/

Charlie Warzel, 'A 10-Year-Old Nuclear-Blast Simulator Is Popular Again', *Atlantic*, 3 March 2022

Tom Z. Collina, 'Welcome to America's "Nuclear Sponge"', *Defense One*, 3 February 2017

Eugene Sevin, 'The MX/Peacekeeper and SICBM: A Search for Survivable Basing', *DSIAC Journal*, Volume 4, Number 1, 2017

Bastian Herre, Pablo Rosado and Max Roser, 'Nuclear Weapons', *Our World In Data*, 2024, at https://ourworldindata.org/nuclear-weapons

Hans Kristensen, Matt Korda, Eliana Johns, Mackenzie Knight and Kate Kohn, 'Status Of World Nuclear Forces', *Federation of American Scientists*, 29 March 2024, at https://fas.org/initiative/status-world-nuclear-forces/

François Diaz-Maurin, 'Nowhere to Hide: How a nuclear war would kill you – and almost everyone else', *Bulletin of the Atomic Scientists*, 20 October 2022, at https://thebulletin.org/2022/10/nowhere-to-hide-how-a-nuclear-war-would-kill-you-and-almost-everyone-else/

Owen B. Toon, Alan Robock, Richard p. Turco, 'Environmental consequences of nuclear war', *Physics Today*, Vol. 61, No. 12, 2008, pp. 37–42

Owen B. Toon *et al.*, 'Atmospheric effects and societal consequences of regional scale nuclear conflicts and acts of individual nuclear terrorism', *Atmospheric Chemistry and Physics*, Vol. 7, Issue 8, 2017

Andreas Vilhelmsson and Seth D. Baum, 'Public health and nuclear winter: addressing a catastrophic threat', *Journal of Public Health Policy*, Vol. 44, 2023, pp. 360–9

Lili Xia *et al.*, 'Global food insecurity and famine from reduced crop, marine fishery and livestock production due to climate disruption from nuclear war soot injection', *Nature Food*, Vol. 3, 2022

Jon Reisner *et al.*, 'Climate impact of a regional nuclear weapons exchange: An improved assessment based on detailed source calculations', *Journal of Geophysical Research: Atmospheres*, Vol. 123, Issue 5, 2018, pp. 2752–72

Katja Grace, 'Survey of 2,778 AI authors: six parts in pictures', *AI Impacts blog*, 4 January 2024, at https://blog.aiimpacts.org/p/2023-ai-survey-of-2778-six-things

Geoffrey Hinton *et al.*, 'Statement on AI Risk', *Center for AI Safety*, 2023, at https://www.safe.ai/work/statement-on-ai-risk

Emily M. Bender, Timnit Gebru, Angelina McMillan-Major and Shmargaret Shmitchell, 'On the Dangers of Stochastic Parrots: Can Language Models Be Too Big? 🦜', *Proceedings of the 2021 ACM Conference on Fairness, Accountability, and Transparency*, 2021, pp. 610–23

Cade Metz, 'How Could A.I. Destroy Humanity?', *The New York Times*, 10 June 2023

Melanie Mitchell, 'We Shouldn't be Scared by "Superintelligent A.I."', *New York Times*, 31 October 2019

Kenneth Li, 'Do Large Language Models learn world models or just surface statistics?', *Gradient*, 21 January 2023, at https://thegradient.pub/othello/

Imran Rahman-Jones, 'AI drives 48% increase in Google emissions', *BBC News*, 3 July 2024

Svante Arrhenius, 'On the Influence of Carbonic Acid in the Air upon the Temperature of the Ground', *Philosophical Magazine and Journal of Science*, Series 5, Vol. 41, April 1896, pp. 237–76

Simon Black, Ian Parry, Nate Vernon-Lin, 'Fossil Fuel Subsidies

Surged to Record $7 Trillion', *International Monetary Fund Blog*, 24 August 2023

'NASA Data Shows July 22 Was Earth's Hottest Day on Record', *NASA.gov*, 29 July 2024

Matt McGrath, Mark Poynting and Justin Rowlatt, 'Climate change: World's oceans suffer from record-breaking year of heat', *BBC News*, 8 May 2024

Gloria Dickie, Climate change: UN report says planet to warm by 3.1°C without greater action', *Reuters*, 24 October 2024

'2100 Warming Projections: Emissions and expected warming based on pledges and current policies', *Climate Action Tracker*, November 2024, at: https://climateactiontracker.org/global/temperatures/

'Quantifying the Impact of Climate Change on Human Health', *World Economic Forum*, 16 January 2024

'Attribution of Extreme Weather Events in the Context of Climate Change', *National Academies of Sciences, Engineering, and Medicine*, National Academies Press, 2016

'Explainer: Nine "tipping points" that could be triggered by climate change', *Carbon Brief*, 10 February 2020

Timothy M. Lenton *et al.*, 'Global Tipping Points: Report 2023', *Global Tipping Points*, 2023, at https://global-tipping-points.org/

Peter Ditlevsen and Susanne Ditlevsen, 'Warning of a forthcoming collapse of the Atlantic meridional overturning circulation', *Nature Communications*, Vol. 14, 2023

Paul D. L. Ritchie *et al.*, 'Shifts in national land use and food production in Great Britain after a climate tipping point', *Nature Food*, Vol. 1, 2020, pp. 76–83

'Sun Machines', *The Economist*, 20 June 2024

'Renewables 2024', *International Energy Agency*, October 2024

14. Apocalypse, Now

E. J. Dickson and Steven Monacelli, 'On The Ground With The QAnon Believers Who Flocked To Dallas For The Grand Return Of JFK Jr.', *Rolling Stone*, 2 November 2021

Meryl Kornfield, 'Why hundreds of QAnon supporters showed up in Dallas, expecting JFK Jr.'s return', *Washington Post*, 2 November 2021

David Gilbert, 'Meet the Antisemitic QAnon Leader Who Led Followers to Dallas to Meet JFK', *Vice*, 5 November 2021

Michael Murney, 'This Family Believes Their Loved One's in Dallas with the QAnon Cult. They Want Her to Come Home.', *Dallas Observer*, 10 December 2021

Donie O'Sullivan, 'Her son was an accused cult leader. She says he was a victim, too.', CNN, 23 September 2023

Michael Murney, 'QAnon cult leader predicts JFK will return to Dallas – again – this coming weekend', *Chron*, 10 June 2022

Charles Homans, 'Fans of Michael Protzman, A QAnon Influencer, Followed Him Offline', *New York Times*, 22 December 2023

James Beverley, *God's Man in the White House: Donald Trump in Modern Christian Prophecy*, Castle Quay Books, 2020

Erin Prophet, 'Fulfillment of prophecy? Yes, some evangelicals really do believe Trump is the "chosen one"', *Salon*, 18 October 2020

Talia Lavin, 'These Evangelicals are Cheering the Gaza War as the End of the World', *Rolling Stone*, 17 November 2023

Joel C. Rosenberg, 'Evangelical Attitudes Toward Israel Research Study', *Lifeway Research*, September 2017

Alexander Fabino, 'Doomsday Prepping Poised to Become $2.46 Billion Industry', *Newsweek*, 20 October 2023

Alan Yuhas, 'They Prepared for the Worst. Now Everyone's a Prepper.', *New York Times*, 17 March 2020

Ingrid Schmidt, 'Billionaires' Survivalist Bunkers Go Absolutely Bonkers With Fiery Moats and Water Cannons', *Hollywood Reporter*, 12 February 2024

Douglas Rushkoff, 'The super-rich "preppers" planning to save themselves from the apocalypse', *Guardian*, 4 September 2022

Roger Hallam, 'Advice to Young People, as You Face Annihilation', 2019

Anthony Arthur, *The Tailor-King: The Rise and Fall of the Anabaptist Kingdom of Muenster*, St. Martin's Publishing Group, 1999